SERVANT LEADER HUMAN RESOURCE MANAGEMENT

Servant Leader Human Resource Management

A Moral and Spiritual Perspective

Gary E. Roberts

palgrave
macmillan

First published in 2014 by
PALGRAVE MACMILLAN®
in the United States—a division of St. Martin's Press LLC,
175 Fifth Avenue, New York, NY 10010.

Where this book is distributed in the UK, Europe and the rest of the world,
this is by Palgrave Macmillan, a division of Macmillan Publishers Limited,
registered in England, company number 785998, of Houndmills,
Basingstoke, Hampshire RG21 6XS.

Palgrave Macmillan is the global academic imprint of the above companies
and has companies and representatives throughout the world.

Palgrave® and Macmillan® are registered trademarks in the United States,
the United Kingdom, Europe and other countries.

ISBN 978-1-349-49141-4   ISBN 978-1-137-42837-0 (eBook)
DOI 10.1057/9781137428370

Library of Congress Cataloging-in-Publication Data

Roberts, Gary E., 1956-
    Servant leader human resource management : a moral and spiritual
perspective / by Gary E. Roberts.
       pages cm
    Includes bibliographical references and index.

    1. Personnel management—Moral and ethical aspects. 2. Servant
leadership—Religious aspects. 3. Management—Religious aspects.
    I. Title.

HF5549.R576 2014
658.3—dc23   2014010003

A catalogue record of the book is available from the British Library.

Design by Newgen Knowledge Works (P) Ltd., Chennai, India.

First edition: September 2014

10 9 8 7 6 5 4 3 2 1

I thank and give praise to my Lord and savior Jesus Christ who is the source and inspiration for this book and gave me my wonderful wife Connie, my beloved mother and sister Joyce and Sharon, and my precious daughters Alyssa, Sandra, and Christin. I thank my many wonderful students for the privilege of serving as their instructor over the years. This book is dedicated to their moral and spiritual education.

Contents

Tables

Chapter 1

Principles of Servant Leader Human Resource Management (SLHRM)

Introduction to Servant Leadership

Human resource (HR) management is one of the foundational "windows on the heart" reflecting the individual and collective values and beliefs of leaders, managers and employees regarding the "theology of work" and its relationship to human nature. Does the HR system honor servant leader principles through shaping the values and incentives to serve, work, lead, and manage in truly a moral and ethical fashion? Are we "hearers and doers" recognizing the great personal responsibility and accountability related to the exercise of power in organizations? This book assists pre-service students and current leaders and managers in assuming the mantle of servant leadership in human resource management (SLHRM), the ethical and moral means for achieving organizational missions.

Hence, this book promotes an explicitly normative and prescriptive framework for HR management setting very high standards of human motivation and conduct. As such, SLHRM is an idealized approach never fully realized in practice given the inherent flaws and limits to human nature. However, the more that organizations and individuals commit to the high ideals of SLHRM, the greater the individual and corporate growth facilitating mission achievement and organizational wellbeing. Hence, it is an ongoing process of gaining wisdom, solving problems, and learning on all levels, moral, intellectual, and spiritual. From the author's personal perspective, progress and growth in achieving SLHRM principles requires a greater authority than self-effort, in this case my Christian religious faith. For readers with other worldviews the sources of power may be different, but individual effort alone is not sufficient.

Why is servant leadership the foundation for this book? There are many approaches to leadership, but only servant leadership emphasizes the necessary balance between morality, mission achievement, and promoting the best interests and wellbeing of the key stakeholders (employees, clients, customers, and the community) (Northouse, 2013). Like yeast infusing bread, servant leadership influences the entire culture of an organization, promoting favorable outcomes on all levels. In essence, it is the Golden Rule in practice. The dual foundation of servant leadership is stewardship, which is achieving the mission by using moral motives, means and ends, and servanthood, which is promoting the best interests and needs of the key stakeholders. Servant leadership manifests both religious and secular roots (Bekker, 2010; Sendjaya, 2010). It is the foundational leadership principle of Christianity as exemplified in the Old and New Testaments with the culmination in the ministry of Jesus as elaborated in the works of Wilkes (2008), Blanchard and Hodges (2005), and from a more secular perspective in the works of Greenleaf (1977). From an ethical standpoint, servant leadership is founded upon the integration of the three key ethical domains, that of deontological principles (moral laws), aretaic or virtue elements imbedded in moral character, and teleological or utilitarian principles that assess consequences (promote the greater good). There is no single agreed-upon conceptual or operational definition of servant leadership with a fixed and narrowly defined set of attributes. A review by Roberts and Hess-Hernandez (2012/2013) identified thirty-nine attributes of servant leadership that include a combination of character attributes (love, humility, and forgiveness), leadership practices (empowerment and active listening), and cognitive attributes (foresight and conceptualization). Research, however, has demonstrated servant leadership is a distinct and unique leadership approach differentiated from the related domains of transformational leadership and leader-member exchange theories (Liden et al., 2008; Schaubroeck, Lam, & Peng, 2011). A more detailed analysis appears in table 1.1 with six global dimensions, the love-based servanthood elements, servant leader stewardship in completing the mission, servant leader character, servant leader behavior, servant leader reasoning abilities, and servant leader spiritual elements. Servanthood is the foundational element and includes the related attributes of altruism, serving others first, facilitating the success and growth of others, promoting healing, egalitarianism, and *agapao* (to love dearly in the Greek) love. Stewardship elements entail accomplishing the organizational mission using virtuous means, building community, and providing an inspiring vision. Key servant leader character attributes include moral integrity, empathy, humility,

Table 1.1 Servant leader attribute literature summary

Servant Leader Attributes: Servanthood Motivational Elements

- *Altruism (2)*: Patterson, K. (2003); Reed, L. L., Vidaver-Cohen, D., & Colwell, S. R. (2011)
- *Altruistic Calling (1)*: Barbuto, J. E., & Wheeler, D. W. (2006)
- *Calling (2)*: Barbuto, J. E., & Wheeler, D. W. (2006); Sun, P. T. (2013)
- *Covenantal Relationship (2)*: Sendjaya, S., & Pekerti, A. (2010); Sendjaya, Sarros, & Santora (2008)
- *Egalitarianism (2)*: Mittal, R., & Dorfman, P. W. (2012); Reed, L. L., Vidaver-Cohen, D., & Colwell, S. R. (2011)
- *Healing (5)*: Barbuto, J. E., & Wheeler, D. W. (2006); Liden, R. C., Wayne, S. J., Zhao, H., & Henderson, D. (2008); Spears, L. (1998); Liden, R. C., Panaccio, A., Hu, J., & Meuser, J. D. (in press); van Dierendonck, D (2011)
- *Agapao Love (3)*: Dennis R. S., & Bocarnea M. (2005); Patterson, K. (2003); Sun, P. T. (2013)
- *Serve Others First (4)*: Boone, L. W., & Makhani, S. (2012); Farling, M. L., Stone, A. J., & Winston, B. E. (1999); Greenleaf, R. K. (1977); Patterson, K. (2003)
- *Needs of Other Over Self (1)*: Laub, J. (1999)
- *Good of Followers Over Self Interest (2)*: Hale, J. R., & Fields D. L. (2007); Wong, P. T. P., & Davey, D. (2007)
- *Positive Effect on Least Privileged (1)*: Greenleaf, R. K. (1977)
- *Put Subordinates/Followers First (3)*: Liden, R. C., Wayne, S. J., Zhao, H., & Henderson, D. (2008); Liden, R. C., Panaccio, A., Hu, J., & Meuser, J. D. (in press); van Dierendonck, D. (2011)
- *Servanthood and Do Others Grow/Succeed (8)*: Boone, L. W., & Makhani, S. (2012); Greenleaf, R. K. (1977); Laub, J. (1999); Liden, R. C., Panaccio, A., Hu, J., & Meuser, J. D. (in press); Liden, R. C., Wayne, S. J., Zhao, H., & Henderson, D. (2008); Spears, L. (1998); van Dierendonck, D. (2011); Wong, P. T. P., & Page, D. (2003)

Servant Leader Attributes: Stewardship Mission Elements

- *Accountability (1)*: Dierendonck, D., & Nuijten, I. (2011)
- *Building Community (4)*: Boone, L. W., & Makhani, S. (2012); Laub, J. (1999); Reed, L. L., Vidaver-Cohen, D., & Colwell, S. R. (2011); Spears, L. (1998)
- *Creating Community Value (3)*: Liden, R. C., Wayne, S. J., Zhao, H., & Henderson, D. (2008); Liden, R. C., Panaccio, A., Hu, J., & Meuser, J. D. (in press); van Dierendonck, D. (2011)
- *Responsible Leadership (1)*: Wong P. T. P., & Page, D. (2003)
- *Stewardship (3)*: Barbuto, J. E., & Wheeler, D. W. (2006); Spears, L. (1998); van Dierendonck, D., & Nuijten, I. (2011)
- *Vision (5)*: Boone, L. W., & Makhani, S. (2012); Dennis, R. S., & Bocarnea, M. (2005); Farling, M. L., Stone, A. J., & Winston, B. E. (1999); Patterson, K. (2003); Wong, P. T. P., & Page, D. (2003)

Servant Leader Attributes: Character Elements

- *Authentic Self (2) and Authenticity (5)*: Laub, J. (1999); Pekerti, A. A., & Sendjaya, S. S. (2010); Sendjaya, S., & Pekerti, A. (2010); Sendjaya, S., Sarros, J. C., & Santora, J. C. (2008); van Dierendonck, D., & Nuijten, I. (2011); Wong, P. T. P., & Davey, D. (2007), Wong, P. T. P., & Page D. (2003)

Continued

Table 1.1 Continued

- *Behave Ethically (3)*: Liden, R. C., Panaccio, A., Hu, J., & Meuser, J. D. (in press); Liden, R. C., Wayne, S. J., Zhao, H., & Henderson, D. (2008); van Dierendonck (2011).
- *Courage (2)*: Dierendonck, D., & Nuijten, I. (2011); Wong, P. T. P., & Page, D. (2003)
- *Credibility (1)*:Farling, M. L., Stone, A. J., & Winston, B. E. (1999)
- *Empathy (4)*: Barbuto, J. E., & Wheeler, D. W. (2006); Mittal, R., & Dorfman, P. W. (2012); Spears, L. (1998); Sun, P. T. (2013)
- *Forgiveness (1)*: van Dierendonck, D., & Nuijten, I. (2011)
- *Hope (1)*: Searle, T. P., & Barbuto, John, E. (2011)
- *Honesty (1)*: Wong, P. T. P., & Page, D. (2003)
- *Humility (6)*: Dennis, R. S., & Bocarnea, M. (2005); Mittal, R., & Dorfman, P. W. (2012); Patterson, K. (2003); Sun, P. T. (2013); van Dierendonck, D., & Nuijten, I. (2011); Wong & Davey (2007)
- *Moral Integrity (9)*: Erhart, M. G. (2004); Graham, J. W. (1991); Mittal, R. & Dorfman, P. W. (2012); Pekerti, A. A. & Sendjaya, S. S. (2010); Reed, L. L., Vidaver-Cohen, D., & Colwell, S. R. (2011); Sendjaya, S., & Pekerti, A. (2010); Sendjaya, S., Sarros, J. C., & Santora, J. C. (2008); Walumbwa, F. O., Hartnell, C. A., & Oke, A. (2010), Wong, P. T. P., & Davey, D. (2007)
- *Trust (3)*: Dennis, R. S. & Bocarnea, M. (2005); Farling, M. L., Stone, A. J., & Winston, B. E. (1999); Patterson, K. (2003);
- *Wisdom (1)*: Barbuto, J. E., & Wheeler, D. W. (2006)

Servant Leader Attributes: Behavioral Elements

- *Active Listening (3)*: Barbuto, J. E., & Wheeler, D. W. (2006); Boone, L. W., & Makhani, S. (2012); Spears, L. (1998)
- *Consulting and Involving Others (1)*: Wong, P. T. P., & Davey, D. (2007)
- *Empowerment (9)*:Boone, L. W., & Makhani, S. (2012); Dennis, R. S., & Bocarnea, M. (2005); Liden, R. C., Panaccio, A., Hu, J., & Meuser, J. D. (in press); Liden, R. C., Wayne, S. J., Zhao, H., & Henderson, D. (2008); Mittal, R., & Dorfman, P. W. (2012); Patterson, K. (2003); van Dierendonck (2011); van Dierendonck, D., & Nuijten, I. (2011); Wong, P. T. P., & Page, D. (2003).
- *Follower Development (3)*: Hale, J. R., & Fields, D. L. (2007); Wong, P. T. P., & Page, D. (2003); Wong, P. T. P., & Davey, D. (2007)
- *Goal setting (1)*: Laub, J. (1999)
- *Initiative (1)*: Laub, J. (1999)
- *Interpersonal Support (1)*:Reed, L. L., Vidaver-Cohen, D., & Colwell, S. R. (2011)
- *Influencing Others (1)*: Wong, P. T. P., & Davey, D. (2007)
- *Inspiring Others (1)*: Wong, P. T. P., & Davey, D. (2007)
- *Persuasion (1)*: Spears, L. (1998)
- *Relationship Building (1)*: Liden, R. C., Wayne, S. J., Zhao, H., & Henderson, D. (2008)
- *Serving and Developing Others (1)*: Wong, P. T. P., & Davey, D. (2007)
- *Shares Power (1)*: Laub, J. (1999)
- *Standing Back (1)*: van Dierendonck, D., & Nuijten, I. (2011)
- *Values and Has Confidence in People (1)*: Laub, J. (1999)
- *Voluntary Subordination (2)*: Sendjaya, S., & Pekerti, A. (2010); Sendjaya, S., Sarros, J. C., & Santora, J. C. (2008)

Continued

Table 1.1 Continued

Servant Leader Attributes: Reasoning Abilities Awareness (1): Spears, L. (1998)
- *Conceptualization (4)*: Liden, R. C., Wayne, S. J., Zhao, H., & Henderson, D. (2008); Spears, L. (1998); Liden, R. C., Panaccio, A., Hu, J., & Meuser, J. D. (in press); van Dierendonck (2011).
- *Foresight (3)*: Laub, J. (1999); Patterson, K. (2003); Spears, L. (1998)
- *Persuasive Mapping (1)*: Barbuto, J. E., & Wheeler, D. W. (2006)
- *Philosophy (1)*: Spears, L. (1998)

Servant Leader Attributes: Spirituality Elements
- *Transcendental Spirituality (3)*: Pekerti, A. A., & Sendjaya, S. S. (2010); Sendjaya, S., & Pekerti, A. (2010); Sendjaya, S., Sarros, J. C., & Santora, J. C. (2008)
- *Transformational Influence (2)*: Sendjaya, S., & Pekerti, A. (2010); Sendjaya, S., Sarros, J. C., & Santora, J. C. (2008)

Note: Number of studies in parentheses.

authenticity, trust, hope, courage, and forgiveness. Foundational servant leader behaviors include empowerment, active listening, goal setting, and relationship building. The reasoning ability elements center on the presence of foresight and conceptualization skills. The final dimension provides transcendental spirituality and transformational influence. The absence of a tightly defined set of attributes is both a strength and weakness. It is a strength in that servant leadership by conceptual definition is holistic, organic, evolving and dynamic combination of heart, intellect, emotions, and spirit. By definition it cannot be distilled into a reductionist and mechanical conceptualization. Conversely, the broad and variable conceptual elements impede uniform measurement and methodological rigor to support reliable and valid measures. However, as empirical research expands in scope, a greater degree of methodological consistency will follow.

Clearly defining the elements of servant leadership is important. The adoption of servant leadership is fully justified on a deontological and aretaic (virtue) basis. However, demonstrating its empirical influence helps buttress its adoption from a utilitarian orientation. In essence, this research is essential in demonstrating that servant leader love and character virtue generates favorable organizational outcomes in terms of employee and community wellbeing and individual and organizational performance (Showkeir, 2002). In essence, is there an increase in the good from the practice of servant leadership?

There is a burgeoning body of literature demonstrating the positive influence of servant leadership on a host of attitudinal, behavioral and performance outcomes (Parris & Peachey, 2013). A review of the empirical literature demonstrates robust, consistent, and compelling evidence on the favorable influence of servant leadership on job attitudes, leadership effectiveness, work behaviors, performance, character formation, desirable personality attributes, and quality of life outcomes. Mayer (2010) proposes that servant leadership attributes increase follower need satisfaction in the key elements that comprise self-determination-theory (SDT), that of autonomy, relatedness and competence (Deci & Ryan, 1985), thereby generating favorable attitudinal, behavioral and performance outcomes.

The table 1.2 provides a detailed summary of the published literature that supports Mayer (2010) and the other servant leader models. Servant leadership is associated with higher levels of organizational commitment, job trust, job satisfaction, procedural justice, and engagement levels, among others. In terms of the leadership outcomes, servant leadership is associated with higher levels of leadership competence, commitment to supervisor, and leader trust. In terms of behaviors, servant leadership promotes higher levels of organizational citizenship, employee creativity and helping behavior, and lower levels of organizational turnover. The favorable influence on productivity is equally impressive with multiple studies indicating higher levels of team effectiveness, team potency, goal and process clarity, and firm performance. Servant leadership enhances essential character attributes such as hope, integrity, and loyalty. Finally, servant leadership promotes a positive work climate, enhances quality of work life, leads to employee wellbeing, and reduces burnout and work family conflict. Only one study demonstrated no consistent influence of servant leadership on organizational performance (de Waal & Sivro, 2012). In conclusion, the conceptual and empirical evidence for the positive influence of servant leadership on a whole host of outcomes is very consistent and positive. However, there are several important caveats. The number of studies is small and their methodological scope and breadth limited, especially when contrasted with other areas of leadership research. There is also potential publication bias for servant leadership.

Studies in closely related domains are consistent with positive servant leader empirical findings. For example, a meta-analysis of emotional intelligence (EI), which incorporates many of the behavioral elements of servant leadership such as empathy, found that EI was a significant and major predictor of job performance (O'Boyle et al., 2011). Another interesting study on companionate love in a long-term care facility found a favorable influence on employee outcomes including job satisfaction, teamwork, absenteeism, and emotional exhaustion as well as beneficial patient effects related to mood, quality of life, satisfaction, and fewer emergency room visits (Barsade & O'Neill, in press).

Table 1.2 Servant leader empirical literature summary

Organizational Studies Supporting Favorable Influence/Correlation of Servant Leadership: Job Attitudes

- *Affect and Cognitive Trust*: Schaubroeck, J., Lam, S. S. K., & Peng, A. C. (2011); Senjaya, S., & Pekerti, A. (2010)
- *Commitment*: Cerit, Y. (2009); Ehrhart, M. G. (2004); Hale, J. R., & Fields, D. L. (2007); Han, Y., Kakabadse, N. K., & Kakabadse, A. (2010); Jaramillo, F., Grisaffe, D. B., Chonko, L. B., & Roberts, J. A. (2009a); Jaramillo, F., Grisaffe, D. B., Chonko, L. B., & Roberts, J. A. (2009b); Liden, R. C., Wayne, S. J., Zhao, H., & Henderson, D. (2008); Pekerti, A. A., & Sendjaya, S. (2010); Schneider, S. K., & George, W. M. (2011); van Dierendonck, D., & Nuijten, I. (2011)
- *Commitment to Change*: Kool, M., & van Dierendonck, D. (2012); Taylor, T., Martin, B. N., Hutchinson, S., & Jinks, M. (2007)
- *Disengagement*: Hunter, E. M., Neubert, M. J., Perry, S. J., Witt, L. A., Penney, L. M., & Weinberger, E. (2013)
- *Empathy*: Washington, R., Sutton, C., & Feild, H. (2006)
- *Engagement*: Parris, D. L, & Peachy, J. W. (2012); Prottas, D. J. (2013)
- *Interactional Justice*: Kool, M., & & van Dierendonck, D. (2012)
- *Interpersonal Trust*: Chatbury, A. A., Beaty, D. D., & Kriek, H. S. (2011)
- *Organizational Trust*: Jones, D. (2012b); Jones, D. (2012a); Joseph, E. E., & Winston, B. E. (2005); Reinke, S. J. (2004); Rezaei, M., Salehi, S., Shafiei, M., & Sabet, S. (2011); Senjaya, S., & Pekerti, A. (2010); Uru Sani, F. O., Caliskan, S. C., Atan, O, & Yozgat, U. (2013); Washington, R., Sutton, C., & Feild, H. (2006)
- *Procedural Justice*: Chung, J. Y., Jung, C. S., Kyle, G. T., & Petrick, J. F. (2010); Ehrhart, M. G. (2004); Walumbwa, F. O., Hartnell, C. A., & Oke, A. (2010)
- *Satisfaction*: Barbuto, J. E., & Wheeler, D. W. (2006); Cerit, Y. (2009); Chung, J. Y., Jung, C. S., Kyle, G. T., & Petrick, J. F. (2010); Jenkins, M., & Stewart, A. C. (2010); Jones, D. (2012b); Mayer, D. M., Bardes, M., & Piccolo, R. F. (2008); Mehta, S., & Pillay, R. (2011); Prottas, D. J. (2013); Schneider, S. K., & George, W. M. (2011); van Dierendonck, D., & Nuijten, I. (2011)
- *Self-Efficacy*: Walumbwa, F. O., Hartnell, C. A., & Oke, A. (2010)

Organizational Studies Supporting Favorable Influence/Correlation of Servant Leadership: Leadership & Supervisor Attributes

- *Commitment to Supervisor*: Walumbwa, F. O., Hartnell, C. A., & Oke, A. (2010)
- *Leader Competence*: Mayer, D. M., Bardes, M., & Piccolo, R. F. (2008); McCuddy, M. K., & Cavin, M. C. (2008); Washington, R., Sutton, C., & Feild, H. (2006)
- *Leader Development*: Melchar, D. E., & Bosco, S. M. (2010)
- *Leader Trust*: Joseph, E. E., & Winston, B. E. (2005); Reinke, S. J. (2004)
- *Satisfaction with Supervisor*: Ehrhart, M. G. (2004)
- *Supervisory Support*: Ehrhart, M. G. (2004)

Organizational Studies Supporting Favorable Influence/Correlation of Servant Leadership: Work Behaviors

- *Collaboration*: Garber, J. S., Madigan, E. A., Click, E. R., & Fitzpatrick, J. J. (2009); Irving, J. A., & Longbotham, G. J. (2007); Sturm, B. A. (2009)
- *Community Citizenship*: Liden, R. C., Wayne, S. J., Zhao, H., & Henderson, D. (2008)

Continued

Table 1.2 Continued

- *Employee Creativity and Helping Behavior*: Barbuto, J. E., & Wheeler, D. W. (2006); Jaramillo, F., Grisaffe, D. B., Chonko, L. B., & Roberts, J. A. (2009b); Neubert, M. J., Kacmar, K. M., Carlson, D. S., Chonko, L. B., & Roberts, J. A. (2008)
- *Empowerment*: de Waal, A., & Sivro, M. (2012); Taylor, T., Martin, B. N., Hutchinson, S., & Jinks, M. (2007)
- *Organizational Citizenship*: Ebener, D. R., & O'Connell, D. J. (2010); Ehrhart, M. G. (2004); Hu, J., & Liden, R. C. (2011); Long-Zeng, W., Eliza Ching-Yick, T., Pingping, F., Ho Kwong, K., & and Jun, L. (2013); Neubert, M. J., Kacmar, K. M., Carlson, D. S., Chonko, L. B., & Roberts, J. A. (2008); Walumbwa, F. O., Hartnell, C. A., & Oke, A. (2010)
- *Organizational Learning*: Choudhary, A., Akhtar, S., & Zaheer, A. (2013)
- *Servant Follower Development*: Parris, D. L, & Peachy, J. W. (2012)
- *Turnover*: Babakus, E., Yavas, U., & Ashill, N. J. (2011); Hunter, E. M., Neubert, M. J., Perry, S. J., Witt, L. A., Penney, L. M., & Weinberger, E. (2013); Jaramillo, F., Grisaffe, D. B., Chonko, L. B., & Roberts, J. A. (2009a); Jones, D. (2012b); Prottas, D. J. (2013); Schneider, S. K., & George, W. M. (2011)

Organizational Studies Supporting Favorable Influence/Correlation of Servant Leadership: Performance Outcomes

- *Firm Performance*: Barbuto, J. E., & Wheeler, D. W. (2006); Jones, D. (2012a); Peterson, S. J., Galvin, B. M., & Lange, D. (2012)
- *Goal and Process Clarity*: Hu, J., & Liden, R. C. (2011); Taylor, T., Martin, B. N., Hutchinson, S., & Jinks, M. (2007)
- *High Performance Attributes*: de Waal, A., & Sivro, M. (2012)
- *In-Role Performance*: Liden, R. C., Wayne, S. J., Zhao, H., & Henderson, D. (2008); van Dierendonck, D., & Nuijten, I. (2011)
- *Profit*: Jones, D. (2012b)
- *Team Effectiveness*: Hu, J., & Liden, R. C. (2011); Irving, J. A., & Longbotham, G. J. (2007); Joseph, E. E., & Winston, B. E. (2005); Reinke, S. J. (2004); Schaubroeck, J., Lam, S. S. K., & Peng, A. C. (2011); Senjaya, S., & Pekerti, A. (2010)
- *Team Potency (Confidence or Efficacy)*: Chung, J. Y., Jung, C. S., Kyle, G. T., & Petrick, J. F. (2010); Hu, J., & Liden, R. C. (2011)

Organizational Studies Supporting Favorable Influence/Correlation of Servant Leadership: Character Elements

- *Hope*: Searle, T. P., & Barbuto, John E., Jr. (2011)
- *Integrity*: Washington, R., Sutton, C., & Feild, H. (2006)
- *Loyalty*: Ding, D., Lu, H., Song, Y., & Lu, Q. (2012)

Organizational Studies Supporting Favorable Influence/Correlation of Servant Leadership: Personality Attributes

- *Agreeableness*: Hunter, E. M., Neubert, M. J., Perry, S. J., Witt, L. A., Penney, L. M., & Weinberger, E. (2013); Washington, R., Sutton, C., & Feild, H. (2006)
- *Extraversion*: Hunter, E. M., Neubert, M. J., Perry, S. J., Witt, L. A., Penney, L. M., & Weinberger, E. (2013)

Continued

Table 1.2 Continued

Organizational Studies Supporting Favorable Influence/Correlation of Servant Leadership: Employee Quality of Work Life & Health Related Outcomes

- *Burnout*: Babakus, E., Yavas, U., & Ashill, N. J. (2011)
- *Employee Wellbeing*: Jaramillo, F., Grisaffe, D. B., Chonko, L. B., & Roberts, J. A. (2009b); Reinke, S. J. (2004); van Dierendonck, D., & Nuijten, I. (2011)
- *Health*: Prottas, D. J. (2013)
- *Life Satisfaction*: Prottas, D. J. (2013)
- *Positive Work Climate*: Black, G. L. (2010); Jaramillo, F., Grisaffe, D. B., Chonko, L. B., & Roberts, J. A. (2009a); Neubert, M. J., Kacmar, K. M., Carlson, D. S., Chonko, L. B., & Roberts, J. A. (2008)
- *Stress*: Prottas, D. J. (2013)
- *Vitality*: van Dierendonck, D., & Nuijten, I. (2011)
- *Work/Family Conflict*: Prottas, D. J. (2013)
- *Work/Family Enrichment*: Zhang, H., Kwan, H. K., Everett, A. M., & Jian, Z. (2012)

Organizational Attributes and Studies Not Supporting Favorable Influence/ Correlation of Servant Leadership

- *Firm Performance*: de Waal, A., & Sivro, M. (2012)

Limitations and Critiques of Servant Leadership

One key element of the discussion is to rebut the varied and conflictual stereotypes and misinformation regarding servant leadership. Three of the most common are that servant leadership is "soft" management with lower degrees of leadership influence and direction, a reduced emphasis on employee discipline, and that servant leaders possess a martyr complex. Servant leadership is love-based, but entails a 360-degree version of love that incorporates grace and accountability, forgiveness and discipline, autonomy and clear boundaries. One cannot be a servant leader and not achieve the mission and discipline the workforce. In effect, servant leaders cultivate a culture of performance excellence that *increases* demands on employees (Reinke, 2004; Irving & Longbotham, 2007; Prosser, 2010; Sendjaya, 2010). Servant leaders facilitate the meeting of true employee needs, but do not cater to their desires and wants that are contrary to their wellbeing and mission integrity. Finally, servant leaders are not martyrs. They actively promote self-care and work-life harmony and balance. In the pages to come, we will more fully define servant leadership in its full balance and harmony.

From a methodological standpoint, there is an absence of agreement on the specific elements and core dimensions of servant leadership (Northouse, 2013). However, this reflects the inherent complexity of servant leadership and its holistic and unique combination of leadership motivation, character, behavior, and reasoning abilities. Hence, it will take many years of sustained study to confirm the basic attributes and the many moderator and mediating relationships.

The explicit prescriptive, normative, and moral emphasis of servant leadership is another source of conflict (Northouse, 2013). It is utopian in essence. However, all theories and approaches of leadership promote a worldview of values, norms, and moral principles. They range from the secular to the religious and spiritual. Hence, there is no neutral or values-free form of management; therefore, they are all similar in this regard. For many who embrace servant leadership, it is a deontological moral imperative, hence the absence of motivation for empirical research. However, a full understanding of servant leadership recognizes the elements of stewardship and mission achievement, hence the need for promoting excellence of performance and character. Empirical research on servant leadership is moving forward and becoming more robust.

Another issue relates to the interface between contextual and cultural elements, leader and follower attributes, and follower receptivity (Northhouse, 2013; Liden et al., 2008; van Dierendonck, 2011). In other words, do employees manifest a universal desire and/or receptivity to servant leadership? Given the contingent nature of leadership (Northhouse, 2013), differing goals due to mutually exclusive truth claims, and inherent human variability, clearly the answer is no. There is limited empirical evidence on the subject, but Meuser et al. (2011) found higher levels of performance and organizational citizenship when subordinates desired servant leadership and lower levels when subordinates lacked interest. For both leaders and followers, the underlying motivational element is critical given the obstacles and challenges associated with servant leadership. Ng and Koh (2010) provide a "motivation-to-serve" model incorporating personality traits such as agreeableness and conscientiousness, which are positively associated with servant leader motivation, while neuroticism is negatively correlated with servant leader motivation. The second element of the model is the value orientation with self-transcendence (benevolence, equality) promoting the motivation-to-serve while self-enhancement (power, achievement, hedonism) attenuates the altruistic motives associated with servant leadership.

Clearly, the receptivity and effectiveness of servant leadership is maximized by a compatible organizational culture fully integrated into the HR system through its mission, vision, and values. In essence, the HR system's decision making process links personnel decision making to servant leader mission, motivation, character, and behavior.

Laub (2005) and Herman (2008) assessed the organizational culture of one hundred organizations, classifying them into autocratic, paternalistic, and servant leader (Laub, 2010). Only 14 percent of the studied organizations received classification as servant leader oriented, as most were a mixture of paternalistic (55%) and autocratic (31%) (Laub, 2010). However, even in those situations in which the culture and employee attributes conflict with servant leadership, the astute servant leader adjusts his or her leadership approach to honor and accommodate subordinate preferences, while not violating key principles such as promoting the best interests of employees. Hence, the leader maintains the core elements of servant leadership while patiently adjusting to organizational climate. Over time, servant leadership can increase trust and build relationships, thereby changing subordinate attitudes, as the vast majority of employees desire dignified and fair treatment. In essence, an organizational microclimate of receptivity to servant leadership organically develops.

One final question relates to the international comparative scope of servant leadership. Servant leadership practice is global in scope, finding support in a variety or religious and philosophical worldviews (Bekker, 2010). The research indicates cultural differences related to power distance, but a high level of consensus on the "Golden Rule" dimensions (Irving, 2010).

Human Resource System Functions

Traditionally, the HR function entails two global components, the first of which is the formal personnel system that supports various line and staff service delivery functions. For larger organizations, a central HR department with a full-time HR director performs these duties and services. For mid-size organizations, the organization typically assigns these functions to a sole HR director. For smaller organizations, an executive director in a nonprofit, a city manager in a local government, or a supervisor in a business assumes the HR mantle. HR functions include employee and volunteer staffing, compensation and benefits administration, health and safety programs, employee rights and discipline, and training and development programs, among others.

The second, and more important, aspect of HR relates to the direct day-to-day management of the service delivery system including individual, group, and organizational performance management and all of the associated functions to lead, manage, and motivate engaged and productive employees. The success of any organization is largely dependent on the conformance of the organization's culture and practice to SLHRM principles regarding the quality of employee selection and training, the provision of an adequate infrastructure (equipment, supplies) and ethical and effective supervision. A high level of employee motivation requires the creation of a workplace that meets the employee's physical, emotional, and spiritual needs in conjunction with an appropriate mix of incentives. Workers who exert the required level of effort in the accomplishment of individual and organizational goals and work outside of their job description (organizational citizenship) when needed to help other employees and clients are indicators of a healthy HR management system.

This book targets both HR professionals and line managers and leaders who must use and navigate the HR system to promote high performance. SLHRM entails developing performance management policies and practices that honor the "triune towers" of support, accountability, and integrity. Employee support entails the adoption of workplace policies and practices that sustain quality of work life and instill hope. Employee support also entails a "speaking truth in love" or "tough love" motivational, conduct, character, and performance-based accountability framework. SLHRM organizations imbed accountability within a value system that infuses the healthy pursuit of excellence with authentic forgiveness and grace policies. Support and accountability, in turn, leans on the pillar of integrity and the authentic implementation of the espoused values.

Human Resource System Integrity

The worst incarnation of SLHRM espouses the values but with a failure to engage authentically and practice those principles. This gap between policy and practice engenders a "witch's brew" of dashed expectations generating a poisoned atmosphere of cynicism, destroying trust and "ship wrecking" the faith of subordinates, peers and clients. As such, this book illustrates the SLHRM policies and practices that produce the positive fruits of an ethical work environment including loving, engaged, and committed employees working with excellence to achieve the organization's mission.

SLHRM unswervingly commits to a covenantal relationship with each employee. The foundation of a workplace covenant is the commitment to a long-term relationship founded upon mutual obligations, accountability, and trust. These include cultivating a high quality of work life including meaningful work, servant leader management, and leadership practices, dignified employee treatment, fair compensation, safe working conditions, and an assurance of long-term job security. From the employee perspective, this entails working skillfully, faithfully, honestly and diligently in all circumstances, working outside of the job description when needed, assuming responsibility for solving workplace problems, honoring the authority and dignity of leaders, treating co-workers and clients with respect, and committing to an appropriate degree of innovation and creativity.

A great example of a leadership covenant is that of John Beckett (CEO of Beckett Corporation, which manufactures oil and gas burners) who models the importance of "word and deed integrity" and the commitment to the "ministry of interruptions" in which we deviate from our schedule to help others. Mr. Beckett takes time from his busy schedule to visit hospitalized employees. When the CEO personally touches employees, it provides validation of the stated policies and becomes the source of positive internal referrals. As satisfied customers can be your best sales advocates, the same principle operates for your employees who become organizational ambassadors with personal testimonies of good will acts of care and kindness.

SLHRM embraces a combination of deontological (principle-based ethics) and teleological (greatest good) attributes. When conflicts between servanthood principles and utilitarian stewardship objectives develop, the SLHRM organization makes the conscious choice to adhere to deontological principles irrespective of the cost. An instructive example is Chick-fil-A founder Truett Cathy and his courageous decision to close stores on Sunday, which strongly conflicted with the prevailing retail and marketing wisdom. By choosing to honor his religious beliefs regarding the Sabbath, Mr. Cathy concurrently demonstrated his care for the wellbeing of employees with a guaranteed day of rest. Chick-fil-A is now one of the most profitable fast-food franchises. When we practice SLHRM integrity in spite of the obstacles, we are demonstrating our genuine commitment. It is important to understand that following the correct path does not always lead to short-term or long-term success. Oftentimes our commitment produces failure as the world defines it, but we sleep soundly with a clear conscious.

A SLHRM-guided organization rejects the compartmentalization of morality, integrity, and ethics at both the individual and organizational decision-making levels. We cannot promote an engaging organizational culture unless our motives, means, and ends honor both the letter and spirit of integrity and obedience. As *we* serve the needs of others, we ourselves grow in maturity, wisdom, and character. The authentic incorporation of SLHRM generates a cultural environment of excellence, innovation, and creativity (van Dierendonck & Rook, 2010). When the organization views employees, clients or customers as instrumental means to an end, it is very easy to move to a relativist ethical position. Maintaining a SLHRM focus requires great faith, courage, and perseverance as managers and leaders are under intense pressure from many sources including:

1. The ascendency of post-modernism and moral relativism.
2. The erosion of civility and professionalism in the workplace.
3. Loss of confidence in the ethics and integrity of organizations in all sectors, given high-visibility scandals.
4. The graying of the labor force and the challenges of succession planning.
5. The challenges of managing generational differences in the workplace.
6. Ongoing fiscal stress and a stagnant economy.
7. Global competition in the market economy.
8. Skill shortages in many highly skilled occupations.
9. The challenges of securing qualified, motivated and long-term volunteers for nonprofits and churches.
10. The increasing levels of competition for the limited pool of charitable donations.
11. Declining government funding in conjunction with increasing service demands.
12. The need to demonstrate clear return-on-investment (ROI) with a declining resource base.
13. Maintaining and building management capacity given resource constraints.

There is a clear need for authentic and passionate leadership based upon SLHRM love and integrity to address these challenges. When the organization is experiencing stress and tribulation, the leader must rise above the confusion and model hope and confidence. The HR function sets the tone and provides the supportive environment for employee engagement.

Crisis is a great test of character. The lesson for SLHRM leaders is to maintain mission integrity in the presence of great fiscal and management pressures and to avoid compromising key values and principles. It is critical to reinforce that organizations can "gain the world but lose their souls (a Christian biblical reference to Mark 8:36)" with the many tempting paths of expediency to relieve short-term pressures. This book reinforces that the ability to maintain a consistent mission focus centers upon two elements. The first is the internal moral integrity of the leaders, managers, employees, and volunteers who have internalized the mission, vision, and values, while the second is a SLHRM led and directed HR system.

In all sectors, it is important to assure employees, volunteers, clients, and customers that their respective investments in the organization are wise and generate appropriate returns. SLHRM enhances management capacity, accountability, and transparency, and is an important means for overcoming the damage wrought by the various well-publicized organizational scandals in business, government, and the nonprofit world. However, instituting SLHRM policies and practices can provide a false sense of security if there is not a sustained long-term commitment to their genuine implementation. External accountability of performance and ROI is an essential element, and those who are committed to excellence of character and competency do not fear or resent the scrutiny of outside stakeholders.

General Principles of SLHRM

I want to reassure the reader that the general principles of SLHRM are not mysterious and esoteric forms of wisdom discoverable and known only to a few after years of search and study; rather, they are Golden Rule values of human conduct written in the heart. The foundation for this principle is the Christian theological concept of "common grace" in which God universally instills rules of conduct that promote harmony and peaceful relations (see http://www.theopedia. com/Common_grace).

The great challenge is authentically implementing SLHRM principles given the many temptations to promote narrow self-interest and embrace the path of expediency and moral relativism. Hence, SLHRM knowledge is necessary, but not sufficient, to endure authentic integration. A sobering reality is that knowledge of SLHRM principles generates a higher level of accountability. It is better to be ignorant of effective SLHRM practices than to espouse them and fail to authentically implement.

Another key element of SLHRM, humility, is recognizing that our knowledge level of good management practices frequently exceeds our ability to implement and practice what we know is right. The only appropriate response is an attitude of humility. We must consistently practice SLHRM in both letter and spirit to produce enduring trust. The insincere application of SLHRM destroys faith and credibility. When leaders fail, it requires a much longer time of sustained excellence to restore confidence and heal the wounds of distrust.

A foundational element of SLHRM integrity requires that motives, means, and ends must be ethical and moral. Frequently leaders and managers embrace a utilitarian view of their role and rationalize that the "ends justifies the means." Leaders frequently fail both to model and teach SLHRM, hence stifling employee growth. SLHRM emphasizes the significance of character, encouraging employees to recognize the importance of authentically practicing altruism and the ability to delay gratification. A foundational element is establishing the basic SLHRM principles of trust based upon relationship credibility, and the belief that the leader doing the communicating is operating from a motive of love. Traditional leadership approaches entail the use of power, judgment, and control to motivate, contradicting SLHRM principles. Even more tragic is that many leaders who espouse servant leadership operate from a situational ethics perspective in which servant leadership is used when convenient, but abandoned when interests are threatened. Adherents of SLHRM must demonstrate in "word and deed" a different spirit that will break down the skepticism and cynicism. When leaders and managers claim that their HR system centers on servant leader principles, but fail to honor the pledge through consistent, good faith application, we in effect discredit our own witness. As SLHRM managers, we are only credible ambassadors through our words of Golden Rule love and deeds. We win adherents by our good works and through "loving our neighbor" in the workplace.

Why is SLHRM such a critical process? Most organizations underinvest in HR, given that they are lulled into a false sense of security based upon their lack of need of it when the organization was smaller. HR problems begin to increase in size and scope as the organization grows. First, the HR system reflects and influences the organization's theology of work and human nature. Our HR leadership worldview exerts the most powerful influence on the quality of work life. For example, does the organization embrace a grace-based and empowerment-oriented confidence in human nature, viewing mistakes, and failures as critical components of the learning process, or does it hold that workers, because of their selfish and egocentric natures, require rigid discipline and close supervision to reduce errors and increase productivity? Do we trust employees to act ethically and morally, reducing the need for detailed surveillance and oversight, or do we possess a cynical view of human nature and a need to monitor carefully every keystroke? Hence, SLHRM is a foundational component of both organizational effectiveness and quality of work life. Unless we treat employees with dignity and respect, the organization labors in vain.

Golden Rule Character is the Foundation of SLHRM

A major focus of this book is on SLHRM workplace character, and one of our greatest temptations is to compartmentalize our allegiance to servant leadership, resulting in moral hypocrisy. In essence, the servant leader character-building process is a holistic, united, and integrated commitment in all life areas. The first step in the character-development journey is a genuine heart conversion to "die to the self." It is important to grasp the humbling breadth and depth of the challenge in order to generate the requisite level of humility. In the paragraphs that follow is a five element model of servant leader character. The foundational elements include:

- *Servant leader knowledge, which is the ongoing growth process of gaining a "heart and mind" familiarity, awareness, and understanding of servant leader moral principles from a theory and practice perspective.* Knowledge is primarily cultivated through active study, modeling and mentoring. One of the key elements of servant leader character resides in the practice of humility regarding knowledge. Knowledge divorced from a humble heart inflates pride and ego leading to arrogance, complacency, and overconfidence. The more knowledge we accumulate, the greater our accountability for its application—along with a higher intensity of struggle to apply what we learn. There will always be a gulf between what we know and our ability to apply and live it consistently, given human moral weakness and limitations; therefore, the only rational response is a modesty and meekness of spirit.
- *Belief is a free-will agreement regarding the legitimacy and efficacy of servant leader moral principles.* However, knowledge and belief is a necessary but not a sufficient condition, as intellectual agreement does not suffice. An example relates to forgiveness. We may know that forgiveness reduces anger and dysfunctional stress and believe that it produces beneficial health and spiritual effects, but choose the spirit of revenge over the moral principle.
- *The motives for our actions are the foundational servant leader moral character elements.* Vain and self-serving motives can give birth to grand and noble actions in the eyes of the world and vice versa. The

foundational servant leader moral motivational principle is the integration of love into all life domains. One of greatest character challenges is cultivating the desire and practice of discovering the true impetus and nature of our motives through ongoing self-awareness analysis. This struggle reflects the continuing powerful nature of self-deception regarding areas of motivation and weakness that accentuate the short-term costs and minimize the benefits for failing to address the true root cause of our problems and motives.

- *The employment of moral means and ends as our actions and behavior should possess deontological (principle-based integrity) and teleological integrity (utilitarian) which promotes the greater good for the key stakeholders.* Servant leaders pursue moral goals and ends out of obligation and duty as well as loving obedience and conviction. Honoring these two principles is very challenging, especially when they conflict. For example, performance appraisal systems frequently clash between the requirements for accurate and honest evaluation from a broad set of sources (deontological integrity for procedural and measurement fairness) while not penalizing employees for factors beyond their control (teleological integrity).

Wisdom is the ultimate fruit of servant leader character. It entails self-awareness, mature decision making, and reasoning skills that honor the higher order principles as we face nuanced value conflict situations. For example, in situations in which there is equal evidence or justification for forgiveness and discipline in the workplace, it is important to ponder and reflect how to promote the higher order principle of accomplishing the mission while meeting the needs for growth, learning, and the best interests of the affected employees. In some instances, the situation warrants forgiveness, while in others, discipline or termination is the appropriate course of action. In many cases, it will be both elements to provide a balance between discipline and encouragement. Fully developed servant leader character is not a final destination but a lifelong journey of growth and learning, incorporating our weaknesses and strengths, our temperaments, gifts, abilities, and accomplishments as well as our abject moral failures. There are many foundational character attributes necessary for success in SLHRM, but six are particularly important (as reflected in the servant leader literature reviewed in table 1.3): love, humility, transparency, forgiveness, hope and perseverance, and empathy and compassion. Our times of trial and the hidden temptations of success are two of the most difficult times for the practice of SLHRM. In the midst of trial, the natural tendency is to remove one's eyes from the moral and ethical compass and focus on the circumstances, while in

Table 1.3 Key SLHRM character elements essential for success

SLHRM Christian Character Attribute Scenarios

Love: The SLHRM led manager embraces the practice of love that is the ability to integrate the goals of achieving the mission with moral integrity while promoting the development, growth, and wellbeing of employees. Love entails righteous and moral motivation and action regardless of emotional state and the manager's personal experiences and feelings toward employees. Love entails the dual elements of delaying gratification and altruism in the course of work duties placing the needs of others first. For example, a City Manager of a small local government must learn to overlook past betrayals by City Council members and department heads who attempt to make deals independently. He must actively mentor and prepare the Assistant City Manager to assume his duties, hence making himself dispensable. In addition, the City Manager must protect his subordinate from undue political interference at the risk of his job security.

Humility: Humility is a foundational character attribute. Humility is essential for servant leaders to avoid the twin poisons of pride and fear. True SLHRM humility is the recognition that success and higher performance is the product of the synergies of committed team members and an inherent understanding of the manager's strength and weaknesses. Hence, humble managers are secure in their identity and perceive no threat when others perform well. In our City Manager example, the humble City Manager actively appoints subordinates that complement his strengths and weaknesses and empower them to succeed.

Transparency: Transparency is a key character element that supports humility. Transparency is the consistent courage to share all types of information, positive and negative, regarding character and performance. When SLHRM managers practice transparency, it sends a clear signal that the manager welcomes open and honest feedback, thereby facilitating problem solving and driving fear from the workplace. For example, when our SLHRM city manager makes mistakes regarding the accuracy of budget forecasts, he accepts responsibility, apologizes for the negative consequences, and openly discusses how he and organizational practices can improve. He does not attempt to externalize the blame or create excuses.

Forgiveness: SLHRM managers understand that personal and organizational wellbeing requires the genuine embrace of forgiveness. Mistakes, failure, weakness, and betrayal are a ubiquitous element of the human condition. Hence, SLHRM managers make the conscious choice to forgive others for their errors, and themselves for their contributions. Forgiveness applied with wisdom drives fear out of the workplace. The wise SLHRM City Manager will publicly recognize employees with good faith attempts that result in failure, thereby helping to promote learning and eliminating the fear of failure.

Hope and Perseverance: The SLHRM manager understands that hope is the foundation of perseverance under stress. SLHRM managers communicate a genuine and contagious optimism and confidence that provides a rationale for employee sacrifices and a vision of a better future. Hence, the SLHRM manager is a "lighthouse" projecting a beacon of hope in the midst of organizational storms. Our city manager demonstrates his solidarity with employees in times of fiscal stress by first absorbing budget cuts through reductions in his and the other executive team's pay levels. He then charts a course of shared shouldering of the necessary budget cuts while empowering employees to restructure service delivery to enhanced efficiency and effectiveness to reduce job losses.

Continued

Table 1.3 Continued

Compassion and Empathy: SLHRM managers understand the importance of understanding the experiences, needs, motives, and problems of their employees. If they are to serve and lead effectively, they need to take into understand the "worldview" of those they serve. For example, our SLHRM city manager understands the workload levels and working conditions of employees, and strives to maintain fair and sustainable staffing and performance expectations that reduce employee stress. This enables employees to avoid the perils of "compassion fatigue" in which they lack either the energy or motivation to help other employees or customers.

---

times of success we remove our gaze as well and focus on our own resources, power, and effort—a pride of self-sufficiency. From a global perspective, all of these character attributes are rooted in *agapao* love, or moral love, which is the inherent desire to do the right thing for the right reason at the right time (Winston, 2002; Patterson, 2010). SLHRM is a motivational system that explicitly rejects using fear as a motivator, and love is the main antidote to fear (Patterson, 2010; Ferch, 2010).

Challenges in the Application of SLHRM Principles

In order for us to be credible SLHRM ambassadors, we must demonstrate in word and deed that SLHRM entails a transformational worldview that changes hearts and minds. The workplace is a wonderful setting to demonstrate unconditional love. Our workplaces are not monolithic. There are many organizations in which managers and employees create a SLHRM "microclimate" work environment embedded within workplace cultures that exploit employees. Increasing income inequity and the erosion of the middle class generates powerful economic pressure on employees, given stagnant wage levels and lower advancement opportunities. In addition, given the high levels of unemployment, employers strive to increase productivity and limit hiring, increasing performance expectations on the remaining employees.

We cannot routinely apply these SLHRM values, principles, and practices as they are neither a mantra that one can chant nor a blueprint applicable in a mechanical fashion. In order for a transformation to occur there must be a genuine commitment. Enlightened managers embrace SLHRM and its associated character traits, values, and principles in all settings. It is a question of a passionate will and heart commitment to stay the course, and pay the inevitable short- and long-term costs associated with adopting a covenantal relationship. As servant leaders, the adoption of SLHRM does not guarantee organizational success; but in many cases, SLHRM is antithetical in our pursuit of short- and long-term career success. Are we willing to pay the price for righteousness?

Hence, a major challenge to SLHRM is that the term "servant leadership" creates mixed feelings given inaccurate understandings of its nature. Servant leadership is not "soft" pandering to employees on one spectrum or a martyr complex at the other extreme. Servant leadership promotes both servanthood and stewardship, thereby positively transforming both individuals and institutions.

We must be cognizant of both the "letter and the spirit" of our management actions and decisions. Organizations adopt SLHRM "best practice" policies for a variety of reasons. Some organizations embrace these tools for their teleological (instrumental) benefits and others for their symbolic and political effects. Organizational researchers Bolman and Deal (2003) developed a framework for analyzing organizational behavior and one of the lenses utilized was viewing the organization as a "theater." Organizations adopt SLHRM practices for external and internal audiences to reassure them that they are progressive, informed, and competent. These practices frequently morph into what are termed "Potemkin villages" that look real from a distance but are merely structural facades with no foundation or root for implementation. It generates what Chris Argyris (1961) terms a discrepancy between espoused theory and the theory in use. Just because an organization lists SLHRM as a foundational element of its mission, vision and values statement, there is no automatic internalization of these values, hence the potential for an institutionalized hypocrisy to permeate the entire organization. Compartmentalization of SLHRM values inhibits growth and change.

One of the underlying reasons for the "policy and practice" gap is that humans are egocentric and are inherently more interested in promoting personal goals and interests over that of clients, employees and other key stakeholders. This battle reflects the never-ending inner struggle with self-interest in conjunction with the pressures of external stakeholders and the conflicting values of alternative management worldviews. If one adopts SLHRM management practices in an organization founded on command and control (Theory X) principles, there is an inherent conflict resulting in "double-minded" practices with disappointing results.

Servant Leader Human Resources Management (SLHRM): Summary of Foundational Principles

SLHRM practices are designed to meet our seven basic needs of (1) conferring dignity, (2) providing the necessary authority to complete tasks, (3) offering encouragement and provision that blesses employees, (4) job and relationship security, (5) clear and compelling purpose and meaning, (6) the appropriate balance between freedom/autonomy and accountable boundaries, and (7) intimate love and companionship (Hillman, 2000). The integration of these principles occurs throughout the remaining book chapters. This list is not exhaustive but, in the author's view, it encompasses the key elements of SLHRM that contribute to the healthy development of all organizational members.

SLHRM Foundational Values, Principles, and Practices

1. *All HR practices should promote the balancing of stewardship in effectively and efficiently achieving the mission with honor and integrity and servanthood by promoting the best interests and legitimate needs of the key stakeholders.* Achieving both goals is necessary for successful SLHRM. To achieve each goal, leaders must separate the "best from the good." It is impossible to achieve stewardship and servanthood without setting clear priorities and following them with laser-like devotion.

2. *Set high standards of performance to communicate, recognize, and cultivate organizational confidence in the inherent capacity of every employee to achieve exemplary levels of human growth and excellence.* This entails setting and maintaining high standards of performance with the appropriate degree of organizational support (resources, time, training, patience, empathy, etc.).

3. *Balance many competing values, recognizing the importance of confronting and resolving conflict in an ethical and moral manner.* The goal is to promote an organizational decision-making process that requires management to analyze fully the broad consequences of organizational decisions from multiple perspectives and values to promote the wellbeing of all organizational members and other key stakeholders. The foundational principle is that the promotion of the good requires the practice of humility. This allows us to listen clearly to the position of others without rushing to judgment and imposing our view of reality on them. Once we more fully understand the motives and contextual circumstances, we

will be in a better position for mutual exploration of the common interests and the identification of the conflicting interests and the short- and long-term consequences for failing to resolve, and the benefits to, a resolution. There must be a firm commitment to resolving conflict ethically, including direct discussion and negotiation. We must always contemplate the consequences of organizational policies from a broad framework. For example, if the work environment is overly demanding, employees often abuse sick time, given the need to take "mental health" days. The aggregate effect of individual decisions to be absent from work imposes costs on the collective workforce. Hence, the value of providing support for employees in times of illness begins to clash with the obligation to provide reasonable workloads. Clearly, the Golden Rule applies here. When an employee has a genuine need for time off (sickness, family crisis), the organization should accommodate. However, if organizational policies are producing excessive stress levels, leaders possess an obligation to address the root cause to avoid externalizing costs to other employees. I am not arguing for a purely utilitarian decision making process, only that balancing values in conflict situations is important.

4. *Practice moral intelligence, which entails possessing a comprehensive knowledge of ethical and moral leadership principles, a heart-based belief in their efficacy, authentically practicing them, and making decisions with wisdom.* Wisdom-based decisions entail the achievement of the mission through moral motives, means, and ends even in the presence of conflicting values and principles.

5. *All HR decisions must pass the Golden Rule love test.* Regrettably, unrighteous motives birth many righteous actions. From a moral accountability standpoint, righteous actions driven by self-interest fail to meet the test. Hence, SLHRM leaders manifest a ruthless commitment to self-examination to discern what is in our hearts. This self-appraisal, though painful, results in the necessary character growth that produces the stewardship and servanthood commitment that places employee needs in the proper perspective, producing great fruit. When employees believe that leadership actively pursues their best interests, they are more patient and forgiving of management mistakes and errors of omission and commission.

6. *The intentional, systematic, and sustained cultivation of moral character to promote a healthy and righteous work environment that fosters employee growth and wellbeing, thereby reducing dysfunctional stress, conflict, and suffering.* The ultimate goal is an

organizational environment that manifests healthy interpersonal relationship characterized by love, joy, peace, patience, kindness, goodness, faithfulness, gentleness, and self-control, the fruits of the spirit as found in Galatians 5:22–23. SLHRM reinforces the importance of character growth and integrity, recognizing that character weaknesses will eventually erode employee gifts and abilities. SLHRM practices must encourage and reward the basic character virtues of love, honesty, transparency, humility, forgiveness, and hope and immediately address character or ethical violations in the spirit of "love the sinner, hate the sin." Competence without character is like a young child behind the wheel of a very expensive and fast car, someone is going to get hurt! Accountability partners are essential elements for SLHRM character growth and are a tangible demonstration of our humility and teachability. We can run from these painful episodes of character development, but we cannot hide. If we are not patient and do not learn from our mistakes, we simply lengthen the time of our development. Self-interest and pride easily corrupts virtue if humility and vigilance are absent. We learn the most in trial and suffering, but are tempted to the greatest degree in success. We must ruthlessly subject our motives to internal review and discernment. Power and success corrupts subtly and incrementally with the heart ungrounded in the truth. Servant leadership is a constant struggle!

7. *Cultivate spiritual transcendence and support through voluntary and non-coercive prayer, meditation, and other related spiritual and religious practices.* Irrespective of one's personal belief system regarding the existence of God or a higher power, all of humanity possesses an inborn need to transcend and find greater meaning and purpose in their work. We are spiritual beings, and it is important to provide means for collective and individual spiritual growth. It is imperative, however, that all spirituality-based initiatives be 100 percent voluntary with no formal linkage to organizational decision making and employee treatment.

8. *Model a passionate commitment to integrity, promoting a harmony between HR policy and practice.* Nothing erodes organizational member trust more quickly than perceived or actual hypocrisy. The foundational element is to use righteous means and pursue moral ends.

9. *Viewing the organizational relationship as a covenant.* A covenant entails a mutual commitment to a long-term relationship with reciprocal obligations and benefits. Management is the "good shepherd" providing a supportive, secure, loving, accountable,

safe, and challenging work environment. In return, employees work with excellence, passion, and loyalty. However, today's labor market is very different from that of the past. The labor market structural and technological changes over the last forty years have reduced the power and influence of unions and the bargaining power of individual workers. Management holds a higher degree of power and influence. However, SLHRM organizations do not exercise arbitrary and capricious power given they recognize that they have a moral obligation to promote the best interests of employees. Given management's enhanced power due to the nature of globalization, there is a great temptation to impose more demanding work performance standards with reduced levels of compensation. This will intensify conflict in the workplace and requires SLHRM organizations to resist the temptation to take advantage of employees with their enhanced leverage.

10. *Provide each organizational member with purpose, meaning, significance, and dignity by clearly linking each position with the greater mission, vision, and values of the organization.* Every organizational member must understand the importance and contribution of his or her job to fulfilling the mission, thereby instilling significance and a clear sense of self-respect. The janitor is as important as the CEO! Servant leadership is the foundation for successful management. It is the "path less traveled." A clear example of this principle is Servicemaster Corporation a company that possesses word and deed integrity in terms of employee treatment. For example, their hospital cleaning staff understands their critical role in hospital mission accomplishment by being the first line of defense against infectious disease (See http://servicemastertr.com/healthcare/). When employees recognize that they are valued not for what they produce, but for who and whose they are, it creates bonds of trust and love. In addition, the good will produced generates tremendous marketing and "word-of-mouth" recruiting, increasing the applicant pool.

11. *Demonstrating trust in organizational members through transparency of management information.* This entails openness regarding the process and outcomes of HR and budgetary decisions. Transparency entails providing access to organizational policies, practices, studies, and databases as well as the ability to engage in ongoing two-way communication. The key is provide sufficient information to inform, but with appropriate contextual explanation to avoid generating undue optimism, pessimism, or complacency. Nature fills a vacuum, and the informal network

(the grapevine) and the rumor mill will fill the gap. By providing an appropriate amount of information on a need-to-know basis, this retards the development of rumor-mongering that sows fear, discord, and distrust.

12. *Aspiring to the highest degree of organizational fair treatment through policies and practices that promote procedural, distributive, and interactional justice.* In essence, SLHRM organizations invest heavily in developing an organizational culture in which the HR and general performance management systems consist of policies and practices that on average produce a fair decision-making process and decision outcomes. This entails conscious and consistent commitment to "testing the spirit" governing the individual, group, and collective influence of organizational decision making. One of the key means of assessing the efficacy of the decision-making process in promoting justice is a systematic and ongoing action-research process consisting of interactive information gathering methods, including surveys, focus groups, and interviews and justice audits, to examine sources of inequity and their remedies. SLHRM organizations generate and use this data to support the organizational and learning empowerment process. Employees participate in gathering and analyzing data while organized into teams to develop solutions to problems and capitalize on opportunities.

13. *The consistent rejection of instrumental worldviews.* People are not resources, and organizations are not living beings. Never reduce organizational members and other stakeholders to abstract instruments or costs of production. When organizations view employees or other stakeholders in an instrumental fashion, it anesthetizes our conscience and permits decision makers to rationalize policies and practices that dehumanize workers and produce a pernicious fruit of human suffering. The pressure of competition enhances the presence and intensity of instrumental worldviews. Hence, it is critical for SLHRM organizations to embrace a moral understanding and application of competition. However, there is much confusion about competition. What is a moral view of competition? These elements include a love-based root motive for all actions, a set of decision rules that promote fair and ethical means to achieve goals, with the ultimate aim to improve the human condition in some aspect, either spiritual or material. As such, competition at any level rarely meets the pure standards of morality. Moral competition stimulates innovation, creativity, and learning in the competing organizations,

rejecting a war mentality of "taking no prisoners." We strive for excellence, but we do not compete against others in a zero-sum fashion. The goal is to perfect our skills, abilities, and character traits as the competition process simultaneously enhances the wellbeing of our competitors. In essence, we are competing against ourselves as we all grow and generate an expanding pie or rising sea benefiting our consumers and clients and the larger quality of life in the community. Hence, competition is a loving and grace-filled exercise in which we realize that we learn as much or more from failure as we do from success. We confuse moral excellence and worldly excellence much too frequently. We must learn that moral "winning" entails humility and practicing forgiveness.

14. *SLHRM leadership entails sacrificial acts of obedience and service.* We cannot learn to lead effectively until we learn to serve. Before leaders ask for sacrifice from other stakeholders, leadership must voluntarily "die to the self," and adopt and apply the policy to their own job situations first. Therefore, when fiscal stress requires service or HR reductions, upper management is the first level to undergo meaningful and painful cutbacks. "Good shepherds" sacrifice for the good of the flock. There is a moral obligation for collective responsibility and sharing of the pain. Without concrete measures of shared sacrifice by management, employees become cynical on any form of management accountability.

15. *Embrace a moral commitment to value the individual employee.* The comforting news is that honoring SLHRM principles does not require us to change the world as individuals operating under our own power. We may not be able to alter the culture of our organization singlehandedly, but we do exercise a potent influence as a manager or colleague as we practice SLHRM within our zone of responsibility and influence. We honor both the letter and spirit of our organization's mission by ministering to our employee flock and providing Good Samaritan assistance to the wounded on our path. Research and personal experience demonstrate that individual managers and groups of employees can create a SLHRM microclimate embedded within the global instrumental organizational culture. Our actions do revolutionize the world of our subordinate employees and peers, one person and small group at a time.

16. *Passionately pursue and practice the moral and good irrespective of the outcome.* To be a true "hearer and doer" of SLHRM principles, we must humble ourselves and unconditionally accept the

results. True SLHRM love trusts not in a result, but in a relationship. If we love our employees, we will choose to pursue righteous actions irrespective of the conclusion.

17. *Promote a holistic understanding of leadership accountability grounded first on high standards of personal accountability.* This entails accepting responsibility for organizational problems and mistakes before focusing on others. Change begins with the leader. SLHRM leaders reject the knee-jerk response to assign responsibility and blame to employees for poor performance and resistance to change, which is frequently the result of ineffective management, the manager's own resistance to change, and other contextual factors beyond employee control. SLHRM managers actively seek out the external factors that inhibit success first before assigning responsibility to employees.

18. *The use of organizational capital punishment (layoffs or termination) is an option of last resort.* The decision to terminate or lay off organizational members entails a profound ethical and values-based dilemma on multiple levels, from the inherent morality of separating organizational members in a time of economic recession, to the impact on families and the community, to the procedural justice implications (the fairness of the process and its associated criteria), and the distributive justice consequences (who is deserving of a layoff).

19. *A key SLHRM principle is honoring our moral obligations to the poor. This entails a commitment to generating wealth for community investment and providing jobs.* This responsibility demonstrates internalization of the Golden Rule to address our loving duty to the needy and the downtrodden. SLHRM organizations do not "glean their fields" and extract every penny of value from their employees. They invest generously in training and employment opportunities to enhance the human capital of their low-wage workers. In the private sector, many investors support the social entrepreneurship model promoting a broader set of values other than short-term profit. This type of investing supports long-term wealth creation and a more responsible business community. We need to invest in others for the long term, not for a quick and superficial "return." The roots of poverty are an amalgam of social, political, economic, cultural and most importantly, spiritual antecedent roots and causes. Hence, poverty is a classic systems issue at the individual, family, community, regional, national, and world levels, reflecting the cumulative

effects of flawed and immoral individual and collective decisions. One implication is undertaking a concerted effort to provide jobs and other income-generating opportunities for the poor. The key is to offer meaningful work to reinforce the dignity, confidence, and self-sufficiency of the poor. Hence, it is important to link poverty and charitable programs to some form of work effort for the able-bodied.

Performance Management Elements

1. *Cultivate and reward the demonstration of SLHRM courage and reasonable risk-taking.* Let us first define SLHRM courage by what it is not. It rejects self-aggrandizing behavior and decisions that promotes personal gain or advancement, notoriety, or adrenaline pumping "organizational mountain climbing." SLHRM courage and risk-taking is another powerful manifestation of love that places the manager's position at risk to promote the altruistic completion of the mission, facilitate the growth and well-being of others, and/or protect them from harm (Meade, 2014). This type of courage and risk taking is a rationale process based upon careful advance planning, a reasonable level of risk, and consultation with others.

2. *SLHRM organizations consistently and genuinely empower and develop their employees.* This entails adopting a systematic succession-planning process, power sharing and delegation, mentoring and coaching programs, individual development plans, and adequate resource support and release time for training and education activities. Below are key elements of empowerment from a SLHRM standpoint.

    a. Commitment to succession planning and leadership dispensability by mentoring successors.

    b. Practice humility by assuming the role of an altruistic mentor consciously developing others to exceed our talent, ability and performance levels.

    c. Reject inappropriate performance comparisons and dysfunctional personal competition that promotes pride, fear, and envy.

    d. Help others unbury their talents and use them appropriately.

    e. Take joy when others succeed and sorrow when they fail, even those that that oppose us.

    f. Serve supporters, detractors, and betrayers with love and excellence.

3. *Promoting servant followership in which organizational members accept responsibility for solving problems, exercising initiative, helping coworkers and clients even when inconvenient or contrary to personal interests.* Servant followership entails committing to excellence irrespective of the obstacles and situation. Servant followers understand their strengths and weaknesses and select jobs or positions based upon their gifting and passions, thereby reducing stress on themselves and others. The true test of servant followership occurs when management or others fail to honor their commitments. Servant followers honor their portion of the covenant by loving others unconditionally and serving just and unjust managers. They "take the road less traveled" and embrace a commitment to mission achievement irrespective of the obstacles and the personal cost.

4. *Cultivating SLHRM excellence over self-promoting management approaches.* SLHRM excellence entails four factors: honoring the macro goals of stewardship and servanthood, the presence of moral motives, giving our best efforts regardless of the circumstances, and learning from our mistakes and correction from others. One of the greatest snares for SLHRM leadership is adopting instrumental standards of success (i.e., goal achievement, power, influence, reputation, money, resources) to replace the stewardship and servanthood standards. It is important that SLHRM organizations reject embracing the criteria of the marketplace to measure their success. I urge SLHRM organizations to embrace the higher standards represented by the Kingdom Business movement that provides a relevant example of viewing profits as means, and not as ends (Regent University Center for Entrepreneurship, 2014). The Kingdom Business movement provides an alternative worldview on the role of commerce and the associated standards of excellence. SLHRM excellence encompasses most of the main elements of secular business success (profit, growth), but we must communicate that profit and sales growth is not a terminal objective or value, but an intermediate performance metric and resource in meeting the important needs of the client or customer, providing jobs, improving communities, and developing employees. A foundational principle is that profit for private business and net revenue for nonprofits and government is not an end, but a means to mission accomplishment. The goal is to improve the physical and spiritual human condition. Hence, SLHRM organizations reject sophisticated marketing campaigns to generate or stimulate superficial desires or to distort and manipulate ethical and moral

motivation. For example, private companies often use marketing by stimulating the passions in three global areas: (1) fear and anxiety over losing quality of life elements such as health, (2) pride, competition, comparison, and a spirit of envy (keeping up with or exceeding your neighbor or peer group), and (3) cultivating a hedonistic and materialistic lifestyle. These marketing passions transform luxuries into necessities, which are really "desires" based upon lusts. For faith-based organizations and nonprofits, the manipulation takes on more subtle forms including: (1) exaggerating the degree of relationship and relevancy between the organization's mission and the donor's interests, passion, and motivation for giving, (2) exaggerating the ROI from donations, and (3) manipulating donor emotions through exaggerated appeals and the use of graphic images of suffering.

5. *Promote sustainable and balanced workload and effort levels that challenge but do not overwhelm employees, thereby reinforcing a balanced set of life priorities.* SLHRM leaders reinforce and cultivate moral life priorities (life balance) rejecting "idol worship" work habits. The organization's mission, vision, and values reinforce a well-ordered set of life and work priorities ensuring that employees possess adequate time and energy for family responsibilities, personal refreshment, and church and community service. SLHRM leaders do not set unhealthy examples of organizational effort, encouraging idol worshiping workaholic behavior. Even though leaders may be able to sustain the 60-hour-week pace, many organizational members will fall by the wayside. An example is vigorously promoting balanced attendance policies that encourage employees to reduce or eliminate presenteeism (working while ill) and remain at home until well.

6. *Promote work-life balance by providing employees with flexible work schedules (compressed workweek, flex time), virtual workplace, non-traditional career paths (job sharing, part-time), regular sabbaticals, and generous family-friendly benefits (child and elder care assistance).* These policies reduce work and life stress for employees and their families. SLHRM employers authentically promote access to these programs and do not penalize employees for participating. Many organizations offer these benefits, but either discourage their use or view employees that utilize them as less committed and loyal. Other elements include providing Employee Assistance Plans (EAP) and wellness programs to promote preventive health care, physical fitness, weight-loss and disease-management programs for existing illnesses.

7. *Driving fear and perfectionism out of the organization through promoting the healthy pursuit of excellence and a culture of forgiveness.* This requires the redefinition of excellence as a long-term character and competency growth building process that by definition requires mistakes, errors and setbacks. Organizations should encourage, recognize, and reward members for good faith failures through forgiveness policies and formally recognize and thank members for their efforts and sacrifice. A workplace based upon fear leads to "burying" our talents because we are afraid of the punishment that comes with mistakes. Management by fear inhibits creativity and produces a climate of compassion fatigue in which we are too tired or fearful to step outside of our protected zone and help others.

8. *Develop challenging but reasonable SMART goals (specific, measurable, attainable, relevant, timely) and standards with employee input and participation.* SLHRM leaders do not impose unreasonable performance expectations regarding the quantity and quality of work, nor do they create role conflict situations (quantity versus quality) in which mutually contradictory expectations frustrate and discourage organizational members. Goal setting is the most effective motivational approach as it incorporates elements of both intrinsic and extrinsic motivation. When we set challenging SMART goals, it focuses limited time and energy and helps employees avoid distractions. When those goals are accomplished, it produces a sense of intrinsic accomplishment and satisfaction. It also provides the foundation for the explicit linkage of goal attainment to organizational monetary and non-monetary goals.

9. *Promoting accurate weights and measures, which is a reference to using accurate metrics in all forms of interactions and transactions, including our interpersonal relationships.* In the performance appraisal process, this entails measuring performance accurately and fairly with minimal amounts of criterion contamination (e.g., includes non-job related factors such as race) and deficiency (fails to include important elements of performance such as quality). Praise and encouragement is not withheld (a form of theft) thereby discouraging employees and tempting them to anger, given the absence of accurate character and performance corrective feedback that demonstrates a genuine love and concern.

Employee Development Principles

10. *SLHRM organizations treat contingent (temporary, contract, and part-time) workers with equal levels of respect, dignity, and support*

as full-time employees. This entails rejecting any manifestation of "second class citizenship." The organization's treatment of contingent and part-time workers is another "window on the soul." Fair treatment equates with internal and external compensation equity, safe working conditions, an effective human capital investment infrastructure (orientation, training, and development), a valid and reliable performance management system, and ongoing encouragement and gratitude for their contributions and performance.

11. *SLHRM organizations treat volunteers with equal levels of respect, dignity, and support as full-time employees.* This entails providing such elements as clear job descriptions, regular performance feedback and performance appraisals, and ongoing encouragement and recognition, comprehensive orientation and training sessions. "Word of mouth" marketing is an organization's best friend or worst nightmare. The treatment of volunteers is another "window on the soul" and a formal volunteer management plan will produce a more effective volunteer program with higher return-on-investment.

12. *Promote a long-term, grace-based view of employee development.* SLHRM leaders patiently coach, mentor, and develop employees for the long term. They empower and encourage them to learn from mistakes and failures, thereby using these painful situations as the catalyst for learning and character growth. Many organizations begin with good intentions, but are not able to escape the implicit value and belief system that focuses on short-term performance at the expense of long-term development. Just as people pleasing and affirmation-anxiety can bind individuals, organizations can be bound to the fear of violating the expectation of clients, customers, donors or other key stakeholders for short-term gain. It requires strength of collective will and character to promote a long-term perspective and delay gratification. Patience is a foundational element of humility and empathy. Without patience, we are unable to reach out to others and take the time to understand their hidden pain and problems. It takes time to develop character, and its absence sabotages all of our gifts, abilities, and accomplishments. It is like a cancer that is starving us from the inside. A major moral intelligence discipline is teachability, and one means for demonstrating our humility is voluntarily placement under the authority of an accountability partner. We must be willing to learn from others and receive discipline and corrective feedback. Forgiveness policies are consistent with

the notion of a covenant relationship with mutual obligations and support. When an employer forgives an employee for a major mistake, it increases trust in management and is consistent with the SLHRM ethos.

13. *Invest in all employees, not only the elite superstars.* SLHRM organizations recognize that every employee is worthy of appropriate growth and development opportunities according to their talents, performance, career and life goals, purpose, and needs. The objective is not a radical egalitarianism, but a celebration of the inherent gifts that each employee brings to the workplace. Long-term success requires the careful cultivation of individual and group work skills, both hard and soft. Success is always a collective, not an individual product.

14. *Place employees in areas of natural gifting, abilities and passions.* Performance excellence is a natural by-product when SLHRM organizations select and place employees consistent with the employee's gifts and abilities. Organizational selection decisions based on matching employee gifts, passion, and ability levels with job requirements produces significantly greater harmony levels. In addition, it is much easier to raise performance in areas of strength and giftedness than to remediate areas of weaknesses. The exception is the talents that we "bury" given the hurts, traumas, fears, and strongholds in our lives. I know this from my personal experience. When I was a freshman in college I took the Strong Interest Inventory test and discovered much to my chagrin that the two highest professions were teaching and the ministry, a strange combination for an atheist! I realize now that the mental illness produced by a stressful family environment bound me with fears and insecurities that kept me from using my talents and gifts. I am grateful to God that I was able to move forward in spite of my fears in such areas as public speaking. The point is that we have many gifts that remain dormant until the appropriate time—and this occurs at all ages. As Bolles (2013) in his classic book *What Color is Your Parachute?* noted, when we operate consistent with our abilities, gifts and passion we are able to meet the critical needs in others that only we can supply.

15. *Adopt a teamwork perspective, facilitating healthy individual employee and team development.* This entails providing team-building training and developing performance management and compensation systems that provide an appropriate balance between individual, team and overall organization performance.

Employees often receive excessive degrees of credit or blame for system and group performance issues. It is a challenging process to separate out the individual from the group influences, but a concerted effort will produce a more valid and reliable performance measurement process.

16. *Engage in systematic workforce planning efforts that entail providing employees with adequate training programs, including individual development plans and individual learning accounts.* SLHRM organizations recognize that employees are the foundation of the organization, hence the need to demonstrate through significant resource investment that the organization is systematically committed to cultivating employee growth. Employees are reassured of their employer's commitment by training and development investment. This is even more important with the erosion of the traditional "psychological contract" of long-term job security in return for loyal and satisfactory performance.

17. *A genuine commitment to an expanded definition of diversity that transcends, race, and gender and includes a full range of human attributes.* This includes religion and spirituality in addition to the traditional elements of race, gender, age, and disability status. The focus is on enhancing awareness and understanding of how subtle cultural conventions and practices disadvantage traditional minorities. The goal is to promote a culture of excellence in which only character and competency are the major factors that promote career development.

The great challenge with these SLHRM principles is not their great complexity of understanding, but with the many obstacles, both internal and external, to their genuine and consistent implementation. Hence, a significant portion of this book addresses the implementation obstacles and means for overcoming.

Conclusion

The master list of SLHRM attributes reflects key principles providing an architectural blueprint for moral motives, means, and ends. The goal is not a legalistic adherence, but a genuine commitment to SLHRM principles. It is a very demanding standard, the path less traveled, but it is clearly the road that produces the most long-term moral value. The other key element is to recognize that adherence to these principles does not guarantee success. In many cases adherence to SLHRM principles results in resistance, ridicule, persecution, and failure. The conventional and SLHRM definitions of success are very different. If you honor SLHRM principles irrespective of the outcome, there will be great fruit produced. The remaining chapters will more fully elaborate and develop these challenging concepts.

SLHRM Leadership Personal Character Reflection: Hope and Realism

But it is not so among you; but whoever wishes to become great among you must be your servant.
        The Bible, Mark 10:43, New Revised Standard Version (NRSV)

Servant leadership is not an "off-the-shelf" management tool routinely and thoughtlessly applied in any setting. True servant leadership is a "pearl of great value" as evidenced by our own lives. How many authentic servant leaders have you known? I can count the number on one hand. It is the path less traveled, requiring a ruthless commitment to serving others while dying to the self. We must be persistent, founded upon a deep-seated commitment to stay the course and pay the inevitable short- and long-term costs associated with adopting a covenantal relationship. Yes, as servant leaders we must love and bless those who persecute us. Can you serve those who betray you? As servant leaders, the adoption of these values does not guarantee worldly achievement, and in many cases, is antithetical to career success in the short or long term. Are we willing to pay the price for righteousness?

The comforting news is that we do not need to change the world as individuals operating under our own power. We may not be able to alter the culture of our employer, but we do exercise a powerful influence as a manager or colleague as we practice servant leadership and followership within our zone of responsibility and influence. We honor servant leadership by ministering to our employee flock and providing Good Samaritan assistance to the wounded on our path. Research and personal experience demonstrates that individual managers and groups of employees can create a microclimate of servanthood embedded within the global instrumental organizational culture. Our actions do revolutionize the world of our subordinate employees and peers. So do not weary in your well doing as that one employee you mentor is of great value and can "pass it forward" to others. A lifetime of employee discipleship efforts will bear great fruit, changing the lives of many. This occurs both through the cumulative numbers of individuals we influence and by the fact that just one person inspired by our example can influence millions. Servant leadership can be contagious!

SLHRM Leadership Personal Character Reflection: Recognizing and Combating Comparison Envy

One of the great cardinal servant leader virtues is thanksgiving for two key elements, our present circumstances and our gifts and abilities. One of the factors that rob our ability to accept ourselves as we are is comparison envy.

I need not remind you that organizations are competitive, even "cutthroat," by design and through human nature. As servant leaders, we are called to compete, but against what and whom? One key to uncovering the truth is grasping the nature of servant leader excellence. Excellence entails four factors: adherence to and effectiveness in achieving the mission, the presence of ethical and moral motives based upon love (the desire of the heart), giving our best efforts regardless of the circumstances, and exhibiting genuine remorse and learning from our mistakes. It is a personal standard of individual accountability based upon how well we use our unique abilities, gifts, talents, and opportunities. Servant leaders do not grade on a curve nor compare their employees against each other! The standard of analysis is not the absolute or relative amount and nature of my talents, gifts, and advantages, but how well I use what I possess given the obstacles, weaknesses, and flaws in my imperfect nature. I term this our "spiritual altitude." Each of us operates within our own unique set of past and present life circumstances that impede or enhance our life fruit. For example, those who are operating with the legacy of childhood abuse operate at higher altitudes with lower levels of spiritual oxygen. Let us take the issue of interpersonal comparison first.

From a moral perspective, the only appropriate standard is that of personal humility. Interpersonal comparison generates pride if we feel superior, envy if we perceive inferior, and complacency if we are at the same level. Our only standard for comparison is recognizing that we are all unique, worthy, and that the process of assessment is inherently fraught with "measurement error."

The deception lurking beneath the comparison process is that people who are more productive, intelligent, charismatic, successful, and attractive (and so on and so forth) are better or more worthy than we are. On the other side, superiority breeds a false sense of security and pride. In essence, we are rebelling against nature by expressing dissatisfaction with how we are. These vain comparisons can become a life orientation that increases our feelings of vulnerability as we conform to the world's standards instead of servant leader ideals. In some instances, we bury our talents out of fear, experience lifelong frustration as we live someone else's life, while in other situations we use our gifts in ways that conform to family or cultural expectations, but violate our own internal passion and standards of excellence. An important principle is to recognize that providence endows each of us with unique talents and abilities. If we deny our inimitable design, we negate what only we can provide to others!

As a final dose of humility, keep in mind none of us can take credit for our accomplishments, gifts, or abilities. Like the analogy of the body, each part (person) is essential to the whole. We need the individual with two talents the same as those endowed with ten or more. Our obligation is to be faithful stewards of what we receive. Do your best and strive to develop your talents to be the best you can be. Learn from others, but do not try to place your round peg in their square hole. Take joy in the accomplishments of your coworkers, as their success does not diminish your accomplishments and talents. Using a baseball analogy, the team needs the reliable .250 hitter as much as it does the superstar with the .350 average. Finally, realize the great value that servant leaders place on those who are humble and promote the interests of others over their own. Servant leaders possess an honest estimate of themselves and their employees! When the focus in the workplace shifts from individual players to a team approach, we experience the freedom and joy of discovering our true selves. So let us all commit to using servant leader faith as the measuring stick for all that we think, say, or do.

Chapter 2

Servant Leader Human Resource Management Organizational Integrity

Elements that Erode Organizational Integrity

One of the great battlegrounds in organizations relates to the integrity issue. The practice of SLHRM is challenging in both the servant leader and greater leadership world. We will face great moral temptations to adopt instrumental standards to achieve success. It requires great character strength to resist the powerful incentives to compromise our values. The human heart is deceptive, and we fail to see the traps, snares, and value compromises that on the surface appear righteous. It is important for SLHRM organizations to work collaboratively to create a culture of virtuous motives, means, and ends in all aspects of HR practice. These enclaves demonstrate the love and power of servant leadership as a viable alternative to instrumental leadership worldviews. However, regrettably, even some SLHRM-espousing organizations practice SLHRM principles and the Golden Rule with less passion and faithfulness than nonadherents do.

One of the most humbling aspects of leadership is to recognize that as shepherds of the flock, we possess a great responsibility not to discourage our employees and tempt them to react in anger. Many managers are oblivious to the fundamental servant leader worldview understanding of leadership that assigns great moral accountability for being the source of temptation. How do managers tempt employees to act on anger and other negative emotions? The answer to that question requires more than a dissertation solely devoted to the subject, but I will endeavor to introduce several fundamental principles. First, we tempt our employees to anger when we fail to provide the necessary encouragement and recognition. In essence, we "steal" the intrinsic heart rewards that are essential for stimulating ongoing motivation and the promotion of hope in difficult circumstances. Most employees report a drought of job-related feedback disheartening to their resolve and eroding of their commitment by the lack of acknowledgment. When we fail to recognize good performance, we are using dishonest scales and stealing from employees! Servant leadership calls us to encourage and support others. In addition, we are failing to use what research deems the most effective motivator: honest and heartfelt praise and encouragement!

Second, we tempt our employees when we fail to provide the necessary discipline to correct poor performance and improve behavior. Servant leaders must discipline; undisciplined employees, like uncorrected children, will operate in a spiritual vacuum, testing the boundaries until they are broken in spirit and body.

Third, we tempt employees to anger and bitterness when we develop in-group and out-groups in the workplace with unequal treatment not based upon character and performance, but upon the manager's arbitrary likes and dislikes. We must be no respecter of persons and treat all according to their character and faith.

Fourth, we tempt employees to higher levels of distrust and cynicism when there is a gap between policy and practice. The absence of consistency between words and deeds shipwrecks the faith of many employees. If we promote empowerment in policy, but in practice only support employee decisions that validate or rubber stamp a preordained management decision, we promote organizational hypocrisy.

We can all relate to flawed human nature at work in our organizations. When there is a higher degree of ethical conduct from non–servant leaders, this serious situation erodes the credibility of our witness. What factors seem to contribute to this paradox? One element relates to the hardness of our hearts impeding our growth. We can be an advocate of servant leadership, but still subject to the same moral and emotional weaknesses as others. Given the higher stakes, there is a great degree of temptation and attacks directed at the weaknesses of servant leaders.

The great temptation for SLHRM-oriented leaders in general is to embrace a cynical and skeptical attitude with the inevitable disappointments and betrayals that organizational life produces. Hypocrisy is one of the most serious and moral and ethical violations from almost any perspective and produces a powerful set of negative emotions, attitudes, and behaviors (Cha & Edmondson, 2006). A major contributing factor for this issue is the absence of emphasis on 24/7 integrity in all life domains. When we compartmentalize and rationalize our actions by selectively choosing when to practice servant leadership based upon the situation and the outcomes, we embrace the ruling worldview, situational ethics based upon self-interest. We all encounter compromising situations and it takes great character strength to stay the moral path when logic and circumstances shout loudly to embrace the more expedient option.

Organizational Justice Elements

What are the key elements that contribute to organizational hypocrisy? Servant leadership demands a higher standard of accountability. Clearly the foundation is a gap between policy and practice, being a "hearer and doer," but in leadership terms, being a "sayer and a doer." A useful research-based framework that relates key aspects of HR policy and practice to hypocrisy is that of organizational justice. SLHRM organizations embrace fairness as a foundational value at all levels (individual, work group, collective). Fair employment laws related to discrimination provide a floor on employee treatment, but do not address the heart-based trust issues related to everyday employer-employee relationships.

The three main components of organizational justice are distributive, procedural, and interactional. Procedural justice refers to the overall fairness of organizational decision making processes (Skarlicki & Folger, 1997; Beugre & Baron, 2001). For example, are performance appraisal decisions supported by a comprehensive array of evidence and sources? Does the employee have the option to participate and rebut evidence or information that is inaccurate? Distributive justice relates to the fairness of the outcome associated with HR related decisions (McFarlin & Sweeney, 1992). Was the pay increase a fair reflection of the employee's contributions? Interactional justice relates to the fairness of employee treatment by supervisors (Cropanzano et al., 2001). Do supervisors bully, harass, and humiliate employees, or are they treated with respect and dignity? The magnitude, scope, and effect of deficiencies in organizational justice dramatically increase if management espouses values of fair treatment but fail to implement accentuating perceptions of hypocrisy. What are some of the common factors that contribute to these visceral feelings of hypocrisy?

One key constituent element of hypocrisy is judgmentalism. Judgmentalism can take many forms. One manifestation is speaking truth not in love to better the relationship, but as means to exalt the self, while controlling and manipulating others. Unless the underlying motive is love as broadly defined to promote the best interests of others, we have a "log in our eye." The sins, problems, and weaknesses of others draw us like moths to a flame, and we fail to see our own transgressions and feebleness. Our "righteous anger" and self-blindness is usually greatest in those areas in which we share the same sin, weakness, or tendency as the person who is the target of our judgment. As stated in Shakespeare's *Hamlet* "thou dost protest too much." We need to assume responsibility for their contribution to a problem before "pointing the finger."

The highly competitive nature of securing financial resources for all types of organizations poses another great threat to organizational integrity, contributing to an "ends justify the means" ethical framework. As customers, donors, and the taxpayers demand more evidence of ROI, there is a corresponding increase in pressure to demonstrate results. This generates greater incentives and temptations to cheat or "fudge" the numbers in terms of program performance, administrative costs, and other measures of financial accountability unless a commitment to moral integrity is at the center of the organization's DNA. These pressures cause employees to lose respect for the integrity of management while providing great temptations for personal moral compromise. Hence, many servant leaders are being subject to greater external oversight. SLHRM-directed managers need not fear the looming hazard of increased oversight from either governmental regulation or other accountability enforcing agencies as SLHRM organizations thrive on transparency and accountability.

Combating the Culture of Apathy and Defensiveness

When employees perceive high levels of management hypocrisy, a pernicious outcome is disengagement and apathy. SLHRM organizations must address and attack this culture of disengagement as reflected in the infamous cliché, "It's not in my job description." Following is a litany of phrases that reflect this poisonous mindset:

- "That's how we have always done things here."
- "I am too busy to help others."
- "I was following orders."
- "It was not in my job description."
- "I have to balance the needs of many competing interests and stakeholders."
- "Helping the client would have adversely influenced mission accomplishment."
- "That's what the rules state."

There are many factors contributing to this malady in addition to hypocrisy, and one key element is the "culture of fear" incentive structure management produces with the imposition of punishment for failures and mistakes. This practice contributes to a culture of defensiveness that reduces motivation, creativity, and innovation. As SLHRM organizations and leaders, we must clearly identify and remedy the long-term self-defeating nature of this culture of fear. Another reason is compassion fatigue that occurs when employees are overworked, overwhelmed, discouraged, and "burnt-out," thereby lacking the energy and compassion to step outside of their job description.

It is a great challenge to overcome employee apathy and the mindset of compartmentalization that problems are "someone else's responsibility." Even if there is an office or a designated person to assume responsibility for a problem issue, SLHRM organizations cultivate values and behaviors that encourage employees to assume ownership and become a champion until the problem is resolved. When management and employees hide behind the rules, it is a collective organizational failure. SLHRM leaders must address several key questions when employees fail to assume accountability and operate outside of their job description.

First, what is the root cause of the problem? In some instances, the problem may not be motivational as much as ambiguous performance management through unclear job descriptions, imprecise standard operating procedures, an absence of performance standards, and blurred lines of authority. However, if these factors are not present and employees are working to the letter of the rules and hiding behind process, then an attitudinal cause is likely.

Another key factor is the degree of value internalization. Crisis is a powerful crucible for assessing our moral foundation. SLHRM organizational culture reinforces the necessity of responding to adversity in a manner consistent with the values of altruism and of placing the needs of the mission and others over self-interest by delaying or denying our self-gratification. Our greatest learning opportunities occur under trial, stress, and interruptions when we are not able to operate on autopilot, protect the ego, or engage in image management. Even under the most favorable conditions the ultimate direction and underlying ethical orientation is only as strong as the character of the participants. Internalizing values is an essential factor to influence positively behavior in a crisis, as there is little or no time to think and reflect given the urgency of action.

Unless the character predisposition of altruism and denying self-gratification becomes second nature, there will be an absence of authenticity. Hence, a key question that management should ask is the degree to which Good Samaritan behavior characterizes management and employees. Do we promote ethical conduct by external processes (rules) or by informal group norms? Conversely, is ethical conduct a function of internal character and integrity (heart-based)?

Varying degrees of ambiguity are inevitable in SLHRM decision making, but a consensus on the foundational principles and shared values is the basis for clear decision rules to guide the decision-making process. For example, when faced with a need to reduce the budget, should we lay off employees (high cost imposed on a smaller group) or freeze wages for all (collectivizing the pain). What does it mean to "love your neighbor as yourself" in this situation? In today's highly stressful workplace with many employees strained to the limits of human endurance, it is very difficult to be altruistic without a common recognition that we are both interconnected and interdependent. For example, the military strives to produce highly cohesive, tight knit groups that will risk their individual lives to accomplish the mission. Individuals are valued, and fellow soldiers will endanger their own lives to save others if there is a reasonable chance of success. We need to embrace this same mentality with our organizations.

One key issue that this problem raises is how leadership worldview influences behavior. Our worldview provides the foundational values and principles that comprise the normative ethics employed in a specific situation. Two common normative ethical positions are teleological, which focuses primarily on promoting the greatest good in a utilitarian fashion, and deontological, which primarily focuses on the ethical correctness of the means (Macdonald & Beck-Dudley, 1994; Takamine, 2002). A balanced, ethical decision maker attempts to satisfy both approaches, often leading to the inherent ambiguity associated with complex decision scenarios. Servant leaders must internalize a deontological (servanthood) perspective, but incorporate relevant teleological reasoning (stewardship reasoning) into our decision calculus. For example, we often face conflicting ethical values related to the employee discipline process. We must balance the principles of grace and correction. In situations that justify suspension according to the rules, we need to weigh the overall context, mitigating circumstances, and the counsel of wise advisors. From a teleological perspective, the suspension may be necessary to promote the overall good order and workplace productivity for successful mission achievement, but an enduring deontological principle of forgiveness and grace overrides discipline in this instance.

The Trust Gap and Its Causes

Trust is a valuable and scarce commodity in today's Darwinian organizational cultures. Trust is cultivated through a long-term relationship. As the dictum states, it is easier to destroy than create. Unfair management actions quickly and efficiently demolish trusting relationships that take years to build. SLHRM managers frequently must clean up the "messes" that management leaves in the lives of employees. It places HR in a difficult position of attempting to assuage angry, hurt, and cynical employees with no decision authority to alter policy. HR managers must exercise high levels of spiritual and emotional intelligence to look beyond the pain and hurt of employees, and help them overcome the negative emotions that inhibit effective management.

Trust is one of the most precious commodities in the workplace and the most important form of organizational "currency." One of the pernicious products of employees stripped of their dignity and low on trust is an apathetic and disconnected emotional state. Employee surveys indicate that only about a third of workers report high engagement with their work (Gallup, 2013), and irrespective of the locus of the responsibility in terms of labor and management, we all pay a high price in lost productivity and poor client services for employees who are alienated for their jobs (Tsui et al., 1997). One of the consequences of the loss of trust is cynical employees that are angry, bitter, and apathetic. As a result, some employees assume an aggressive or passive-aggressive posture, engaging in overt and covert rebellious or aggressive behaviors to restore a semblance of control and vindicate "eye for an eye" behavior. Hence, even when the employer demonstrates good faith, the cynical attitude taints how employees view all management actions given that negative attributions are more salient.

When a climate of distrust is present, employees interpret an ambiguous situation consistent with their overall global attitude. For example, in a union and management conflict situation, labor views the organization's fiscal problems as a ruse or a pretext to squeeze more concessions from suffering employees. Hence, management only cares for the bottom line and views employees not as human beings but as costs to reduce in order to increase profit and shareholder value. Conversely, if there are harmonious relations, employees perceive the exact situation differently. Fiscal stress becomes an opportunity for joint problem solving to preserve the health of the organization as a whole. Communication and transparency are key factors in shaping trust and accurate perceptions. What are some of the factors that reduce trust?

One pernicious practice is the "disposable employee" syndrome adopted by many organizations in all sectors. The "throwaway worker" policy is the equivalent to "slash and burn" agriculture. Employers demand great work effort and high levels of performance but fail to "fertilize the soil" with a sustainable workload, fair treatment, comprehensive investments in employee training and development, long-term job security, and the cultivation of work-life balance. This produces a pernicious product of burned-out, cynical employees lacking trust, leading to high organizational turnover. The absence of job security creates and elevates long-term stress, reducing employee motivation, morale, and performance. A natural discouragement effect reduces confidence and trust. Hence these organizations seek to maximize short-term gains for the lowest present investments (low present costs for high present benefits), while SLHRM organizations are covenant investors understanding that long-term success requires higher upfront costs in supporting and sustaining employees for greater long-term fruit (ROI).

A second trust-reducing practice is the absence of management transparency in conjunction with micromanagement and high management surveillance levels and/or electronic monitoring. An employee has a reasonable right to privacy, and it is important that employers do not demand an excessive and intrusive level of oversight that communicates management distrust of employee motivation, ability, or character. With an absence of employee privacy, it generates a global affective and cognitive atmosphere of insecurity and vulnerability. It is critical for employers to possess a more comprehensive information base for decision making, but not at the expense of employee privacy and dignity.

A third factor is the absence of servant leadership in which management fails to accept ultimate responsibility for overall performance and management's specific and global contributions to problems and poor performance. We are unable to see the truth until we "remove the log from our own eyes" and apply the same value system to ourselves. The human tendency is to externalize blame. It is interesting that from a religious perspective, Jesus reserved his harshest criticism for the hypocritical Pharisees (religious leaders of the day), for good reason. When leadership and managerial practice diverges from stated policy, the visible contradiction generates disappointment, distrust, and cynicism toward those in authority. It reduces employee motivation and organizational citizenship behaviors associated with vibrant, productive, and healthy work environments. Employees are less likely to exert the necessary effort and creativity to solve problems and make necessary changes when they lack trust in the integrity of management. For example, when managers utilize the "tell and sell" approach to performance appraisal, employees rightly perceive manipulation if there is no employee input and no transparent acknowledgement of management's contribution to performance problems (remove the log first from your own eye) and those factors beyond the employee's control that affect performance.

Another key trust inhibitor is the absence of "honest weights and measures." If the performance management system manifests an unsatisfactory level of reliability and validity with bias in the measurement and decision making process, employees fail to receive the corrective and encouraging feedback necessary to improve and cope with challenging circumstances.

A common example is in the performance appraisal process with rater bias. The presence of nonperformance factors contaminates appraisal ratings producing a fruit of perceived and genuine unfairness in the rating process and its outcomes, which in turn links to adverse behaviors such as lower job satisfaction and higher turnover. The various forms of appraisal bias serve as a major fertile source of workplace discrimination or equal employment opportunity (EEO) complaints and court cases involving contested personnel practices linked to performance appraisal. Rating bias occurs with the contamination of appraisal ratings by nonperformance related factors.

Conclusion

The great challenge for management is to recognize and assume responsibility for the valid resentment and distrust produced by ill-treatment, which is the first step in beginning the slow healing and confidence-building process of genuine support and encouragement. Following chapters will detail the specific SLHRM strategies to overcome distrust and provide authentic care for employees. When human beings become mere instruments, we are engaging in a dangerous game at the altar of short-term gain. The key is to commit to a covenant, and like any relationship, there will be times of pain and conflict that test our commitment to our espoused ideals. The depths of such character testing reveal our heart's motives. If organizations self-promote their adherence to SLHRM values through aggressive public relations "branding," hollow or specious claims will only lead to the development of cynical employees disengaging from the employer, further reinforcing the downward spiral.

SLHRM Leadership Personal Character Reflection: Elements of our Job Description

One of the main job duties of our SLHRM "job description" is the development of high moral character. The development of servant leader character requires a lifelong process of growth. Below are reflections on how servant leadership entails "trial by fire" character building:

- *The development of humility:* The greater our knowledge, maturity, and responsibility level, the greater the standards of character accountability. The more I learn, know, and grow, the greater the difficulty in living a life of wisdom and "practicing what I preach." This reflects a powerful servant leader principle that knowledge frequently outstrips our application capacity given the omnipresent deficiencies in our character and wisdom levels, and most importantly, the inherently corrupting nature of success through self-sufficiency, complacency, and ultimately pride. The only appropriate response is an attitude of humility, recognizing that all of our successes embed within a collective web of accountability. One key element is the practice of servant leader transparency, the action side of humility producing great fruits. How can we be humble when we fail to authentically interact and communicate a realistic view or ourselves in all settings, weaknesses and all? The practice of transparency is very difficult given our fleshly impulse to hide our flaws and the need to control how others view us, given the risks of disclosing weakness. However, the absence of transparency grants our conscious permission to attack us with condemnation and shame as we live in fear of discovery. In addition, there is great freedom and peace when we discard the crushing weight required to maintain the façade of command and control.
- *Workplace trials are a blessing as they increase our patience, perseverance and the ability to engage in servant leader love.* Irrespective of how well we handled the trial, the circumstances reveal great

truths to better equip us for the future. An important lesson is that judgmentalism toward others leaves us blind to the "log in our own eye." Like moths drawn to a flame, we see the weaknesses of others, but we fail to visualize and grasp the breadth, depth, and power of our own failures and imperfections. From a spiritual standpoint, the human tendency is "far sightedness" in which we see clearly the weaknesses and problems of others while possessing blurred vision when gazing upon ourselves in our mind's eye. We use distorted lenses, with the most common tendency to demand "justice" for others and grace or mercy for our weaknesses and failures.

- *The commitment to support our supervisors is an important form of servant followership.* Managers have great responsibilities, and we all benefit when our boss completes his or her duties with excellence. It is important that our supervisor, in turn, earn the trust, confidence, and respect of his or her supervisor and other key organizational stakeholders thereby ensuring "upward influence." When managers are in the "out-group," subordinates frequently suffer, given the diminished fiscal, information, and emotional resource support. Hence, it is an essential Golden Rule attribute to take joy when our supervisors succeed and be sorrowful when they struggle and fail.
- *The importance of patience reinforces that we can run from painful areas that promote character growth, but we cannot hide.* Patience is a foundational character element along with humility and empathy in our relationship with others. Without patience, we are unable to practice the ministry of interruptions and take the necessary time to understand the pains and problems that others hide.
- *The absence of servant leader character will sabotage all of our gifts, abilities, and accomplishments.* It is like a cancer that is destroying us from the inside. Without servant leader character and the integrity of means, ends, and motives, our work will be built upon flawed foundations. Hence, it is important to seek self-knowledge regarding our motives through ongoing reflection and fellowship with mentors.

We must be willing to suffer persecution and endure uncertain outcomes as we practice servant leadership. When faced with workplace trials and persecution, it is easy to become discouraged. Oftentimes the benefits of our actions do not bear fruit until years later, after we have left the organization. Do we have the courage to stay the course?

SLHRM Leadership Personal Character Reflection: Recognizing Strongholds

Our servant leader walk is a glorious adventure but with hidden spiritual warfare dangers. One of the most pernicious is strongholds. Oz Hillman has a very clear definition of a stronghold:

> A stronghold is a fortress of thoughts that controls and influences our attitudes. They color how we view certain situations, circumstances, or people. When these thoughts and activities become habitual, we allow a spiritual fortress to be built around us. We become so used to responding to the "voice" of that spirit, that its abode in us is secure. All of this happens on a subconscious level. (Hillman, 2014)

Strongholds produce strong passions and emotions including fear, anger, jealousy, and rejection, among many others. Strongholds frequently go unrecognized given that they habitually center on moral or ethical activities and motives. I struggle with work-related strongholds of perfectionism and affirmation addiction in which "the job" sometimes becomes a "god" giving a foothold to anxiety, fear, and insecurity. What are some of the key indicators of a stronghold's presence? One telltale factor is the drive to succeed, irrespective of the cost.

Servant leadership leads firmly but gently, while strongholds compel us with an exaggerated sense of duty, obligation, and compulsion that extinguishes the joy, peace, and satisfaction of our work and service. In effect, the stronghold becomes our master, as we begin to rationalize that our personal needs are synonymous with the interest. A second factor is that the stronghold becomes more important than the mission itself or the wellbeing of organizational members. When our work becomes a "god," we refuse to surrender our personal agenda and become reluctant to sacrifice what is most precious to us for the greater good. We prefer living in bondage with our known stronghold than facing the fear of an unknown future with the stronghold "splinter" removed. In essence, we must ask the question, "Do we really desire freedom?" Often the answer is no. We always have an excuse, as we grow comfortable and accustomed to the pain.

A third element of a stronghold is an unrelenting rumination, obsession, and "what-if" focus dominating our thinking patterns. In essence, "where your treasure is, there is where your heart (and thoughts) is also." I hearken back to a very challenging time in my life with my wife's breast cancer. I engaged in an ongoing battle for the allegiance of my heart as my work took precedence at a mental thought frequency level. Strongholds overwhelm our spiritual peace creating guilt, doubt, and insecurity with an endemic double-mindedness. When I was with my wife, my thoughts frequently focused on the work that needed to be done, and when I was working, I experienced guilt over neglecting my wife.

What is the underlying root cause of a stronghold? The motives are always self-promoting, and in my case, it was the fear of failure at work and the perceived negative judgments of others in combination with my need to gain approval, acceptance, and affirmation of my identity through job performance. In contrast, *agapao* love is the sole foundation of servant leader motives, the unselfish placing of the needs of others over our own.

Each stronghold possesses a unique set of root factors, but the underlying motive is relying on a secondary and inferior source for *agapao* unconditional love, forgiveness, affirmation, and significance. For example, when affirmation anxiety is the prime motivating factor, appearance becomes the most important element—"What would my colleagues think?" When we are committed to success irrespective of the cost, and find our thoughts dominated by the issue, the first stage to freedom is to recognize its presence and commit to change. The first step in overthrowing a stronghold is to identify its presence through self-reflection, counseling with trusted mentors and other sources of external feedback. This is much more difficult to implement in practice given our proclivity for denial and the stronghold's resistance to discovery, identification, and eradication. We need to recognize that strongholds require a higher level of change commitment than we are able to muster through self-effort alone. We cannot gain freedom based upon intellect, self-will, and effort alone.

The good news is that when we recognize and challenge our strongholds, we grow in servant leader character. When we obtain freedom, these experiences become a great source of growth, and our experiences are foundational in assisting and guiding others sharing similar struggles. So please do not weary in your well doing, and you will reap a mighty harvest!

Chapter 3

The SLHRM Change Management Process and the Barriers to Effective Change

One of the great management challenges is cultivating long-term organizational culture change. There are many key decision points in the success of such a complex effort, and hence many "veto" opportunities to impede change progress. In this chapter, we present a diagnostic change resistance typology that identifies the various motivational attributes that contribute to opposing change. This chapter concludes with an outline of a change management process to overcome resistance and obstacles. It is important to embrace the belief that the power to change organizational culture begins with committed servant leaders who love their employees and other key stakeholders.

Servant Leadership and Change Management

Where does servant leader love begin? It begins with a dynamic and holistic integration of love of mission and love of key stakeholders in dynamic relationship. In organization theory, we use a term called "reification" to describe the tendency to ascribe human characteristics to inanimate objects. We impute human attributes to organizations when we use such phrases as the "personality" of the organization. Hence, love begins with a dynamic and vital moral foundation that recognizes the inherent dignity of human beings within the confines of the organizational relationship. Servant leader growth and sanctification requires a combination of individual effort and communal fellowship and accountability. As servant leaders, we possess both individual and corporate responsibility for justice.

So where does organizational change begin as a servant leader? Clearly, the genesis is the restoration of the leader's human heart based upon an inner moral harmony. Unless our life demonstrates a harmonic balance between our values and their application, the credibility of our witness is tarnished. Once our hearts are oriented in the proper direction, we possess the power and credibility to begin facilitating the restoration of the hearts of our employees both individually and through collective organizational policies and programs that promote mission achievement and organizational justice and fair treatment. Hence, we begin at the executive and/or leadership levels and then focus on the base. Hence, the question becomes how do we foster disciples instead of followers? Clearly, there is no specific formula, but every single instance of organizational change requires varying degrees of effort in each of these areas.

However, I must provide a "realistic job preview" as it is difficult to apply SLHRM principles to "worldly" organizational cultures founded upon instrumental and utilitarian values, irrespective of the sector. A "values"-espousing organizational status does not guarantee a SLHRM culture. Macro- and system-level change is always difficult, but the focus for SLHRM is changing hearts at the individual level in order to promote enduring change. With integrity, SLHRM leaders become empowered to be "light and salt" in their employees' lives. One genuine and passionate SLHRM leader can make a profound and long-term difference, with a co-worker, with a work group, with a department, an organization, an entire industry, and then the world. Organizations are not monolithic; they provide opportunities for the development of change and the creation of "microclimates," an oasis of servanthood in a sea of self-interest. Even if we are a lone voice crying in the wilderness, our SLHRM actions for our co-workers generate positive outcomes.

We begin with a cardinal rule of SLHRM, that we first remove the log from our eye before we remove the speck from our brother or sister. The human tendency, when faced with the many complex individual and system performance and ethical issues related to organizational change, is either to rationalize away or externalize the locus of responsibility. We desire forgiveness, patience, and grace for ourselves, but justice for others. The nature of moral evil entails deception and disguise, and unless executives demonstrate servant leadership in word and deed, the organization encourages moral drift on the part of employees. Management must first set the tone and accept responsibility for tempting employees to engage in various forms of protective and self-serving behavior, in essence for "gaming" the system. The foundation is the understanding that there is no victimless organizational moral or ethical violation.

Barriers to Organizational Change

Organizations reap what they sow in regards to employee treatment. When employees trust management, HR organizational change efforts are much easier to implement given the willingness of employees to exert extra effort even when the rationale is not completely clear. Hence, one of the important initial elements of the change process is to assess the attitudes of the key stakeholders toward the organization. A helpful framework for conceptualizing the change process is to visualize a continuum of attitudes from high levels of trust to neutrality, to a skeptical state that requires proof, to a state of cynicism in which trust is lost. When employees lack trust in management, it engenders varying degrees of skepticism and cynicism. Skeptical employees will cooperate with clear evidence that the change promotes the mission and employee interests. When employees have lost all confidence in management, no amount of logic or persuasion can force employees to engage in good faith efforts. When employees are cynical, they possess low motivation levels and exert minimum effort while rigidly adhering to the job description (the letter of the law and not its spirit). The goal is simply to "wait out" the change initiative; hence, irrespective of its effectiveness or necessity, the change effort recipe produces failure. Cynical employees may actively sabotage the HR change effort as well. Indicators of cynical behavior include lack of confidence in HR and other organizational initiatives or programs, a belief that management "goes through the motions" and exerts minimal effort in solving workplace problems that affect employees, dissenting employees are punished or disadvantaged, management is not concerned about employee welfare, management does not listen or respond to employee change or problem solving recommendations, management is hypocritical toward employees, management only supports employees when they agree with existing decisions, and management lacks the needed skills to solve problems (Reichers, Wanous, & Austin, 1997).

If the employees or other stakeholders possess high to moderate cynicism levels, it is important to address the underlying causes before beginning the HR change implementation process. The key is to regain trust, which is a long process that we will discuss later in the chapter. However, some changes cannot wait until attitudes improve. Every change effort can be an opportunity to "bridge the gap" and begin the process of thawing cold hearts and challenging rigid views on the ethicality and morality of management. However, it is vital to apply the same assessment to yourself as a manager or leader. Oftentimes it is management and leadership itself that is a powerful source of hidden opposition to change. We pay "lip service" to change, but our hearts resist. Hence, as with other areas, we must test ourselves relentlessly to identify our visible and hidden personal fears, insecurities, and other source of resistance to change. Unless we are truly willing to "count the cost," our motivation will be superficial and we will lack the integrity to lead others. In fact, our subordinates or others will quickly perceive the discrepancy between our rhetoric and our actions.

However, it is important to recognize that there are valid and invalid rationales for pursuing or not pursuing an HR organizational change initiative. Based upon the work of Nutt and Backoff (1995), inappropriate reasons for rejecting an HR change effort include the unwarranted lack of top leadership confidence in organizational and employee capability, unrealistic expectations relative to success (perfectionism), a belief that the organization is too small to benefit (organizational size mismatch), the HR change effort overlaps with other organizational HR planning efforts, the inability to identify a clear starting point, and the greatest threat, organizational complacency given past and present success. Conversely, Nutt and Backoff suggests several legitimate reasons for opposing HR change efforts including leadership instability, lack of top-level commitment, cynical and/or hostile labor-management relations and the organization lacks resources and expertise.

Categories of Resistance to Organizational Change

The key is to first assess the sources of resistance by the important stakeholders. A framework for diagnosing the underlying motivations for opposing organizational change appears in table 3.1. Managers must automatically avoid equating change resistance to disloyalty, sloth, or an absence of vision. The first set of factors is valid servanthood and stewardship reasons why employees oppose HR organizational initiatives and effective servant leadership proactively addresses these legitimate concerns. The other two categories are more problematic as they represent dysfunctional and unethical or immoral self-interested motives for opposing change. The psychological resistance factors embody the general tendency to fear the unknown. This fear increases with an absence of trust, faith, and

Table 3.1 Source of resistance to organizational change

Servanthood and Stewardship Organizational Change Resistance Factors

1. Conflict with or adverse impact on mission achievement (deflects from core mission, for example)
2. Conflicts with foundational organizational values
3. Deontological conflict (ethical impropriety)
4. Stewardship: Adverse impact on the efficiency or effectiveness of program, product or service delivery
5. Adverse impact on key stakeholders (clients, employees)
6. Absence of adequate employee support (training, resources, time)

Psychological Organizational Change Resistance Factors

1. Lack of trust through high levels of skepticism and cynicism. For example, the organization engages in pseudo-participation in which managers ask for employee input but never use it or punish employees who make recommendations contrary to management desires (I will let you participate as long as you follow the "party" line)
2. Fear of the unknown
3. Lack of efficacy (confidence) to cope with the demands of the new situation
4. Fear of failure
5. Disruption of comfortable routine
6. A perfectionist spirit that inhibits innovation and trial and error learning

Ego and Political Organizational Change Resistance Factors

1. Loss of power, resources and influence
2. Loss of prestige
3. Lack of trust in organization
4. Personality conflicts and power struggles and the desire to punish through failure and delight in the misfortune of others

---

reliance in the motivation, credibility and intentions of others. Fear is the counterfeit to faith, as employees develop insecurities that inhibit growth. The third category, ego and political factors, is more pernicious given the employee's motivational intentionality in the promotion of selfish interests over the mission and the wellbeing of others. Ego and political resistance is the dark spiritual antithesis of servant leadership. These barriers can appear anywhere in the organizational change process.

These three categories of change resistance require varying strategic and tactical change management approaches. However, the foundational line of attack remains increasing stakeholder trust. When employees trust the organization, they are willing to exert extra effort, take more risks, and give the organization the benefit of the doubt in ambiguous, stressful, and challenging circumstances. When trust is present, it reduces employee and other stakeholder stress levels, providing more energy to devote on productive pursuits.

When employees and other stakeholders begin to see a sustained change effort that begins with SLHRM leadership, the mountains of cynicism and skepticism gradually erode. The various sources of change resistance reinforce the complex nature of the relationships and the number of unknown variables. Given the deception of the human heart, the governance structure in all forms of social institutions consists of various combinations of external controls through rules, policies, sanctions, and electronic or traditional forms of surveillance to provide clear boundaries and accountability mechanisms. The most efficient and effective means for securing organizational change compliance begins with leaders and employees possessing internalized SLHRM character. A key factor with managing organization change is inviting the key stakeholders into the decision making process. When there is conflict and distrust, begin with cooperation in areas in which there are mutual interests and clear, verifiable and transparent decision rules. For example, middle managers are key stakeholders in organizational change situations. Their cooperation is essential, and it is important to determine the breadth, depth, and source of their resistance. Is it a form of apathy linked to years of failure or neglect, the absence of empowerment, or the hard shell formed from ongoing disappointment or exploitation? It is important to assess whether you have skeptical versus cynical middle managers. Skeptical middle managers will engage and buy in with reasonable evidence, but cynical employees possess a more entrenched negative worldview that repels most forms of reason.

Hence, a key element is developing a learning organization. As the dictum states, those who forget the past are doomed to repeat its mistakes. One of the challenges associated with organizational change efforts is retaining the institutional knowledge of those who exit the organization while embracing present and future innovation. Another related test is discounting knowledge that lacks relevance for the future. Hence, what do we need to remember? It is important from a servant leadership standpoint to honor and remember past achievements. All policy changes possess both intended and unintended consequences, and a careful evaluation of the plan's implementation and outcome effectiveness is necessary. Group-based differences in perspectives are important to analyze given as what appears effective at the design stage frequently manifests serious problems at implementation.

The next section summarizes important strategies to increase trust.

Strategies to Increase Trust and Provide a Solid Moral Foundation for the Change Effort

If the organizational change effort is to succeed, employees must possess confidence in management motives, means, and goals. Key action steps to begin this process include:

1. *Leadership and management should begin by a detailed introspective analysis to identify leadership's contributions to the problems, weaknesses, and failures before assessing the contributions of other stakeholders.* SLHRM organizations set high standards for leaders, and if any sacrifices are required, it begins first with leadership.

2. *Implement the change effort at the executive leadership and management levels first while observing the same or higher performance standards than those applied on other stakeholder groups.* SLHRM organizations need to "walk the talk."

3. *SLHRM managers share the burdens and the sacrifice in very tangible ways demonstrating both symbolically and practically their empathy and common interests with employees.* A great historical example was Lee Iacocca assuming leadership of a bankrupt Chrysler Corporation during the late seventies and accepting a salary of a $1 until the company returned to profitability while rewarding employees for agreeing to wage and benefit concessions (Herbst, 2007). His efforts set a high spiritual bar that increased employee trust and were the catalyst to save the corporation. Management must model and apply SLHRM "Golden Rule" values by listening to employees, demonstrating transparency, and making a commitment to joint problem solving.

4. *Staff the change effort wisely with passionate and skilled change champions and facilitators.* Ensure long-term commitment and continuity in the change process through a clear succession planning process.

5. *Practice transparency and humility through a realistic "change" preview in which there is a clear and systematic communication regarding the individual, group, and organizational benefits and costs using a multi-method and media campaign.* In essence, a key element is illustrating the costs of maintaining the status quo while clearly emphasizing the long-term nature of the change process with higher upfront costs for great downstream benefits.

6. *Cultivate the formation of an ethos embracing the "healthy pursuit of excellence," encouraging employees to take chances and learn from mistakes and forgive themselves and others for failures and difficulties.* It is important to avoid blaming employees for factors beyond their control. This entails actively seeking out contextual information that identifies the external factors that inhibit success.

7. *For all stakeholders, and especially for those employees whose resistance to change is ego and politically oriented, the key is to persuade the recalcitrant that either the costs of maintaining the status quo are higher than the costs of changing and/or the benefits of the change exceed the benefits of inertia and remaining the same.* In addition, it may be necessary to transfer or even terminate cynical and politically resistant employees as a last resort option to avoid contaminating the attitudes of other key stakeholders. A place to begin is securing broad-based input through surveys coupled with direct representation by selecting credible change leaders and influencers among the rank-and-file. If the level of opposition is too great, it remains in the interest of the organization to begin laying the foundation by clearly defining the costs of not changing and the associated benefits.

8. *Promote employee and other stakeholder input and empowerment in the change process thereby aligning interests, facilitating ownership, and improving effectiveness of the change process increasing trust.* The implementation of employee empowerment/partnership strategies will improve service delivery efficiency and effectiveness. It is important to empower the key stakeholders in the implementation process to enhance ownership and buy-in through convening implementation teams responsible for ongoing improvement efforts.

9. *Provide employees with adequate physical, mental and spiritual support during the change effort and transition (training, equipment, financial resources, ongoing coaching, counseling, and wellness programs).* Many organizational change efforts lose credibility and employee trust when change efforts add new duties with no infrastructure assistance or additional personnel.

10. *The need to establish and reinforce SLHRM values and competencies through careful employee selection, management development, and reward practices. Systematically reinforce the new attitudes, behaviors, and performance goals through the HR system by linking rewards and corrective actions to results.* Systematically link the various reward systems (budget, compensation, recognition)

at all organizational levels to the achievement of change effort goals, objectives, and metrics. The key is to reward participants for process compliance and outcome success.

11. *Provide financial and other means of support such as innovation grants to support change efforts.* The key is to select pilot projects with a high probability of success (pick the low-hanging fruit) and publicize these early successes in order to inspire supporters and overcome opposition. By engineering early successes, the organization increases employee confidence in the change effort. In effect, these become powerful testimonials that enhance the credibility of the change process (a form of word of mouth marketing). Organizational change efforts require a delicate balance of centralization and decentralization, hierarchy and empowerment—in other words, a harmonic mean of top-down and bottom-up planning. Organizational change efforts are by definition inefficient and time-consuming, especially with multiple stakeholders. The costs are high upfront, with the benefits realized downstream. Hence, patience is required. It is very important to set measurable goals at the early stages and to provide a clear demonstration of success, progress, and momentum. A general rule of organizational change is to select solvable problems of mutual interest and partner with employees *early* in the change process. Early success is critical in demonstrating the sincerity of management in their claims of practicing SLHRM "Golden Rule" employee treatment values. For example, appoint a joint-labor management team to solve an employee-parking problem and demonstrate good faith by reducing the number of management designated parking spaces, freeing up more spots for employees.

12. *Need to develop realistic performance expectations with ongoing, specific, behavioral, and timely performance feedback on change effort progress through a balanced scorecard set of standards and metrics for all levels, beginning most importantly and visibly with leadership and management.* It is important to set high but reasonable SMART goals (specific, measurable, achievable, relevant, timely) and provide feedback that is corrective, encouraging, and respects the dignity of employees. It is critical that key stakeholders participate in developing the action plan, SMART goals and metrics to enhance acceptance, relevancy, validity, and commitment. It is important for both employees and the organization to exercise patience and recognize that it requires a season for employees to develop. The overall value ethos is to instill a long-term investment value system versus a short-term return

focus. It is important to recognize that the costs of many change efforts are "upfront" with the benefits "back-loaded."

13. *Organizations are operating blindly without early warning systems. The most effective "canary in the coal mine" is ongoing communication based upon a climate of trust, but database systems are important as well.* This increases employee trust, and can be the focal point of joint labor-management quality improvement and problem solving efforts. "Keeping a finger on the pulse" of the organization is critical from both a change management and employee confidence and support perspective. This entails a systematic data gathering process that includes surveys, focus groups, town meetings, suggestion systems, and a balanced scorecard. Based upon the feedback received, the organization makes adjustments in the communication and implementation of the change effort. These methods also provide the foundation for a multi-method means for providing two-way communication and feedback on the change effort. Through a process called "action research," the organization responds to the feedback and demonstrates good faith attempts to review and make appropriate adjustments. The stakeholders will not demand that the organization adopt every suggestion or recommendation, but only that management make a good faith attempt to provide honest and transparent responses and a full discussion of their feasibility. There are two approaches, the first entailing direct face-to-face communication, which includes town hall meetings (in-person and virtual), employee work-group meetings, interviews, focus groups, and "management by walking around," and the second category of anonymous communication, which means including suggestion systems, surveys, and blogs. A multimedia communication campaign directed at the key stakeholders to provide ongoing updates on the status of the change management process is another critical element in engendering support and overcoming opposition. One of the SLHRM objectives is to reduce unnecessary stress on employees through information vacuums. If the organization fails to keep the key stakeholders informed, it generates a vacuity that demands fulfillment through rumor and speculation, thereby increasing employee anxiety and fear.

14. *Systematically evaluate the effectiveness of the change process and adjust the implementation process and/or goals based upon the evidence.* Promote a flexible approach to the change process that recognizes the need to make adjustments based upon evolving

circumstances and conditions. The key is to develop the appropriate balance between persistence and consistency to avoid the errors of stubborn rigidity or excessive reactivity. Provide ongoing evaluation of the organizational change progress. SLHRM organizations integrate organizational change into the fabric of managerial decision making through conducting yearly assessments of the plan's progress and engaging the key stakeholders in the evaluation process. Implementation teams accomplish this through reviewing change evaluation data and making recommendations for adjustments in the change goals and implementation plan.

There is clearly no formula or checklist that can assure an effective change management process. The strategies above are critical in overcoming resistance to HR system change, and their embrace is necessary, but not sufficient.

Other Change Management Challenges

There are many other challenges to practicing change management from a SLHRM foundation. These include overcoming the ubiquitous obstacles of adhering to servant leadership values in the midst of decisional problem pressure and uncertainty, including lack of clarity on the nature of problems or challenges and their causes, resource scarcity (time, information, money), and stakeholder conflict. Servant leader values are the moral compass for our managerial decision making journey. The management challenges include:

• The challenge of maintaining a uniform SLHRM culture as the organization grows in size, expands its number of work sites and geographic scope, and diversifies its services. This begins with developing management policies and practices to systematize the internalization of foundational system values while encouraging an appropriate degree of autonomy and empowerment.
• The personal leadership challenges of maintaining a consistency of policy and practice as an organization grows and managerial decision making scope and responsibilities broaden. Often managers promote a personalized management approach emphasizing empowerment for the immediate staff, but retaining an excessive degree of decision making authority as the organization grows. The SLHRM practices that are effective with smaller organizations (management by walking around, town meetings) become a liability if the chief

executive officer fails to delegate these tasks to subordinates and lower levels. From a servant leader standpoint, it is critical that leadership reinforces the importance of delegating management authority and duties.

Servant leadership/followership is the foundation for our organizational "temple."

Best-Practice SLHRM Organizational Change Character and Behavioral Attributes

Effective organizational change requires an unswerving commitment to mission achievement. All the involved stakeholders must work together to in a spirit of cooperation, patience, and a willingness to sacrifice personal interests for the common good. Just as tone of voice and body language contributes to the majority of meaning in verbal communication, the organizational change process requires attention to key servant leader character elements, which ultimately determine long-term success. Behaviors matter. The table 3.2 provides a list of key elements that SLHRM managers must embrace.

These standards are challenging, but their ongoing implementation enhances employee trust and confidence in leadership.

Table 3.2   Principles of SLHRM strategic change management servanthood

1. Unwavering commitment to achieving the organization's mission.
2. Practice humility by promoting the needs of others over the self and the greater collective good over narrow special interests.
3. Demonstrate a spirit of forgiveness for good faith mistakes. Encourage employees to innovate and be creative, and acknowledge that organizational learning involves blunders and trial and error.
4. Practice empathy to understand the positions and views of others by active listening (do not interrupt, listen instead of thinking of your reply when others talk, frequent paraphrase and probe when you don't understand).
5. Reduce status differences between executives, management, and employees to promote honest, two-way communication.
6. Be a polite listener and avoid side conversations when others are speaking. Be mindful and self-aware of our body language and avoid exhibiting distracting facial expressions such as frowning, rolling eyes, snarling, snickering, and shrugging of shoulders in our interactions with others. Monitor our tone of voice to identify and suppress impatience, anger, hostility, impatience, and judgmentalism.
7. Practice the Golden Rule and always treat the other person respectfully. Respect and dignified treatment is a foundational character virtue and reflects the principle that we assume that others are inherently worthy of respect.

Continued

Table 3.2 Continued

8. Embrace and promote a collaborative approach to conflict resolution that identifies the mutual underlying interests and a trust that a solution will be found. The key is to recognize areas in which both sides can achieve common goals and needs.

9. Practice a spirit of openness to the views of others through a non-judgmental spirit and assume a humble posture recognizing the existence and validity of other perspectives and views and that our own personal perspectives are limited and error-prone.

10. Disagree in a polite and loving manner. It is critical to separate the person from the position; we must differentiate the individual from their behavior. Hence, when we personalize disagreement and conflict, especially with the strong emotions produced by a history of personal conflict, betrayal, and competition, it clouds our judgment about the merits of the issues. Hence, it is critical to practice emotional regulation and reject personal or personality based attacks, and a rigid cynicism of the person's motives. In those situations in which we cannot achieve consensus, agree to disagree. Do not personalize the discussion, forgive others for their mistakes and transgressions, as we desire forgiveness for our own. The human tendency is justice for others, but forgiveness or mercy for ourselves. It is vitally important to reject the critical spirit.

11. Embrace the marketplace of ideas in which truth emerges from an honest discussion and debate. We learn from others and views that are different from ours. However, this does not entail compromising key values and principles. We acknowledge that some conflict is necessary and inevitable given the servant leader worldview, which embraces the existence of moral standards and principles and the existence of mutually exclusive truth claims.

12. Enter the process with an open mindset that avoids fixed agendas or preset outcomes. Embrace a genuine commitment to the process which means accepting the consensus of the group (within stewardship and servanthood guidelines) if it diverges from your own views or preferences. If the executive shapes the outcome, participants will feel manipulated thereby reducing trust, acceptance, and support for the plan.

13. Avoid self-censorship of our views to avoid the groupthink phenomena in which a group reaches a premature consensus and resists ongoing feedback, discussion, and alternative views. Encourage in others a questioning attitude to provide honest feedback and opinions. Assume the courtroom perspective and subject your own views to cross-examination in an attempt to understand the views of others from their perspective (practice empathy). Assume the role of the other side and attempt to communicate and support their views to gain a more detailed understanding.

14. Commit to a spirit of excellence and diligence in completing all assignments (read assigned materials, attend meetings, be on time, offer opinions).

15. Demonstrate personal commitment to the organizational change process by attending all meetings, provide adequate support resources and release time, and appoint skilled facilitators to conduct the planning process.

16. Develop realistic standards of success and embrace the inherent inefficiency of the organizational change process, upfront costs and down-stream benefits.

Conclusion

As in the old comic strip Pogo, often "we have met the enemy and he is us" in the organizational change process. SLHRM change efforts begin with a self-inventory of our commitment level and the sources of resistance. Unless we can first manage ourselves, we will lack the vision, strength, and credibility to serve others. To complicate matters, we judge on appearance, and unless we relentlessly seek the truth through ongoing testing and reflection, our change efforts will be ineffective.

SLHRM Leadership Personal Character Reflection: The Knowing and Doing Gap

Across the various life domains, there is no shortage of information on "best-practice" principles. Irrespective of whether we are addressing areas such as personal wellness, financial planning, or management practice, the well-informed consumer possesses a wealth of data from a variety of sources with the two most influential being life experience and formal education. There are several preconditions for successful knowledge application. The first is the possession of the appropriate information base. One of the great challenges of the modern age is separating the "wheat from the chaff" given the proliferation of knowledge sources and the exponential increase in the quantity of information. The second is the formation of the character to apply the knowledge in an ethical and moral fashion. Our family history, education, influential mentors, and the integration of religious and spiritual beliefs, among others, influence this capacity.

We gain knowledge by instruction and constructive feedback from our life circumstances. The bridging of the "knowing and doing gap" (a person of integrity) rests upon the calculated integration of knowledge into our ongoing decision making and behavior. In essence, we become "hearers and doers" of the servant leader principles and values. Knowledge that is applied becomes wisdom when processed through the lenses of our moral and ethical value systems as we learn and experience life and critically reflect on our experiences, positive and negative, success and failures, and all in between. We all are familiar with the frustration that ineffective knowledge application produces. One of the markers of servant leader character is an awareness of the various knowledge application barriers that sabotage our best efforts. Below are several important barrier categories:

1. *Self-deception regarding our motives for actions.* Psychology and our various religious belief systems agree on the presence and power of

the human heart to disguise and misperceive the motives of others and ourselves. A behavior frequently possesses multiple motives that operate both at the conscious and unconscious levels. There is pronounced human tendency to focus on socially desirable motives at the surface level while underlying selfish and sinful motives are less salient or suppressed to the subconscious. For example, we may understand that employee empowerment is essential for employee growth and organizational effectiveness, but we subtly and subconsciously sabotage empowerment efforts due to a variety of weaknesses including pride (cannot accept others getting credit or recognition) and insecurity (fear that employees will take our job or "outshine" us).

2. *Cognitive distortions such as emotional reasoning in which we make decisions not on the objective situation, but on our "fickle" feelings.* For example, we may understand that providing honest employee feedback to our subordinates improves their performance, but such situations activate strong emotions of fear or helplessness based upon past traumatic experiences related to authority figures over interpersonal conflict. Hence, we feel incapable of handling the stress of confrontation situations and thereby avoid the threatening situation by providing muted or favorable feedback.

3. *Subconscious wounds and insecurities.* We all manifest the adverse effects of various traumatic life experiences. These life experiences sabotage our efforts to apply knowledge at the conscious level. For example, a lack of forgiveness toward an authority figure such as a father can translate to a general tendency to distrust superiors and resist correction (performance feedback), which is a form of rebellion against authority.

One of the key indicators of the presence of the knowledge-practice gap relates to differences between self-perceptions and those of others. For example, managers frequently espouse allegiance to participatory management, but only if employees choose means consistent with management desires. Over time, employees discover the discrepancy between stated policy and the policy "in use," thereby generating perceptions of employee manipulation, disillusionment, and cynicism. Another common example is differences in perceived performance feedback quality and quantity between managers and employees. Managers perceive that they invest time and provide employees with ample specific performance feedback. However, from the employee perspective, this feedback frequently assumes a generic form ("good job") that provides reduced corrective or behavior reinforcing information. Employees desire a more sustained, specific, and

genuine relationship and hence experience superior-subordinate interactions very differently.

What are the solutions to these problems? The first element is to
commit to an ongoing self-reflective process of analyzing our motives,
both proactively and reactively. The goal is to illuminate the underlying motives of the heart, uncover the wounds and dysfunctions that
bind us, and provide the requisite guidance and strength to make the
necessary changes in our behavior. The second element is to be under
the authority of a more experienced accountability partner who can
help us analyze more clearly the underlying motivational dynamics.
Unless we are dedicated to uncovering the truth about our identity,
we cannot apply the knowledge at our disposal. A third key factor is
comparing our perceptions to those around us. This can assume the
form of a 360-degree feedback process. All of these practices require
humility and recognition of our vulnerability to deception. This
requires great courage, but the fruit produced is very pleasant as we
grow in self- and emotional-awareness.

SLHRM Leadership Personal Character Reflection: Affirmation Anxiety/Addiction

Our collective journey into the realm of servant leadership carries
us to many uncomfortable places. Our self-awareness regarding our
weaknesses and faults is most acute when stripped of our conventional
defenses that provide a false sense of comfort and security. For those
of us who experience what is termed "affirmation anxiety," the performance evaluation process is clearly a "step on the water" experience.
Affirmation anxiety is the term used for the apprehension associated
with the need to receive positive feedback and recognition. We all
experience this condition at one time or another given the inherent
human need for affirmation, support, and direct evidence regarding
the fruit of our labors.

Servant leadership requires us to recognize, support, and encourage employees to cultivate hope and confidence. Concurrently, we
must provide accountability (tough love), which entails setting standards and providing corrective feedback. It is important to seek
out and be responsive to external feedback, but resist control by it.
When we place more weight on the praise and feedback of men than
adhering to moral, ethical, stewardship and servanthood values, we
are vulnerable to a whole range of dysfunctions. If we assign more
importance to pleasing others, it becomes an idol and a source of
fear and insecurity. Natural affirmation anxiety frequently morphs into

affirmation addiction. The root lie is that in order for us to achieve meaning, self-purpose, and success, we must "earn" the approval of others and achieve worldly definitions of success. In essence, we defer to human standards and judgment the foundational definition of our self-worth and the meaning and degree of our success, discounting servant leader standards of attainment and obedience, character and love. We thereby lose control of our emotional and spiritual peace. In effect, we delegate our sense of self-worth and wellbeing to the frequently fickle, unreliable, and invalid assessment of human wisdom and judgment.

Servant leadership calls us to work to the best of our ability and to seek excellence while maintaining a sense of perspective and priority. When we recognize the primacy of servant leader performance standards, we understand implicitly that our desires will not produce outcomes that stand the test of time unless the foundation rests upon servant leader love. As the Apostle Paul states in 1 Corinthians 13, we can possess all knowledge, wisdom (and we can infer worldly success and the praise of men as well), but without love it profits us nothing. When we place workplace performance feedback in its proper perspective, we are better able to learn from our mistakes and improve performance, be more emotionally stable, and pursue excellence rather than perfectionism, which inhibits growth from fear of failure robbing us for our joy.

I am a "work in progress" in this area, as I am learning to allow myself to fail and exhibit weakness. A good example relates to my vocation as a college professor and teaching ratings. The perfectionist in me gets discouraged when one or a small group of students provides a low rating. The servant leader perspective is to recognize I do not have to be perfect to be a good instructor. My goal is to be open to feedback and make improvements (the teacher must be teachable!). I am improving in this area, but it is an ongoing challenge given our inherent tendency to focus on the negative. Let us all commit to place servant leadership at the center of every area of our life and adopt the associated liberating achievement standards.

Chapter 4

Employee Empowerment and Discipleship Making Principles

Empowerment is a vitally important element in the successful implementation of SLHRM and requires the possession of virtuous character, maturity, and spiritual intelligence. Empowerment begins with followers who embrace the role of conscientious servants. Hence, it is important for SLHRM organizations to cultivate the principles of servant followership as both the foundation of servant leadership and empowerment. Employees need to demonstrate the maturity, ability, and character to be faithful performers in small and great aspects of their work. Servant followership is a great safeguard to leadership self-deception, as servant followers provide honest feedback, which is frequently a "shock" to leadership self-image and beliefs, forcing leaders to re-evaluate the foundation of their actions. That is why servant followership in tandem with employee empowerment are such powerful tools for overcoming resistance to change at all levels as it forces leadership to interact with the key stakeholders exposing them to alternative views, thereby altering how leaders assess the situation and the roles and intentions of others. Peter Drucker's advice in his 2006 book *Managing the Nonprofit Organization* is to ask staff and volunteers what areas require help, assistance or improvement and how to solve the problems. Employee feedback provides important information to adjusting our perceptions that inform our decisions. As servant leaders, our goal is to shine a bright light of hope, direction, and security in the midst of the dark storms and chaos that affect employees (light in a dark place). In essence, servant leadership is that "city on a hill" that provides a hopeful vision of a better future on clear days, and a lighthouse on dark nights that points the way to safety. Servant leadership is the brightness that illuminates the sources of support and is the preserving salt for life-sustaining foods during the organizational desert experiences. Servant leaders understand the motives, goals, and tactics of power politics in various organizational settings, but embrace a gentle but firm trust approach that enables them to reject Machiavellian power tactics. Servant leaders are able to function effectively in systems with a variety of worldviews and ethical perspectives without embracing or adopting those values, tactics, or strategies. Organizations assume an important role in this regard by minimizing the motivation and contextual circumstances that tempt our employees to take ethical shortcuts. Management becomes complicit when we make it easy for employees to act on their self-serving needs and wants.

SLHRM empowerment entails a covenantal approach with mutual obligations. This includes instilling a collective recognition regarding the team nature of success, cultivating forgiveness and grace, taking joy in the successes of employees and empathy for failure, and assigning the locus of responsibility for accomplishments externally while assuming management responsibility for failures and weaknesses. SLHRM empowerment entails the cultivation of key character elements such as altruism, the ability to defer gratification, and the desire to promote the needs of others over the self. A major element of the framework is the development of policies and practices that: (1) link leadership effectiveness and advancement to success in developing employees, thereby helping employees identify and "unbury talents" and apply them in an appropriate manner, and (2) preparing successors that are more successful, thereby promoting genuine succession planning and making leaders "dispensable." The next section more fully explores the foundation of servant leadership, the heart of a disciple follower.

Servant Followership

Improving our leadership skills is a lifelong pursuit. From a servant leader worldview perspective, when we seek leadership skills first, we are placing the proverbial "cart before the horse." Servant followership gives birth to servant leadership in which employees develop the essential character traits that enable leaders to use their gifts and skills in a humble, responsible, mature, and unselfish manner. Servant followership entails such key attributes as enduring trials and tribulations patiently, learning from mistakes, teachability, obedience to authority, accepting responsibility for solving problems, exercising initiative, and helping co-workers and clients even when inconvenient or contrary to personal interests. Another key element is self-awareness and knowledge. Servant followers understand their motives, strengths, and weaknesses and select jobs based upon their gifting and passions, thereby reducing stress on themselves and others.

Servant followership entails committing every aspect of our work to excellence irrespective of the obstacles and situation. Even when we work for unjust superiors, it is important to give our best efforts as patiently enduring the offenses. We are then able to achieve the challenging balance between enduring unfair conditions and persecution silently and exercising voice to correct the injustices. We need to reflect carefully and craft a response that balances "voice, endurance, and exit." Which strategy to employ requires a careful moral, strategic, and tactical reflective process that entails seeking confirmation through other counselors.

These character elements require a conscious and deliberate dedication to growth. When we practice servant followership in today's troubled and stress-filled workplace, we become that candle in the dark shining light, hope, and love into the gloomy recesses of our workplaces. I have listed below important key attributes of servant followership.

Twenty-Six Key Attributes of Servant Followers

Principle 1: The Great Commandment

The first principle of servant followership is to commit to complete all of your job responsibilities with excellence, employing moral and ethical motives, means, and ends irrespective of the obstacles. This high moral and ethical standard requires great courage, emotional intelligence, and patience.

Principle 2: 360-Degree Forgiveness

The practice of 360-degree forgiveness in which we forgive all those who disappoint or fail us is a foundational character attribute. An absence of forgiveness is a powerful impediment to healing, growth, and healthy interpersonal relationships at the physical, spiritual, and emotional levels. A prison of toxic emotions holds us captive when we are unable to surrender the wrongs committed against us as we repeatedly relive the events precipitating the pain. Forgiving the person who wronged us demonstrates our commitment to loving others unconditionally. In the workplace, the absence of forgiveness produces a host of pathologies including the inability to learn from mistakes, a hostile climate toward innovation and creativity, and a repression of growth. A lack of forgiveness is a form of relationship pollution producing toxins that destroy the fabric of healthy human interactions, creating elevated mental and physical stress. With the ongoing practice of forgiveness, there is a higher degree of transparency, honesty, problem solving, and conflict resolution.

Principle 3: Serve Just and Unjust Masters

The third principle of serving just and unjust superiors with excellence is a very demanding standard. One of the greatest tests of character is to serve with excellence when those in authority attack, malign, betray, marginalize, ignore, and humiliate. How do we respond when our efforts are not valued or are distorted and our good deeds are punished or unrecognized? Do we plot revenge, engage in silent but passive-aggressive resistance, or simply disengage? Or do we strive to make the best of the situation and maintain excellent performance and love our supervisor in spite of the provocations and the pain?

Principle 4: The Exercise of Situational Leadership

One of the great distinguishing characteristics of a mature servant follower character is asserting leadership when the situation warrants our intervention. In today's more complex and rapidly changing environment, SLHRM organizations encourage and require employees to exercise leadership in solving work-related problems on their own initiative. One of the great impediments to a genuine servant leader witness is adopting a defensive and legalistic approach to our jobs. When we are reluctant to use our talents, assume responsibility, and exercise leadership in solving problems, we impose costs on our co-workers and clients, and depreciate organizational effectiveness. One of the great servant follower character attributes is the embrace of the "ministry of interruptions" in which we take time from our busy schedule to assist others. We all have natural job descriptions written by our employer, but of greater importance is our moral job description that entails loving our neighbor as ourselves.

Principle 5: Embrace the Healthy Pursuit of Excellence

SLHRM organizations understand that growth is a long-term process entailing mistakes, errors, and failure. The healthy pursuit of excellence is the orientation to institute high but realistic standards of performance, accepting the inevitability of mistakes and embracing the value of trial and error in the learning process. Perfectionism is the antithesis to the healthy pursuit of excellence. Perfectionists "game the system" and do not take the risks needed for personal and organizational growth. Our moral job descriptions call for us to work with excellence. What does excellence entail from a servant follower standpoint? The key element of excellence is love-based obedience. We perform to the best of our ability and treat others according to the Golden Rule, but recognize that we can only do our best and trust for a good outcome. This enables us to rest in peace irrespective of the situation and associated consequences, thereby reducing stress, anxiety, and fear. When we fail, we "fall forward with grace," confident that we will learn and grow from the situation, given our trust that we can learn from all situations. SLHRM organizations reinforce this principle by "going against the grain" through such management practices as positively recognizing individuals and work groups for good faith efforts that resulted in failure. When management demonstrates appreciation for efforts as well as results, it reinforces confidence in employees and strengthens trust and credibility.

Principle 6: Practice Initiative and Creativity
Servant followers understand that there are instances and seasons when status-quo job performance is not sufficient. Hence, solving problems requires novel approaches. Traditional problem solving will not work, and there is need for "outside of the box" thinking. Hence, employees must work both within and outside of their normal job description and work requirements. The goal is to use all employee creative gifts and talents to take authority over our work environment and be fruitful in our job domain. When we consistently make the choice to withhold our skills, time, and talents, we impoverish the work environment.

Principle 7: Reliable and Conscientious Work Performance in All Situations
Servant followers understand the importance of being faithful in the routine and exceptional, in the minor and major job duties, and in the unobserved "behind the scenes" and the highly visible public settings. Good and faithful servants possess a passionate conviction to promote servanthood and stewardship interests as we must strive to perform our job to the best of our ability and serve irrespective of the circumstances.

Principle 8: Honor Your Employer by Providing Honest and Constructive Feedback

Servant followers understand the importance of speaking truth in love and reject walking in a critical or cynical spirit. As servant followers, we must provide clear information on performance issues, both positive and negative. Withholding, distorting, or selectively presenting information to promote gain or avoid punishment for self and others impedes truth and problem solving. It requires great courage and wisdom to honor this requirement.

Principle 9: Commit to Supporting your Leaders, Subordinates, Peers, and Clients

It is vital as servant followers to support every member of the organization through a mindset that earnestly hopes for their success and prosperity. When others succeed, we rejoice, and when they fail, we are sorrowful. If we are to develop the courage, wisdom, and discernment to love others, to complete our work duties with excellence, and resist the darker impulses and pressures to compromise our ethical and moral integrity, we must commit to a positive and supportive mental attitude toward others, even those that we dislike or that dislike us. The call especially applies to those who are difficult to love, the "sandpaper people," those who resist, persecute, and hold ill will toward us. The only effective weapon is to respond in love, and an attitude of support is the foundation. To promote the best interests of our enemies is a powerful statement of forgiveness and faith.

Principle 10: Practice Gratitude for Past, Present, and Future Blessings

Servant followers are grateful for the blessings in their lives. A great means for ensuring inner peace and tranquility is to assume a mindset of contentedness irrespective of the circumstances. We can only embrace this principle if we truly believe that all the experiences of our lives can eventually produce good. We must look beyond what we see and feel, and by faith believe that we will never be tested or tempted beyond our ability to bear, a biblical reference to 1 Corinthians 10:13. As servant leaders, we go beyond the "half-full" principle. We are realists in that we see that the glass is half full, and we are grateful that it is not empty, but by faith we have an earnest expectation of hope that the glass will become full and overflowing in due time.

Principle 11: Commit to the Success of Your Supervisor
and Co-workers

Servant followers understand and are comfortable in their identity as team players and the necessity for others to "shine brightly." One of your prime work duties is to help others around you to achieve their work goals. There are times when we "must decrease so others can increase," a biblical reference found in John 3:30. An active embrace of support entails such factors as helping others when they are over-whelmed with quantity or quality of work, require assistance in learning new tasks, provide moral support and encouragement in stressful situations, and simply take time to listen. When we take time to assist others, we release a spiritual power that brings encouragement, love, and support to the workplace. A mark of maturity is our commitment to helping others unbury and develop their latent talents and to use them in appropriate ways.

Principle 12: Resist the Human Impulse to Rejoice When Our
Enemies, Competitors, or Those We Dislike Experience Difficulties,
and Commit to Returning Good for Evil

The "path less traveled" is to take joy in the success of others while being sorrowful over failures, even with the "tough love" and "sand-paper" people that we dislike or those who abhor us or view us as enemies. One of the most human emotions is to take joy when those who have hurt us fail or suffer. As the saying states, "misery loves company." When we make the choice to "love our enemies" in spite of our feelings, our obedience to this principle changes the work cli-mate in a very profound manner. It clearly releases a power that melts hardened hearts as it requires courage to surrender our natural self-protective mechanisms.

Principle 13: Discover and be Content in Your Unique
and Priceless Identity

One of the great sources of ineffectiveness in the workplace is to live someone else's life. It requires a tremendous amount of energy to direct and channel our gifts and abilities away from our natural pro-clivities, like forcing water to run uphill. When we misunderstand and misperceive our purpose, gifts, and abilities, we are never "good enough" and are always searching for fleeting confirmation and reas-surance. The goal is to learn from colleagues, not to assume their identity. One of the great psychological warfare weapons is for our misplaced focus to steal our genuine distinctiveness thereby impeding our ability to fulfill our purpose and calling, hampering the distinctive purpose and attributes that only we can provide in meeting the unique needs in others. We find great peace when we accept our gifts and roles both individually and as part of a team.

Principle 14: Do Not Compare Yourself to Others

Being content requires us to reject comparison. Comparison leads to many deceptive emotions, beliefs, and actions from envy, jealousy, and lust to fear, anxiety, pride, complacency, and judgmentalism. Misguided comparison is the source of much misery, stress, and strife in the workplace as we use inaccurate standards and knowledge to assess others. We judge the surface, missing the key contextual details and those of the heart. As any lawyer will state, inferring intent in others is a very difficult standard. The goal is to learn from others, but not to allow our perceptions of their strengths and weaknesses to control how we view ourselves. We all have a tendency to hide our weaknesses and showcase our strengths, making accurate assessment under any circumstances challenging. We can learn from others, not judging them or us.

Principle 15: Humility Is a Foundational Servant Follower Virtue

We must recognize both our God-given gifts and strengths, as well as our weaknesses and limits. Humility is not self-depreciation, degrading, or discounting of our strengths and accomplishments. It is a humble but grateful recognition that all of our capabilities and successes did not occur in a vacuum and we are all part of a collective, integrated system. Conversely, humility acknowledges that every human possesses weaknesses but we reject identity definition by our failures or shortcomings. We must recognize that there are no "self-made" men or women and that we are debtors to many. Humility recognizes that we have much to learn, and embraces a teachable spirit as we seek out feedback to help us grow.

Principle 16: Servant Followers Passionately Embrace Truth Telling

Servant followers speak "truth to power" through honest feedback (voice) to protect the integrity of mission achievement and the interests of other key stakeholders, and demonstrate their love of their supervisor by providing input to avoid mistakes. One of the greatest tests of character in the workplace is mustering the courage to inform superiors of performance problems, interpersonal dynamic dysfunctions, or waste, fraud, and abuse. Can we speak truth when the risks are high? This requires great courage and trust.

Principle 17: The Practice of Personal Transparency

Servant followers recognize that they are not perfect and that others can learn from their mistakes. When we admit our weaknesses in an appropriate fashion, it demonstrates our humility and trust. Clearly, this practice requires a climate of faith, mutual respect, and confidence in the integrity of co-workers and supervisors. We must be prudent in our disclosures to avoid needless attack or disadvantage. However, when we are open about our mistakes and problems, it encourages others to practice transparency and improves the climate for learning and problem solving greatly. From a broader perspective, one of the great truths of servant leader character is that proclamation without works is dead. The same principle applies to the relationship between humility and transparency. Humility requires an "open window on the heart" commitment to transparency. How can we be humble unless we share our weaknesses, failures, and fears to others? As the saying goes, "we are only as sick as our secrets," and when we retain our weaknesses, we deny the world the benefit of our experience in managing the trials and tribulations of life. The absence of transparency is especially damaging as our weaknesses are eventually exposed in one form or another through the inevitable march of "armor piercing" everyday life experiences and events. We pay a high personal price for the absence of transparency as the use of image management creates a fertile ground for self-condemnation and burnout. Managing as if we are in complete control and possess all the answers requires a tremendous amount of energy and time. We become alienated from ourselves and others as a prideful spirit rules us and severs the link with the life-giving vine of teamwork and sharing the burden. The love and joy that provides passion and energy dries up, and we are in the desert. The absence of transparency inhibits problem solving, decision making, growth, character development, and managing change. When we repress negative information about ourselves, it creates a climate of distrust in which other employees engage in image management leading to managing by fear and risk aversion inhibiting creativity and innovation. One of the pernicious effects of an absence of transparency is compassion fatigue, as self-absorption reduces our time, motivation, and ability to help others, one of the key means for freeing ourselves from this psychic prison. When we are more concerned about our image and how we are viewed by others, most of our energy is devoted to maintaining the façade of control, and very little is left for others. The antidote for this poison is to disclose our weaknesses and lack of self-sufficiency. Once you embrace transparency, begin to share your problems with trusted others. Gradually expand the scope of your candor to the larger workforce. Others may occasionally use your weaknesses against you, but the benefits of transparency far exceed the cost.

Principle 18: Reject the Temptation to Harden our Hearts and Externalize Blame

Servant followers understand that the natural response to failure is to blame others or circumstances beyond our control. We desire grace and forgiveness for our mistakes and moral transgressions, but for others desire justice and accountability. As Adam blamed Eve for eating the forbidden fruit, humanity is always searching for reasons to avoid responsibility. One of the great enticements is to fault others or external factors for our mistakes and failures. To resist this tendency we must assume personal responsibility for creating and solving problems. The key is to relentlessly review our motives and actions to first determine our contribution to the problem. In effect, servant followers search a situation and reflect on their contributions before addressing other factors, regardless of actual personal responsibility levels. Another key tendency is what scientists term the "fixed response bias" or tendency to remain excessively loyal to our initial decision or belief which protects our egos and self-image (few of us enjoy being proven wrong); in essence, we seek information that confirms our decision and view and more readily discount information that contradicts our beliefs (Tversky & Kahneman, 1974). Hence, this is a form of "hardening our heart." To overcome this tendency, we must learn to seek information that challenges our views and assume "an innocent until proven guilty" perspective given that this is a higher standard of proof.

Principle 19: Be Patient and Faithful in Trials and Tribulations

Servant followers persevere through the trials and communicate hope and optimism while avoiding complaining, grumbling, and faultfinding. Be willing to "pay your dues" and wait patiently for recognition and promotion. When we make the decision to be thankful in the midst of our trials and suffering, we are making a very powerful statement that our faith and hope in a better future is greater than our fear of present and future problems. A very effective strategy is to embrace an "attitude of gratitude" reflecting on our blessings even as we experience the "body blows" of difficult situations. Complaining demonstrates a lower degree of faith and impedes our ability to cope and adapt. When we become discouraged, begin to complain, or respond in anger, we are worshipping the problem and stating implicitly that the circumstances and problem are more powerful than hope for a future solution.

Principle 20: Learn to Live in the Present

Servant followers are mindful of the "precious present" and fix their internal vision and attention on how to both enjoy the moment and to trust for a better tomorrow and future. This attitude of trust promotes patience and perseverance. One of the great tools of spiritual warfare is to focus our mental and physical energy on reliving the trials, traumas, and failures of the past while rehearing and projecting doom, gloom, and fear into the present and future. When we permit the past or the future to rule the present, we fail to live fully in the moment and love others. It provides a fertile ground for both pride and fears to rule our emotions and generate powerful forces that deflect our attention from the precious present. When fear and anxiety dominate our thoughts, this torment impedes our ability to solve problems and address the needs of the now. When we nostalgically live in the past, we overlook the problems of those bygone times, the blessings of the present and the hope of the future. When we live continually for the future, we forget the lessons of the past and the blessing and advantages of the present. We must actively seek to be content in our present situation while praying for the future in faith, pursuing healing from the traumas of the past, and avoiding resting in complacency in the present.

Principle 21: Practice Unconditional Altruism

Servant followers assist fellow employees in need (mentor and coach new employees, support and assist co-workers) even when inconvenienced or disadvantaged. When we make the choice to assist others in spite of the obstacles and the costs, it demonstrates our commitment to esteeming others greater than ourselves. It is also provides the foundation for a "Golden Rule" workplace in which others take time to help us when our time of need arises.

Principle 22: Practice Courtesy, Tact, and Politeness to All

Servant followers respect and treat others with gracious and loving esteem. One of the great contributors to workplace stress is the loss of civility and respect. Servant followers assume that others are inherently worthy of respect and do not have to earn fair treatment. This foundational Golden Rule attribute reduces tension, defensiveness, and aggressiveness in the workplace. Honoring this principle is especially important during interpersonal conflict and interacting with difficult personalities. Other employees will be watching, and such principles as "A soft answer turns away wrath" (Proverbs 15:1 NRSV) will defuse many confrontations.

Principle 23: Practice Active Listening

Servant followers hear with the heart as well as the mind. The key is to be content in listening more than we speak. Active listening is a powerful demonstration of "other centeredness" and a manifestation of Golden Rule love. Active listening reinforces through words, body language, and tone of voice the importance and high priority attached to the other person's views and needs as we concentrate intently on understanding and developing empathy. Empathy and understanding does not imply agreement or the condoning of what others say, but is a powerful form of humility that rejects overt judgementalism. Active listening entails paraphrasing to demonstrate understanding, probing to generate enhanced detail, a posture in which we listen more than we speak, avoiding interrupting or make leading statements, and resisting forming rebuttals in our mind while the other person speaks (we can think much faster than we or others can speak). Active listening requires practice and commitment, but the fruits are considerable.

Principle 24: Supporting Co-workers through Encouragement and Accountability (Tough Love)

Servant followers embrace the harmonic balance between high standards of performance supported by encouragement and grace. Excellence of character entails love in its full form. Discipline and corrective feedback is a form of love. Providing correction with the appropriate motive to promote the best interests of others is a foundational element. When we are dedicated to servanthood, irrespective of the nature of our personal relationship, it sends a very clear message that we are persons of character and can be trusted.

Principle 25: Do Not Exploit Your Employer

When in a position of bargaining strength relative to your employer, do not make excessive or unreasonable demands that take advantage of an employer's vulnerable situation. Servant followers commit to a long-term employment relationship founded upon trust, and grasp that the relative positions of strength and weakness can change. The goal is to promote the mission and honor our moral job description. When we restrain our natural impulses to extract concessions at times of bargaining strength and the vulnerabilities of our employers, we demonstrate a commitment to the higher order Golden Rule principle.

Principle 26: Practice Unswerving Honesty
Servant followers are uncompromisingly conscientious and honest in using organizational resources (money, time, equipment, supplies, etc.). When we are faithful in the small things, we earn the trust and confidence of our employers and those around us. When we resist the temptation to avoid work or use organizational resources for personal gain, we shine brightly and set a tone that encourages others to honor moral conduct standards.

Application

The challenge is to embrace these attributes from a love-based relationship standpoint, not purely out of obligation. Servant followers will often pay a high price, but they are confident in their ability to cope and adapt to changing circumstances. We focus on the problems of the day and reject worry regarding the future outcomes. It is clearly a challenging proposition to embrace a life of trust, but servant leader character is the foundation of our confidence. Servant followers take the road less traveled!

With the foundation of servant followership established, servant leaders genuinely understand that empowerment requires an internal ethos in which the mission requirements and the needs of others are more important than the leader's ego, reputation and personal needs. This requires an inner patience and contentment to focus on the mission regardless of the circumstances or conditions. It also entails the courage to reject a comparative and competitive orientation that focuses on what employees lack while embracing a patient confidence that they will grow and develop in a unique but equally or more effective fashion. In the empowerment process, servant leaders must resist the impulse to micromanage and avoid investing in others to retain indispensability and control. Servant leaders understand that one of the most important elements of their natural and moral job description is to develop disciples that will significantly exceed them in skill, success, power and influence. Hence, they must decrease, so others can increase and do greater things. Servant leaders possess the ability to identify hidden talent and gifts as well, helping others to appropriately use and channel existing misused talents. Hence, they seek out opportunities for subordinates to prosper and succeed in new organizational territories. They are always training their successor and endeavor to provide them with all the necessary resources. In order to lead effectively, servant leaders understand the importance of setting priorities for themselves and their organizations, to focus on the "best" while reducing emphasis on the "good but not critical" elements related to organizational success. A great challenge is to make the difficult decisions to reject desirable activities that reduce time and effort devoted to the core priorities. Another aspect is to model and grant permission to subordinates to reject "fire-engine management" with urgent but trivial items. One of the key character elements of servant leaders is to serve and empower those who for whatever reason oppose, dislike, attack, humiliate, or persecute us. The key character element is the ability to take joy when others succeed, and be sorrowful when they fail. Finally, servant leaders generate a passionate enthusiasm for the mission, their clients, and their employees, providing meaning, purpose, and dignity to all.

Encouragement and support are two major pillars of servant leadership empowerment and basic elements of our moral job description in all life domains. We all need affirmation and encouragement; however, servant leaders recognize that our need for encouragement and recognition can become an idol with an insatiable addiction. The ideal state is to welcome recognition and affirmation when it comes, but not to depend upon it to validate our worth and self-esteem. In essence, we hope that our relationships will be supportive and loving, but we do not require human affirmation to feed our soul and spirit.

A basic servant leadership/followership principle is that each person assumes personal responsibility and accountability for his or her contribution to relationship or performance related problems. We first must "remove the log in our eye" and then make the necessary sacrifices and actions to solve the underlying factors. Implementing this principle is very difficult in practice, especially with relationship trauma from past wounds and intense performance and financial pressures. Given today's fiscal and other performance pressures, employees and managers are in desperation mode, and the typical Darwinian survival of the fittest cultural mindset dominates. For every organization that remains true to the ethos and values of SLHRM, many more have taken the "low" road. Servant leadership/followership is a precious character attribute.

A great challenge for organizations is how to select and develop servant leaders who inherently desire to empower others. Is an orientation to servant leadership empowerment a function of a relatively fixed and stable human growth and development process, a genetic attribute, or is it a learned set of behaviors? In reality, it is likely all of these. There are several key facets at the heart of servant leadership. We should be assessing both character and competence, but there are both legal and ethical challenges to character assessment. One frequent error is to focus selection efforts on recruiting the "star" performer. Research and servant leader principles agree that focusing HR recruitment strategies on the best performers ignores the reality that the success of our "stars" is dependent on the team (Groysberg, Nanda and Nohria, 2004). Hence, it is more effective to assume a long term developmental approach.

Another key SLHRM practice is the intentional cultivation of servant leaders who embrace empowerment through formal succession planning and mentoring. Servant leaders who were themselves developed and mentored are more likely to make disciples themselves! Servant followers understand that they require instruction by "masters" with greater levels of experience and understanding. The development and mentoring process is central, but given the limited time and number of SLHRM managers, how practical is it? The first element is carefully to select mentors and offer organizational support, training, and boundary expectations. One option to increase the number of mentors is to redefine a senior mentor to include one or two levels above, but that may not provide sufficient distance in expertise and experience level for some employees.

When we select managers who will empower employees, it is crucial that they possess desirable character traits such as conscientiousness and honesty, and manifest a strong internal motivation to serve with excellence, meet the needs of others, and promote the mission. With the establishment of character, the next set of selection factors include a composite criterion consisting of technical skill related to the core job duties and responsibilities along with behavioral, personality, and attitudinal "fit" with job requirements, well-developed and honed interpersonal skills, and positive peer input regarding teamwork and interpersonal skills. Another key element is to empower middle managers. We often focus on the lower and upper levels of management to the exclusion of the mid-levels with fewer direct subordinates. It is important to assume a balanced approach of engagement with middle managers while at the same time bringing in outside expertise to provide new perspectives. The key is to forge a partnership to retain the valid institutional knowledge.

The empowerment process entails a reciprocal set of obligations. Servant leaders understand that empowerment is not cultivated in a vacuum. It is important to systematically plant, nurture and water, the seeds of empowerment. To support empowerment, we need ongoing human capital investment in group processing skills including the competencies associated with self-directed work teams such as goal setting, feedback, and empowerment, conflict resolution, performance planning and ongoing team-building exercises. Effective empowerment requires also the development of a performance management support system of valid and reliable performance standards and metrics that assess teamwork skills and periodic recognition of exemplary teamwork skills (e.g., an awards ceremony for the "solid citizen"), interpersonal skills evaluation, work process and outcome performance metrics, and a balanced system of group and individual rewards.

However, the foundation is always the cultivation of positive character traits and identifying and proactively remedying negative traits, attitudes and behaviors. One strategy is to implement a spiritual intelligence support program. Spiritual intelligence counseling identifies cognitive distortions and replaces with healthy coping thinking and behavioral patterns. These distortions include unrealistic performance standards and goals, judgmentalism, the martyr syndrome, perfectionism, pride in various forms including viewing performance as overly dependent on individual abilities, comparison envy that contributes to jealousy, and externalizing blame and failure in lieu of assuming personal responsibility. Healthy spiritual intelligence principles include promoting a foundational humility in which we measure ourselves only by progress from our starting point and an appreciation of our gifts and abilities and the abilities and gifts of others. Other key elements include being joyful over the success of others, and viewing mistakes and failures as essential learning and character development experiences. Another key element is cultivating shared values through team activities such as community service and social events. The ability to develop a team, work as a team member, and manage a cohesive group is an invaluable managerial competency that is increasing in importance as the nature of the production and service delivery process evolves from a hierarchical to a shared and organic process.

We impede the healthy development of empowerment by common organizational practices such as not enabling job candidates to meet with supervisors thereby losing an opportunity for additional information gathering, in effect, a form of realistic job preview. Another key weakness is the absence of a systematic management training and development program and the lack of managerial accountability for employee development and advancement. Organizational solutions include the use of 360-degree feedback to hold managers accountable, and in the selection process arranging for candidates to meet with direct supervising managers.

Servant leaders guard against the spirit and practice of compartmentalizing our servanthood and stewardship obligations into a narrow manager and employee dichotomy. In essence, the servant leader embraces 360-degree servanthood and believes passionately that demonstrating love and excellence in all situations is in our "spiritual job description." Cultivating a workplace of spiritual excellence entails an unswerving commitment to mission, an altruistic spirit of self-sacrifice, and a commitment to ethical integrity of motive and action. The levels of accountability for remedying these problems include organizational level policies and practices that promote accountability (training, performance management process oversight, mediation, counseling), moral SLHRM character in managerial behavior (support, forgiveness, clear expectations), and promoting servant followership oriented peer group relations (support, collegiality, and assisting and helping co-workers).

Conclusion

As we conclude this chapter, recognize that empowerment is a signature element of SLHRM. There is no recipe-like formula guaranteeing success. Empowerment capacity develops slowly through the crucible of ongoing development and growth in our level of character, job knowledge, and general life experience. However, organizational policies and practices can either accelerate and accentuate or impede and suppress empowerment values and skills. Let us dedicate ourselves to this noble quest and take the path less traveled!

SLHRM Leadership Personal Character Reflection: Humility and Vainglory

Unbridled pride is the great moral and ethical character killer. Humility is the antidote to the poison of pride. Humility is the recognition that none of us is an island, and that the image of a "self-made" man or women is an illusion. All success entails the product of a team effort from our families, to our teachers, to our mentors, to our peer group mentors. However, the counterfeits to humility are very subtle. It is very easy to become prideful with a surface meekness. Those who are emotionally intelligent can subtly use the behavior associated with humility to manipulate perceptions of others. The play "How to Succeed in Business without Really Trying" clearly illustrates this principle. The main character J. Pierrepont Finch uses a book to use desirable character traits such as humility in an instrumental fashion to carefully market and construct an image of altruistically caring for others when in fact his goal is manipulation to promote self-advancement.

I too struggle with this issue. How do we know that false humility is present? A key indicator is the presence of vainglory, or our secret desire to receive praise, recognition, or benefits from others for our good deeds and surface acts of humility. Hence, we take conscious pride in our decisions to place the needs of others first. For example, we may give others the credit for an achievement, but we are hoping that they will "return the favor" by praising us for our role and are disappointed if they do not. Another clear example is subtlety broadcasting our good works to be "seen by men." We arrange or "stage manage" our acts of service to be visible or discovered. Another element is simply taking pride in our reputation as a "humble person" thereby building relationship "capital" (trust) with the goal to influence others to promote our own interests. Our behavior may be ethical, moral, and desirable, but the perversion enters the picture when we engage in surface altruistic actions to produce long-term personal benefit.

When we most keenly focus our attention on encouragement or positive feedback directed toward us, this is a powerful indicator of the presence of vainglory. I know that I struggle with this passion greatly. I am always looking first for the part about "me" and place less focus on others. If I do well and receive "good press," I am less concerned with overall mission achievement or how others are affected. This is a very serious, but hidden, character flaw.

What is the remedy for this pernicious attribute? First is to learn how to receive encouragement in proper perspective. As servant leaders, we should encourage each other and protect others from depression, discouragement, apathy, and hopelessness, thereby motivating other to maintain good behaviors in all situations, especially when we are weak and wounded. We are never to use the feedback to exalt or promote ourselves, only to serve and solve problems. The key is our response to positive feedback and comments. The appropriate reaction is gratitude but also realizing that recognition is fleeting and the ultimate source of our success is a team effort. There is no self-made man or women. As such, we receive the compliment with gratitude, but recognize that we are not solely responsible for the success.

When we recognize the presence of vainglory, the first step is simply to acknowledge its presence and commit to change. The goal is not to stop altruistic actions and behaviors, but to identify the source of the stronghold and "tear it down." When we find ourselves engaging in vainglorious thoughts and actions, change direction immediately. The foundational element is the ongoing temptation to define our worth and self-identity in performance and the approval and views of others. Make a concerted effort to monitor your thinking patterns and reject the temptation to manipulate and practice "image management." Practice altruistic actions that benefit others with no expectation of notice or recognition. Our battle with pride and vainglory is a great challenge, but with steadfast commitment, we can make great progress in slaying this goliath.

SLHRM Leadership Personal Character Reflection: Self-Deception

Self-deception is one of the "signature" attributes of moral failure. The ubiquitous spiritual warfare surrounding self-deception entails various forms of rationalizing and externalizing responsibility in combination with ignorance and lack of self-awareness. This principle is illustrated in the Bible. When Adam and Eve ate from the Tree of Good and Evil, they engaged in the first form of self-deception by vainly assuming that they possessed a better understanding of their needs and interests than God (a very presumptuous attitude!). This posture can be likened to a rebellious teenager committing the cardinal mistake of "second guessing" the wisdom of their parents in setting boundaries. In effect, self-deception is a foundational element of our attempt to promote self-interests.

Interestingly, self-deception is only possible because of our free-will decision-making authority, a paradoxical outcome given the inherent irrationality of pursuing evil over good. We follow this self-fraudulent path given that moral failure actively misleads and disguises both its root and consequences. Moral failure by its very nature assumes control of our decision-making processes reducing our degree of self-control and autonomy. With continued transgressions, the ability to resist moral failure weakens with the searing of our conscious and we become slaves to our desires. Self-deception is rooted in our own selfish desires, in effect, the disguise to place a "sugar coating" on our motives and actions.

What is the remedy for self-deception? The key it is the employment of 360-degree testing and assessment. Our walk as servant leader is like peeling away the layers of an onion as we die to the self. There is no need for self-condemnation, only conviction and self-awareness in this struggle that is never complete. As human beings, we judge both our personal motives and those of others using deficient and contaminated standards and criteria,

As we mature as servant leaders, the process of self-discovery is very painful and humbling as we ascertain to our surprise and chagrin that the foundations of our "noble" actions are made of substandard building materials. Our moral values become our building inspector and provide both the motivation and means to remedy our "code" violations. I am experiencing the gentle but firm conviction firsthand in many ways. The first response is to ask for wisdom and discernment in testing our hearts.

A foundational question for servant leaders is identifying our motives for service. As a faculty member, I realize that a spirit of vanity drives and operates through the need for personal recognition and affirmation. If we actively seek appreciation and acknowledgment from others, their fickle attitudes and actions control our ever-increasing ego needs. When we die to the self, we understand that the only enduring and truthful recognition and affirmation comes from "letter and spirit" integrity. If we receive recognition and affirmation from others, it is a "bonus," but we do not expect kudos for our actions, gaining freedom from anger when others reject the law of reciprocity and its associated notions of fairness by overlooking or criticizing a good deed or excellent performance. It is a great joy to be free of the "personal rights" mindset. One test for fleshly motives is the types of thoughts and emotions produced when our performance is not recognized or is criticized.

For example, because of my insecurity with public speaking, I have a strong need for affirmation after every speech. If I do not receive it, I assume that I was not effective and I ruminate on the always-present flaws (no speech is ever perfect). Did I let my nervousness show? Why did I forget that important point I wanted to make? Why did I not answer that last question clearly? Round and round we go in the mixed motive merry-go-round! Did the audience like me? With moral motives, we only assess the speech in terms of its effectiveness in achieving a moral objective and benefitting the audience, whether we gave our best effort, and how we can improve. A successful speech with effusive praise is the other end of the spectrum. If we are only concerned about our performance and the praise we receive, pride and vanity control us. Servant leadership requires only our obedience in achieving mission objectives, while we desire to be justified by our personal agenda and efforts.

Chapter 5

Employee Fair Treatment Principles

SLHRM organizations possess a passionate commitment to dignified employee treatment. Employees are not just "resources," but human beings with emotions, families, and souls. Promoting employee rights is a foundational servant leadership principle. How we interact with employees is an essential interface between core servanthood and stewardship values in an organizational decision-making environment that typically possesses a schizophrenic view toward employees. In one perspective, employees are human beings with souls while from another standpoint they are instrumental "costs" of production that must be minimized in our hypercompetitive marketplace. Which of these views prevails? For SLHRM organizations, the response is simple: employees are not costs, but the human flesh and blood foundation of the enterprise.

We recognize, however, that servanthood mission objectives sometimes require staff reductions and/or changes in the terms and conditions of employment and that some degree of employee-management disagreement and conflict is inevitable given conflicting interests and human frailty. However, these differences need not metastasize into the violation of dignity leading to the abuse of rights producing dysfunctional and destructive behavior. These abuses of dignity take three forms: management violation of employees, employees violating management, and employees violating the dignity of each other. When any form of abuse occurs in the workplace, it distorts the moral fiber of both the offender and the recipient.

Leadership Abuse of Power

Let us begin first with leadership abuse of employees, which is the most pervasive and serious. Historically, leadership exploitation and abuse contributed to the need for employment and safety laws and the advent of unionization. These institutional accommodations are a reaction to abuse of employee rights and dignity through the exploitive operation of the employment-at-will doctrine and the instrumental view of labor as another cost of production. The instrumental view of employees dehumanizes the workplace, impedes employee growth, and hinders workplace transcendence. It is a form of idol worship deifying financial goals (teleopathy) over human welfare (revenue over human needs). An instrumental worldview fails to promote a public interest perspective and the necessary altruism to be our "brother's keeper" within the organization, with clients, and the larger community of stakeholders.

Instrumentalism is the product of the underlying casual character and moral violations of pride, greed, fear, envy, jealousy, power, control, and narcissism, among others. The fruit of these organizational spirits are arbitrary employee treatment and the abuse of authority exacerbated by the absence of due process protections and the inequality in power between individual employees and management resulting in exploitative and unsafe working conditions and performance expectations, wrongful terminations, and unfair discipline. When management views workers as instruments, it is easier to rationalize the imposition of labor cost reduction strategies that increase work effort and reduce compensation.

What are some of the risk factors that contribute to potential unfair treatment? A major influence is the absence of servant leadership and employee empowerment, gradually leading to a higher level of distrust and varying degrees of overt, covert, and passive-aggressive conflict and resistance. The final stage is an open and sustained conflict-infused employee-management relations climate generating an accelerating cycle of distrust and retaliation for perceived or actual wrongs. Each side views the other as the "enemy" and devises military-like strategies to "defeat" their opponent. This creates a culture that impedes the development of a learning organization in which leadership views all stakeholders as worthy of dignity and respect. This toxic environment impedes effective organizational problem solving as each side withholds information to gain an advantage in the employee-management "wars." The result is the "house divided" that cannot stand given the absence of a shared ethos of a mission and relationship altruism orientation in which the needs of others assumed precedence. Organizational history demonstrates that this pathology of conflict can so thoroughly dominate attitudes and behavior that employees and management are willing to sacrifice customers, clients, and the mission integrity of the organization rather than cooperate or admit defeat. This was a major factor contributing to the demise of Eastern Airlines in the seventies (Zainaldin, 2004). The pernicious effects of a poisoned employee relations climate impedes good faith attempts to solve problems given that the other side is always wary of a "catch."

Another risk factor is a blatant power imbalance. When either employees or management achieve dominance, the potential for abuse is greater. As the dictum states, absolute power corrupts absolutely. Employees can impose unreasonable terms and conditions on employers if they lack a commitment to servant leadership and mission achievement. There are many examples of labor and management working synergistically providing a competitive edge if both sides are dedicated to mission achievement and a spirit of humility. Southwest Airlines and the City of Indianapolis are best-practice organizations that are heavily unionized (O'Reilly & Pfeffer, 2000; Rubin & Rubin, 2006). The common denominator is the embrace of partnership perspective based upon trust, mutual commitment, a common set of mission and vision values, and recognition of their mutual dependency.

Servant Leader Character Development and Employee Fair Treatment

How can SLHRM organization begin the long march back to regain employee trust? It begins with character development, a lifelong and intermittently painful process. We can all relate to the central role of trial and tribulation in the shaping and restoration of the heart. A "mountaintop" experience inspires given the breadth and depth of vision, but the close-quarter spiritual warfare combat involved in the maturation process is waged on a daily basis in the dense undergrowth of the organizational jungle with limited lines of sight. We must rely on our moral compass for direction, strength, and wisdom to resist the hidden dangers of ambush by the idols of this world. The great enemy to our success is the internal mental and physiological effects of the internal battle of the mind, the fog and confusion produced by negative thoughts and emotions such as fear, anxiety, discouragement, anger, and lack of forgiveness, among others. When servant leaders are fighting their own internal battles, it reduces the time, effort, and energy for the necessary external focus to cultivate individual and corporate relationships and practices that address the risk factors for unfair employee treatment. We must be intentional in addressing the root cause of our mental warfare temptations, as there are specific actions we must embrace while trusting providence for the overall outcome. One key element is the need to rebut negative thoughts and emotional states with the countervailing words of encouragement and hope. The development of such a balance is a major challenge in our servant leadership walk. When we assume an excessive degree of responsibility for outcomes, the "yoke of legalism" engenders excessive levels of self-effort and a reduction in empowerment, further exacerbating the situation and producing another wave of guilt and condemnation. When we fail to assume the proper degree of shared ownership for outcomes, we shirk our responsibilities to promote mutual growth. Achieving the harmonic mean is an ongoing life challenge.

A major element of servant leader character development is empathy for others. One means for increasing understanding of line employees and their interests is through job rotation. Many corporations rotate their new management or professional hires among service or production level positions to enhance their understanding of the business and develop empathy with line employees. At many companies, professional employees serve in various blue-collar positions. This enhanced knowledge of the production process, employee needs, and problems increases networking contacts.

When trust in a relationship is low, there is a concurrent increase in anxiety and stress. There are two categories of employee responses to a stressful superior-subordinate relationship. The first dimension relates to coping strategies that provide internal psychological adaptations to the stressful situation. For example, there is a calming influence by acknowledging and agreeing with religious faith principles of protection through times of trial. We may have little to no influence regarding the external situation, but we can influence how we react. This is a fertile area for servant leader growth as we experience the challenges that contribute to character development. The second dimension relates to what stress researchers term "adaptive responses" that entail changing the external environment through a physical or interpersonal intervention such as engaging in a principled negotiation strategy to reduce dysfunctional conflict by identifying mutual interests. As servant leader employees and managers, we need to develop a career management toolkit inventory of coping and adaptive strategies. A key factor is identifying the underlying mutual interests that meet the legitimate needs of manager and employee. A third dimension for thought is the development of institutional safeguards to reduce the frequency of dysfunctional work relationships including stress audits to identify the sources of conflict. We address this topic in more detail in Chapter 6. SLHRM organizations proactively reduce employee stress through a variety of organizational practices.

Organizational Practices to Enhance Workplace Justice

This section addresses key organization practices to enhance workplace fair treatment from a macro labor-management perspective. The key element is maintaining an ongoing commitment to promoting a just and fair workplace. As noted in Chapter 2, one very useful framework for viewing employee fair treatment is through the lens of procedural, distributive, and interactional justice. Research demonstrates that employee perceptions of fairness influence a whole host of attitudinal, behavioral, and performance outcomes (De Cremer et al., 2010). Procedural justice entails employee perceptions of the fairness of the organizational decision-making process, including elements such as the presence of due process, the degree of employee input, voice and participation, the presence of clear, specific, fair and transparent decision rules, unbiased and fair decision makers and the comprehensiveness and accuracy of information. If employees are confident the process was fair, they are more willing to accept actions and decisions, even if they disagree or fail to promote their interests. Distributive justice is the perceived fairness of the outcome produced by the decision itself, for example the size of a pay increase or a promotion. Interactional justice refers to the fairness of interpersonal relations and dignified treatment of employees. Clearly all three forms of justice are essential to SLHRM organizational integrity. What are selected key policies and practices to prevent and solve the conditions that contribute to unfair treatment?

Provide Broad Spectrum, 360-Degree Feedback

A powerful means for proactively identifying present or future organizational justice-related problems or liability areas is through a diagnostic "early warning" qualitative research system including employee attitude surveys, focus groups, and retention/exit surveys. Organizations are operating blindly without such systems. However, the most effective "canary in the coal mine" remains open, two-way communication based upon a climate of mutual trust. The qualitative research methods can serve as a focal point for joint labor-management quality improvement and problem solving teams. When the diagnostic instruments identify problematic trends, the organization can implement interventions to address the underlying problem. For example, if the attitude surveys demonstrate employee frustration with high caseloads, labor and management can jointly work together to reduce time invested in less essential tasks to increase the focus on the core functions. However, if information is gathered and "sits on a shelf" unused as a key resource in organizational change, employees develop a cynical approach, reducing their incentive to provide honest feedback.

Managers who terrorize subordinates, clients, and other stakeholders impose great costs in terms of employee wellbeing and organizational effectiveness. The presence and influence of "rogue" managers erodes employee trust and increases vulnerability to lawsuits. SLHRM organizations address this issue through such means as 360-degree feedback systems with subordinate appraisals. FedEx is a "best practice" organization in the use of 360-degree feedback, as managers cannot advance with poor subordinate assessments (FedEx, 2013). In addition, the organization must clearly demand fair and dignified employee treatment in all aspects of the HR system and that employee abuse is grounds for severe discipline and termination. Of course, the same level of accountability is important with employees, given the widespread presence of employee abuse, bullying, and harassment.

Provide Employee Voice

These serious ethical treatment issues place tremendous pressure on employees. SLHRM executives and managers possess a deontological obligation to protect employee interests and integrity. When there is a violation of fiduciary obligation, employees must make difficult decisions to address their cognitive and affective ethical dissonance. Organizational dynamics frequently place significant barriers to a righteous organizational response. A major factor that influences an employee's course of action is the degree of employee loyalty to the organization (See the work of Hirschman, 1970). When loyalty is low, employees are more likely to embrace either active or passive exit. Active exit is leaving the organization, while passive exit entails a "checking-out" at work as the employee psychologically disengages thereby reducing job effort and performing at a minimum level. When loyalty is high, the employee is more likely to attempt voice, or an active process of intervention to change the organization. Employee voice is effective when the following three conditions are present (Hirschman, 1970): (1) there exists an effective means to express employee discontent, (2) the organization possesses the time and resources to change direction, and (3) the organization possesses self-interested reasons to take seriously employee attempts at voice and exit.

There is an inherent quandary at both the employee and customer levels with the interface of a closely linked attitude, that of loyalty. Organizational loyalty is a function of trust, and reflects a cumulative form of psychic capital that can cause employees to overlook the ethical implication of a policy. Hence, employees may overlook or rationalize away misgivings based upon their confidence in the intentions of the organization (psychological trust). In other words, they are excessively liberal in giving the organization the benefit of the doubt. For voice to be credible there needs to be a legitimate perceived threat of exit. When employees possess few employment options, or are subject to easy replacement, voice is muted (Hirschman, 1970). The same thing occurs at the customer level if new clients readily replace dissatisfied customers. As servant leaders, it is our duty to actively seek employee voice and hold ourselves accountable irrespective of the bargaining power held by employees. The best-practice organizations in all sectors possess many formal and informal policies and practices (360-degree feedback systems, employee empowerment, suggestion systems, among others) to increase employee input in order to promote the organization's long-term wellbeing and interests. When organizations embrace employee voice, a bountiful crop of goodwill is harvested, thereby enhancing organizational problem solving and learning.

Labor-Management Collaboration

One goal is to develop an employee-management paradigm shift toward a consensual and collaborative problem solving approach. The key elements for success include recognizing that a just and ethical workplace consists of an ironclad covenant between labor and management. Both sides must be committed to the success of the mission and a means and ends integrity that recognizes their mutual dependency and must assume the attitude of a servant. It requires servant leaders and followers from both labor and management who are willing to risk personal job security and reputation to bridge the conflict gap. There must be champions on both sides, as occurred in the labor-management cooperation initiatives within Indianapolis city government (Rubin & Rubin, 2007) Servant leaders must be willing to love the truth more than the praise of men. As noted previously, a great historical example was Lee Iacocca assuming leadership of the

Chrysler Corporation and accepting a salary of a $1 until the company returned to profitability, thereby demonstrating his empathy, support, and solidarity with employees agreeing to wage and benefit concessions (Herbst, 2007).

Another key but sobering learning point is that the ethical conduct levels can never be taken for granted given our human tendency to rationalize our actions to promote self-interest and the inherent discrepancies between self-image and perceptions of others. We must ruthlessly commit to integrity in all areas of our lives and admit when we fall short. As such, managers must first acknowledge their contributions to the problem before assigning blame to others. Another area in which we must remove the "log from our eye" is by assuming our personal responsibility for the management and work system contributions to the organization's problems. As servant leaders, we must model accountability. Externalizing blame by attributing problems to the employees and other stakeholders accentuates negative job attitudes, apathy, discouragement, conflict, resistance, and distrust. Employees resent being held accountable and responsible for factors beyond their control. Leadership must first analyze its contribution to the fiscal and management problems. Total Quality Management (TQM) guru Edward Deming noted the tendency of management to attribute to employees a much higher percentage of the responsibility for poor performance than warranted (Deming, 1986). Deming believed that 90 percent of productivity problems were the responsibility of systems, hence an overlooked management accountability area. Whether the actual figure is 90 percent or 1 percent employee responsibility, the trust restoration process begins with a critical self-appraisal of leadership's contributions to the problem, to remove the log from our eye first. Only then can we reverse the human tendency to demand justice for others, but grace for ourselves.

Secondly, leaders must "humble themselves" and reach out, acknowledging that the relationship is broken and I am a major problem contributor. This lays the foundation for the next stage, searching for the areas of common ground of mutual interest and gain. When these areas are located, propose a jointly empowered process to develop a solution to a well-defined and readily solvable problem, thus searching for the "low-hanging fruit." The area selected should be limited in scope (start small) with the decision rules mutually developed with accountability and evaluation mechanism equally verifiable. A very effective summary of this approach is Ury, Fisher, and Patton's (1991) classical book of *Getting to Yes.*

When we achieve success in small areas, it begins to melt the glacial and hardened hearts with hope. The next stage is the development of employee-management teams to solve jointly the common problem areas. Employees and management should be jointly empowered to make changes in work processes, work rules, staffing practices and supervisory spans of control (reduce management staffing). It is critical to provide training to support the problem solving efforts from both a technical (quality improvement techniques) and process perspectives (group functioning) learning from best-practice examples of other employee-management partnerships. It is important as well to publicize actively the results of these efforts to reinforce perceptions of progress in building trust and reducing cynicism. Another key reinforcement practice entails explicitly linking the results of employee-management cooperation initiatives to the performance management and appraisal system. It is essential to develop standards and metrics for management that emphasize the promotion of harmonious employee relations and a high quality of work life. To reinforce a climate of innovation, one effective approach is to reward employees for cost reductions and productivity increases through a gain sharing (sharing a portion of the savings) and bonus system (Arthur & Huntley, 2005).

A collaborative employee-management approach is truly the road less traveled, but provides a great opportunity to change the culture of an organization to promote a more ethical and moral climate. Even in the areas of unionization which is anathema to many organizations, it is important to resist automatic opposition to unions. Even Sunbelt cities like Tampa, Memphis, and Atlanta manifest strong support for unions based upon high levels of community and political system support for social justice oriented employment policies that benefit minorities through the higher wage and benefits levels of union living wage jobs. Are labor unions antithetical to SLHRM values? I believe the answer is no. There are numerous examples of mutually beneficial labor and management partnerships across the public and private sectors (O'Reilly & Pfeffer, 2000; Rubin & Rubin, 2007). There are numerous examples of successful companies, such as Southwest and Lincoln Electric, that partner with unions (Handlin, 1992; O'Reilly & Pfeffer, 2000).

Compensation Elements

Another "window on the heart" related to distributive justice is the distribution of profits and revenue, or how the fruits of employee labor are distributed. Compensation should be fair and generous, and research demonstrates organizations that pay higher than market wages (leaders) manifest higher retention levels among other benefits (O'Halloran, 2012). In all sectors, there is a moral and ethical obligation to share the fruits of the labor with employees. It is my belief that if organizations adopted a salary, compensation, and working condition "market leader" policy, they would be even more successful and profitable over the long run. One question that is important from a wage and social justice standpoint is whether it is better to employ fewer workers at a living wage or more workers at subsistence levels. Should SLHRM organizations choose to pay higher wages than the market? One approach is that employees must assume responsibility for human capital development and obtain advanced skills and training if they expect a living wage. However, employers can demonstrate their commitment to employees by providing training and education subsidies to employees that can prepare them for advancement within the organization or other employers. Some organizations will provide education and training benefits in non-job related areas in effect preparing them for new careers, such as teaching, that benefit the employee and the community (Raines, 2012). This demonstrates love and respect for employees. I believe that choosing to pay above market wage levels demonstrates trust, confidence, and recognition that the organization's success is a product of a team effort. In essence, it reflects the choice to adhere to the letter versus the spirit of the compensation system law.

Performance Management Fairness

Performance management is a core SLHRM function area that addresses the interface between core servanthood and stewardship values in a decision-making environment characterized by ambiguity and intense time pressures. Performance management is the set of organizational policies and practices to ensure effective employee performance including strategic planning, performance measurement and appraisal, and the progressive discipline process. A fair performance management system begins with a requisite level of reliability and validity to support HR decision making. When performance management systems are biased, it increases the potential for legal liability issues such as wrongful discharge, negligent hiring and retention, and adverse impact by race, age, and gender while lowering employee trust and confidence in management. There should be a systematic decision-making process employed to identify areas of inefficient allocation of human resources and to separate poorly performing employees. As we shall explore later in the book, many performance management systems lack the requisite level of reliability and validity to support HR decision making, increasing legal liability for wrongful discharge and adverse impact on protected groups (race, age, gender) while lowering employee trust and confidence in management.

Fairness in the performance management process begins with a developmental and coaching-based process of clear and specific performance goals and standards, specific and timely performance feedback, and the opportunity to provide input into work goals and standards. When performance problems develop and reach a level in which formal management action is necessary, corrective and progressive discipline is the foundation. When management disciplines or discharges employees for cause through the inability to meet performance standards, rule violations, or ethical and moral transgressions, procedural justice requires providing a: 1) disciplinary process based upon the principles of "just cause" including advanced employee notice and warning, 2) the violation's clear connection to safe, efficient and effective operations, 3) a detailed, complete, timely, and investigatory (discovery) process with comprehensive employee input and participation, 4) sufficient evidence to support the action, and 5) a consistent and unbiased rule application process (Chief Human Resource Office, 2014). The final ideal element is a fair appeals process ideally before an unbiased and independent review board or official (Folger & Cropanzano, 1998; Jackson & Schuler, 2006).

Many organizations fail to provide an objective and independent appeals process, eroding trust and fairness.

Organizational Termination Decisions

As a servant leader, we approach all forms of organizational separation decisions with humble "fear and trembling." Employees possess souls, and we must engage in deep moral reflection regarding the appropriate course of action. As management author Michael Zigarelli (2003) notes, downsizing or firing per se is neither unethical nor contrary to servant leader principles. Servant leaders are genuine "realistic optimists," embracing the belief that good is produced from all situations, and there are instances in which this form of "tough love" discipline is necessary for the best interests and wellbeing of the employee. We certainly do not state this flippantly, recognizing the breadth and depth of the consequences for the employee and his or her family.

The various separation categories include fiscal, performance, and mission-based mass layoffs, and performance or conduct-related individual terminations. SLHRM managers should begin by analyzing the implications of layoffs relative to four key areas: (1) morality, ethics, and values, (2) HR implications in terms of employee attitudes and behavior, (3) financial integrity, and (4) performance/mission impact. A key question is how the layoffs will influence organizational trust. The decision to terminate or lay off employees entails a profound ethical and values-based dilemma on multiple levels. These include the inherent morality of separating employees in a time of economic recession, the impact on families and the community, the procedural justice implications (the fairness of the process and its associated criteria), and the distributive justice consequences (who is deserving of layoff). When narrow fiscal self-interest drives the decision-making process, it impedes the genuine expression of love and support in the workplace and contributes to moral compartmentalization (e.g. "I am not responsible for the consequences of organizational actions relative to the lives of employees"). Layoffs generate stress, fear, and "survivor's guilt" for those who remain. The addition of higher workloads increases job demands and pressures, contributing to job disengagement and burnout. Employees who are stressed and afraid develop a defensive posture that reduces compassion in the workplace (helping others), and contributes to minimal levels of work effort ("not in my job description" syndrome). Chronic job insecurity is a source of employee job stress adversely influencing employee job satisfaction, commitment, work motivation, productivity, and citizenship behaviors (compassion fatigue), hence a vicious circular casual path (Hellgren, Sverke, & Isaksson, 1999; Marchand & Blanc, 2011).

Layoff decision rules should incorporate financial viability. However, economic criteria are necessary, but never a single sufficient criterion from a SLHRM perspective. From a servant leader worldview, an organization provides services and goods that promote society's greater purposes and good. SLHRM organizations understand the importance of a long-term covenant, and are willing to incur significant short- and long-term financial loss and hardship and lower levels of long-term profit or net revenue to honor core relationship obligations. From a servant leader worldview, if love is the ultimate "currency," then relationship viability is the moral key and end goal necessary for mission success.

SLHRM organizations imbed layoff decisions within the achievement of greater purposes. Hence, the financial standards that justify immediate or future layoffs for SLHRM organizations are very demanding. It is important to assess both the short- and long-term effects and the consistency with SLHRM values. Hence, they frequently contribute to a conflict between traditional financial metrics and servant leadership values. For example, are the short-term financials improving? If so, this provides evidence to support delaying layoffs until clear evidence of sustained long-term negative fiscal trends emerges.

As with mass layoffs, individual performance or conduct-based terminations should be the option of last resort and only after the institution of a progressive discipline process. As Michael Zigarelli (2003) notes in an article on the termination procedure, grace with accountability should be the default decision-making approach. One reason for this attitude is that the necessity to terminate reflects a collective failure apportioned between the manager (e.g., the absence of mentoring), flawed organizational systems (e.g., poor selection and training practices) and the employee's behavior (e.g., failure to receive and integrate performance feedback). SLHRM organizations grant employees ample opportunities to correct deficiencies, but employees possess a concurrent good faith obligation to be teachable and make good faith efforts to apply the feedback and guidance.

However, SLHRM organizations do terminate, and a highly personal example (my own termination story) illustrates that we must assume a long-term perspective. A workplace termination for any reason or cause can be a very traumatic and humiliating experience, especially if one manifests prideful perfectionist tendencies. I completed my Masters in Public Administration degree with a 4.0 average, and obtained an excellent entry-level career position as a HR representative at a paper mill in Alabama. There are many career lessons related to my experience, but the most profound related to that final interview as the plant manager terminated me. The "straw" that broke the camel's back related to what I considered to be a "minor" job duty. As personnel representative, I coordinated the recognition events for work teams that exhibited zero accidents for a designated time. Working in a paper mill is dangerous, and safety is a life and death issue. When work teams avoid injuries, there is great pride and joy for both rank-and-file and management. At one of these events, the recognition cake did not arrive from the bakery. As personnel representative, I had completed all of my required duties for the event, however my attention was focused on conversations with other employees, and I was too distracted to notice that the men and the supervisor were greatly upset. It was not in my job description, so why be concerned? I was too oblivious to notice the consternation and anger of the supervisor. Later that week, on a Saturday, the plant manager called me into his office. He politely but firmly stated that they must reluctantly terminate me for ongoing performance deficiencies including my lack of "common sense" and initiative related to the "cake incident." He left me with words that forever will be with me. He said "Gary, what you did at the recognition event is like driving down a rainy road at night in the midst of a storm. You see a large log in the road in the middle of your lane and are able to stop and drive around it. You miss it, but what about the next person? What if that person was your wife or daughter? You could have stopped and cleared that log and saved a life." Those words resonated in my spirit, and humbled me in a profound manner. I was crushed by the termination, but I learned powerful life lessons that benefit me to this day and I now commit to working outside of my job description and assume responsibility for problems. When I see debris or road hazards, I stop and clear them, or call the emergency road hazard number. Logs in the road are in my job description! I admit that I do not stop at every road hazard, but I take action when I can. At work, I am cognizant of the "road hazards" and strive to take responsibility for problems that I did not make, but in which I can help others. As servant followers and leaders, solving problems and helping others is a permanent duty.

In deciding on the correct course, we have the benefit of hindsight and many years of research to shed additional light on the situation. Servant leadership requires a 360-degree stakeholder-by-stakeholder justice assessment to identify the consequences of the layoffs (employees, shareholders, and the community). This entails addressing the procedural and distributive justice implications of termination decisions for all relevant stakeholders. Another important principle is that as managers we are the shepherds of the flock. None of us wants to stand before our Maker with ineffectual excuses as to why we failed to protect the interests of our employees, their families, and the community. As such, it is our responsibility to protect our employees to the best of our ability, even if it means significant personal loss. There is an increasing body of research demonstrating that the various forms of downsizing (layoffs and contracting out) as a cost reduction and profit-maximizing strategy is ineffective and actually delays a return to profitability (De Meuse et al., 2004; van Dierendonck & Jacobs, 2012). What is clear is that there are a host of dysfunctional consequences such as higher levels of employee stress, a loss of institutional memory reducing productivity, and higher degrees of anxiety and insecurity (Brandes et al., 2008).

The indiscriminate use of layoffs violates the implied psychological contract between employees and management, resulting in a loss of trust, lower levels of job satisfaction, survivor's guilt, reduced organizational commitment, higher levels of turnover, loss of institutional memory, and elevated employee stress levels due to the increased workload. The establishment of a servant leadership covenantal relationship (as with Southwest Airlines) entails the adoption of a policy in which layoffs are a last resort remedy. This entails empowering employees to increase efficiency and effectiveness and use the creative energy of employees to solve organizational problems. When employees are active participants in the quality process, they are more likely to accept layoffs when there are no other options. Accountability begins with management making the initial sacrifices through reductions in compensation, bonuses, and stock options before engaging in downsizing. When organizations view the employment relationship as a covenant, there are reduced reliance on layoffs and a greater embrace of strategies such as hiring and salary freezes/reductions, voluntary furloughs, early retirement, and employee layoff "volunteers."

If financial conditions mandate layoffs, servant leadership requires that we support employees adversely impacted by organizational stewardship decisions. This sends a clear message that the organization values employees and actively considers the consequences of its decisions. In a layoff situation, the organization should entail ample advanced notice of the layoffs, a comprehensive outplacement support program that includes severance pay, job placement and counseling, transitional paid health insurance for a reasonable period, and educational and retraining assistance. The decision to terminate employees entails a profound set of ethical and values-based issues including the procedural justice implications (the fairness of the process and its associated criteria), and the distributive justice consequences (who is deserving of layoff). The ethical challenge is especially acute in a time of economic recession given the impact on families and the community. How an organization manages this process reflects essential character and integrity issues for leadership and the organization as a whole.

The list below provides a summary of the main principles related to SLHRM downsizing decisions. These principles are "ideal" type and foundational to a workplace culture that places employee and human relationships at the center. We cannot love our neighbor as ourselves if we treat employees as mere instruments of production. These principles clearly increase the short-term costs of operations, but we must sacrifice short-term gain for the wellbeing of all stakeholders.

- *Establish a workplace covenant that embraces job security as a foundational value with layoffs as a strategy of last resort.* SLHRM organizations cultivate an ethos of mutual sharing of the financial pain and loss between employees and management. This reinforces the commitment of the organization to its employees and its employees' commitment and humble submission under management's authority. Hence, management and employees should share the costs and burdens of economic problems. The strategies of "first resort" include:
- *The key factor for the servant leader is the confirmatory evidence provided by moral and ethical reflection.* Management and leadership empower employees to engage in continuous improvement to enhance organizational efficiency and productivity. Employees should share in the benefits of increased efficiency and effectiveness (a gain sharing system that provides employee bonuses, for example). This will improve the organization's effectiveness to reduce the probability of downsizing.
- *Empower employees at all levels to develop solutions.* This entails productivity improvement suggestions, new product development, and innovative marketing efforts. Tap the expertise and good will of employees to develop creative solutions. In addition, higher levels of employee input reduce employee stress and anxiety while increasing organizational trust.
- *Empower employees to develop a collective commitment to sharing the costs and the associated pain.* It is unlikely that employee efforts to develop creative solutions will solve the problem in the short term. At this stage, it would be wise to empower employees to devise methods for sharing the burden, including hiring freezes, pay reductions, early retirement options, relaxation or work rule restrictions, work hour reductions, and voluntary reductions in grade or job classification systems, transfers, or reassignment to lower-skilled positions, among others. These options must be carefully managed and balanced to avoid a loss of institutional expertise and disrupting established work relationships and routines of the production departments.
- If reducing costs and increasing efficiencies are insufficient, consider voluntary/involuntary furloughs and salary and benefit

reductions as the next stage for leadership, management, staff, and line positions.

- If downsizing must occur due to a serious and prolonged fiscal crisis, adopt a fair and transparent protocol for separations with the following attributes:
  - Openly share the fiscal or other mission-related rationale with employees, including access to budget, financial, and performance data to validate the financial exigency. Organizational leaders then consult with employees who provide input into the downsizing implementation plan. This reinforces management trust in employees.
  - Leadership commits to ensuring that as many terminations as possible will be accomplished by attrition or other non-coercive means (e.g., a hiring freeze, buy-outs, early retirement, etc.).
  - Ask employees voluntarily to assume the role of a contractor or part-time employee with a commitment to rehire when business warranted. This would work most effectively if done on a voluntary basis. If organizations mandated this step, most employees would view it as exploitative.
  - Leadership provides as much advance notice as possible for all layoff decisions (ideally at least three months).
  - Leadership clearly communicates the impact and scope of the separations and how remaining employees will be affected and supported.
  - Provide a relevant severance package including education and training assistance.
  - Provide job counseling services, job training, and outplacement assistance Provide life transition or mental health counseling.
  - Provide paid benefits for six months or until the employee obtains a new position.
  - Provide viable reinstatement options if the economic conditions improve.
  - Promote pensions and health insurance portability to reduce fiscal and family stress.
  - Provide each separated employee with a personal thank you and statement of regret from leadership.

Many will "roll their eyes" over such an extensive list, but organizations that "walk the extra mile" and truly "count the cost" reap precious fruits of support and trust. A great historical example of these principles is Malden Mills, the Massachusetts textile company.

In 1995, the plant burned to the ground, and the company was faced with closing its doors and laying off 3,000 employees with devastating consequences to the community (Leung, 2003). The owner of the company, Aaron Feuerstein, rejected the path of expediency, embraced the Golden Rule, and paid the employees while the plant was rebuilt, generating tremendous good will and loyalty leading to long-term prosperity. If more employers would embrace a covenantal, long-term approach, we would create a more just, equitable, and prosperous workplace and society. Hence, when servant leaders take the path less traveled, it produces a treasure trove of employee benefits.

The Recruitment Process

SLHRM organizations frame the workplace in the terms of a covenant. This entails establishing a set of mutually recognized and observed obligations and benefits that govern and order workplace interactions, terms and conditions. In essence, the employment relationship is one of the most important life roles. Managers are shepherds of the flock, possessing a humbling and fearful level of accountability while employees must work diligently. The recruitment process establishes a foundation for the communication and demonstration of the organization's values.

Organizations are often tempted to terminate newly or recently hired employees when fiscal problems emerge. From the employee's perspective, it is a breach of faith when a candidate accepts a job offer and the organization suddenly informs them that their services are no longer required. Employees accept organizational offers of employment in good faith. An early termination imposes high costs on employees relative to relocation expenses, the stress of job change and moving, lost income and most importantly, adverse career development effects. The organization violates the psychological contract, generating a pernicious fruit of anger and dissatisfaction. In addition, employees can suffer adverse effects related to their reputation, even with economic layoffs, given the widespread practice of using fiscal exigency as a convenient excuse for terminating problem employees.

Contingent Labor

It is important that SLHRM organizations use contingent labor in a moral fashion, adhering to servant leader principles and values. Contingent labor consists of contract, temporary and part-time employees. Contingent labor when used judiciously is an effective means for providing services at lower costs. The benefits of contingent labor for management include lower staffing costs, a more accurate assessment of employee ability and performance before a permanent hire, and increased staffing flexibility. For employees, the advantages include the promotion of work life balance (job sharing, part-time work), enhanced learning and career development opportunities, and the flexibility to "test-drive" careers or employers before a long-term commitment.

The use of contingent labor is becoming standard practice in today's flexible, "just-in-time" service delivery and manufacturing processes. Many employers are reducing the cadre of permanent employees while utilizing contract employees at times of peak demand. However, it is also a great source of temptation to replace full-time employees simply to reduce labor costs. This increases the job insecurity of permanent employees. In addition to the lower wage and benefit levels, contingent employees frequently endure higher workloads and reduced investment in employee training, health, and safety. In addition, managers and full-time employees frequently view contingent employees as "second-class citizens" creating an "in-group and out-group culture" in which the organization refrains from the communication and relationship investments needed to adequately empower, support, encourage, and mentor their contingent labor. In essence, the organization denies contingent labor the requisite level of dignity ascribed to full-time workers. Temporary workers are frequently disengaged given the lack of investment in their future (Boyce et al., 2007). Managers possess a higher degree of position power relative to contingent labor given their contractual, at-will status, but this coercive power to terminate does not engender genuine, heart-based motivation. Employers have the power of sword, but fear produces only minimal engagement, commitment, and motivational levels. The lower adherence of temporary and contract employees to the mission is a very real and present danger.

Attendance Policies

One key aspect of SLHRM ethics is the systematic assessment of how organizational policies influence the attendance incentive and motivational system of employees. Are we tempting our employees to rebel by abusing sick time? The important issue here from a servant leadership perspective relates to the mutual responsibilities of employees and management. The research clearly indicates that the majority of unscheduled absenteeism is not for employee sickness (Bonacum &

Allen, 2007). The decision to call in sick is the employee's alone, but does the employer bear any responsibility for the underlying incentives? Clearly, the answer is yes. When organizational workloads are excessive, supervision ineffective, support and encouragement absent, and abuse and bullying is rampant, employees are looking for "mental health" days.

Another issue that increases the complexity of absentee management programs is the interaction between the Family and Medical Leave Act (FMLA) and the Americans with Disabilities Act (ADA) in relation to mental illness and stress-related illnesses. These conditions are more difficult to diagnose reliably and hence can be an area in which employees can manipulate the system. Clearly, stress illnesses are reaching epidemic proportions but the actions of a minority of manipulators are making it more difficult for those with legitimate problems to receive help.

In an ideal world, the internalization of servant leader moral values is the essential immunization as employees recognize that honesty is the best policy, and that employee character flaws will ultimately sabotage both their personal success and that of the organization. It is very tempting for employees to abuse paid time off, and easy for management to look the other way. However, there are significant monetary and nonmonetary costs to unscheduled absenteeism and it is essential to communicate clearly the nature, magnitude, and effects of those expenses in terms of their ethical and utilitarian aspects. These include that misusing sick leave imposes a tax on all employees through higher workloads and the associated mental and physical stress in addition to the increased labor and production costs. It is important to recognize that when there are chronic attendance problems, there is a collective systems failure. If employees abuse the system, the organization must carefully assess the factors that encourage employees to abuse paid time off. In many cases, it is the unrighteous treatment of employees through unrealistic performance expectations, unfair supervision, poor compensation, abusive and dysfunctional relationships with supervisors, peers and/or clients, sexual harassment, and other forms of discrimination. In other instances, it simply reflects a lax moral climate in which management and HR fail to monitor the system.

Hiring for character is a major element of an effective servant leader SLHRM system, but given prolonged temptation, even virtuous employees succumb to paid time off abuse. The formula requires treating employees with respect and dignity but requiring a concurrent level of integrity and responsibility. Many employers provide immature employees with unwarranted and unwise degrees of freedom and autonomy, thereby providing the means to support their own ongoing moral failures. Permitting chronic leave abusers to manipulate the system provides additional rationale, motivation, and temptation for others to act upon their negative impulses. The key here is to set high ethical standards, provide incentives for correct behavior, and administer appropriate discipline. Absentee control responsibility is a partnership with employees and management with each side possessing important obligations and roles. It is always easier to blame the other party before looking in the mirror. The key is to train managers to administer the system in a uniform but flexible manner that takes into consideration mitigating circumstances. There should be no compromise on foundational principles and ethics, but reasonable grace. It is important to move beyond the confines of the absenteeism control plan to address the key intrinsic motivational issues. The long-term solution is to change the underlying value orientation of employees by increasing the job's intrinsic motivational attraction through job enrichment work redesign enhancing task significance, task identity, skill variety, knowledge of results, and job autonomy (Hackman, & Oldham, 1976). This encourages the development of group norms and values that reward and reinforce servant followership.

Attendance policies encapsulate the clash of competing motivational philosophies. Should we reward employees for meeting a basic term and condition of employment such as showing up for work? If the answer is yes, this runs the risk of reducing intrinsic incentives for attendance. The answer to that question partially relates to a person's worldview. A teleological behaviorist worldview adopts the utilitarian approach of embracing practices that produce the greatest good. Recognizing employees for high levels of attendance clearly communicates a greater level of employee regard and appreciation. A deontological principle approach states that rewarding people for doing the correct thing ultimately weakens motivation. This occurs when the reward is no longer provided (extinguished), hence the motivational force behind the behavior loses its power. I believe that intrinsic motives are more effective, but an effective system clearly requires both extrinsic and intrinsic incentives. In many cases, the heart of the issue is character and ethical integrity, hence system behavioral management only addresses the symptoms, not the root cause, and there is always room for manipulation by negatively motivated employees.

Managers bear responsibility for anticipating attendance-related motivational temptations and how the system affects employees and their incentives for maintaining proper conduct. However, leaving adjustments solely to managerial discretion can produce an undesirable level of variance in accommodating legitimate employee needs leading to differential working conditions and perceptions of unfairness. We cannot change the heart of our employees, but we can provide moral role models and boundaries that protect employees from their negative impulses. Using positive reinforcement for improvement in the behavior of the chronic abusers has its place, but unless they demonstrate good faith and improvement, it is in management's best interest to terminate with due process.

However, given human nature, abuse of paid time off frequently occurs. Managing to both the letter and spirit requires a greater depth of thought and reflection. Given the hectic "fire-engine" management environment, most managers react on autopilot. If there is a pattern of abuse, what are the options? In most cases, management needs to enforce existing rules rather than develop new draconian policies that penalize employees. It is sometimes easier to institute a new policy than to directly confront the employees that are abusing the system. Management must muster the courage to overcome the resistance and rebellion of the "prodigal" employee and use loving discipline to re-orient mindsets. Hence, from a systems perspective, there is an important need to involve the supervisors in diagnosing the causes and solutions to chronic absenteeism and tardiness. Front line supervisors bear the greatest burdens in terms of absenteeism control, and their input is critical from a diagnostic standpoint in identifying the cause of absenteeism as well as potential strategies for addressing the problem.

There needs to be a balance of flexibility and standardization in absenteeism reduction systems. However, there are significant administrative and legal complexities generated by a flexible system. How can the organization balance the two interests? First, clearly reinforce a point of "servant leader 101," that moral conduct is the most effective path. Concurrently, servant leaders provide a clear rationale for the policy's negative consequences, discipline employees that fail to honor standards, and most importantly, provide forgiveness and grace opportunities to demonstrate a genuine change of heart and behavior. A sole reliance on a punishment and rewards system is operant conditioning, a hedonistic worldview strategy.

The absenteeism area provides a promising venue for increasing trust between unions and management. A very important element when trust is absent is providing mutually agreed upon decision rules and mutually verifiable information and data. When there is suspicion of the motives and intent of the other party, it is important to begin relationship restoration with an issue such as absenteeism that lends itself to transparent and mutually verifiable analysis. Absenteeism is an issue in which both sides possess mutual interests and a potential "win-win" bargaining position. Providing data on the negative consequences of an absenteeism control plan is a key element of a partnership in solving the problem. For example, consider developing a paid time off system that lumps together sick, personal, and vacation days, compensating employees for unused time. These systems provide more flexibility for employees and reduce management monitoring requirements. Employees can take time off for any reason with advanced notice, and then use the days for unscheduled absenteeism as well. These systems remove management from having to police employee behavior while reducing the temptation for employee deception. However, from a servant leader worldview, is this simply another policy decoupling moral responsibility from decision making? I understand and generally embrace the use of positive incentives, but my question relates to our obligation as employees from a servant leader worldview. Servant followers and leaders understand that we obey not to receive rewards, but to honor moral principles. Hence, we do well and right as part of our ethical nature, knowing that when we violate standards, there are consequences.

Employees need to receive clear and specific communication and training on the various key HR policy areas including absenteeism and its consequences and sign an accountability pledge committing them to honoring both the letter and spirit of the policies and practices. As servant followers, we possess an obligation to "honor the king" and review the relevant policies and procedures that govern our terms and conditions of employment. When employees do not take the time to review the information, they place themselves at risk. It is important that employees read the employee handbook and absenteeism policies and discuss the policies in orientation and training sessions. In this regard, having employees sign an agreement that they have reviewed the handbook and the various attendance policies is another means to reinforce employee moral responsibility.

Presenteeism

The opposite end of the continuum of paid sick time abuse is presenteeism, or working while sick (Bonacum & Allen, 2007; Cocker, Martin, & Sanderson, 2012). Both presenteeism and absenteeism contribute to organizational ineffectiveness, though presenteeism is more difficult to measure. Recognize that all attendance policies possess a foundational motivational worldview that reflect and operationally define the organization's view of human nature. In making the decision to work while ill, should workers be trusted with autonomy, or do they need strict controls? Another key element is the type of error and cost produced when working while ill. In many settings, it is more costly to have workers on the job who are sick and not 100 percent productive than in others. In other settings, the absence from work has serious performance implications thereby enhancing the importance of both attendance rewards and accountability. Hence, the absentee policy may be more effective with less stringent controls and reduced penalties for unscheduled absences. Management and employees need to grasp the many ethical issues surrounding chronic employee absenteeism. There are significant costs related to the employee who needs to take time off, but will not. Employees can become legalistic when work assumes the status of an idol. Employees become addicted to the affirmation and recognition related to their essentiality and thereby believe that their presence is essential for success. Only a more balanced view of life and a greater understanding of moral and negative performance effects of working while ill break this vicious cycle. Are we being our brother's keeper when we come to work sick? What are the costs on other employees and productivity? Will working while sick impede recovery? Employees must grasp that their decision to work while sick has broader consequences.

The chapter will conclude with a discussion of the key principles related to promoting a climate of fair employee treatment in relation to servant leader business principles and competition.

Servant Leader Business Principles: Competition

Servant leader principles embrace and promote social justice, but reject radical egalitarianism for equal opportunity and the inequality of rewards. Providence endows human nature with a diversity of gifts, talents, and resources. However, this diversity of gifts will produce a diversity of outcomes. SLHRM organizations embrace a competition grounded within a spirit of humility and agape love. If our motives are anything but love, they fail the servant leader morality test. Our pride and self-interest corrupts virtue. We must ruthlessly subject our motives to the review and discernment of moral reflection. Power and success corrupts subtly and incrementally in the heart ungrounded in the truth. Define success in servant leader terms in which growth in revenue and budgets are a means to support larger more noble ends.

There is much confusion about the nature of competition. Servant leaders are called to excellence, but we do not compete against others in a zero sum fashion, but to perfect our individual and collective gifts, talents, and character traits to accomplish the mission more effectively and serve others with a greater degree of efficacy. In essence, we are competing against ourselves as we grow in servant leader character. The competition, however, is a loving and grace-filled exercise in which we realize that we learn as much or more from failure as we do from success. We confuse servant leader excellence and worldly excellence much too frequently. We must learn that servant leader winning entails humility and practicing self-control. Morality requires a tripartite set of conditions. The competition should possess a moral root motive, employ a fair playing field, use righteous means, and be directed at a goal that improves the human condition in some form, either spiritual or material. As such, competition frequently fails to meet these standards of morality. Moral competition stimulates innovation, creativity, and learning in both organizations and individuals. Servant leader competition rejects a destructive "take no prisoners" mentality but embraces the pursuit of excellence to achieve the mission and contribute to the greater good of all the stakeholders. Moral competition is a form of motivation and learning at the individual and group level, elevating character and performance. It is like a rising tide that lifts all.

As the body is composed of many parts of different size and purpose, we all possess a unique mission function that requires a variety of resources to accomplish the tasks set before us. The real key is the stewardship issue, that we follow moral principles in how we use our diverse resources, gifts, and talents to promote integrity in word and deed. From a servant leader perspective, work is a foundational life domain, and therefore job creation is a prime criterion for a servant leader led organization.

Servant Leader Business Principles: Job Creation

SLHRM organizations embrace job creation as a foundational mission element. Two private sector companies that provide excellent lessons are Cardone and Pura Vida as both demonstrate a high form of mission integrity while protecting different elements of the servant leader worldview. Pura Vida is a company that grows fair trade, organic coffee while supporting many charities. Its business plan provides letter and spirit integrity regarding its emphasis on community investment and promoting social justice. It is a collective expression of shared values across many different producers. Pura Vida reinforces the principle that a servant leader organization invests in the spiritual, emotional, and physical wellbeing of workers, their families, and the larger communities in which they operate.

A second company that can provides a great role model is Cardone Industries, one of the leading remanufacturers of car parts in the world. The company models biblical values by espousing and practicing servant leadership as a foundational value of their workplace covenant, a moral psychological contract. Employees share generously in the fruits of their labor, and management views employees as precious souls, not as instrumental numbers. A signature element of Cardone is their commitment to employee growth and wellbeing through education and training. Cardone is a more centralized company than Pura Vida, but given federal laws relative to religious discrimination, they must provide a broader tent of more generalized Golden Rule values. It requires a passionate commitment to common grace Golden Rule values plus the personal devotion of a cadre of leaders at all organizational levels. Cardone possesses word and deed integrity in terms of employee treatment. When employees recognize that they are valued not for what the produce, but for who they are, it generates bonds of trust and love. Kingdom Businesses do not manufacture "needs" which are really "desires" based upon lusts. Hence, they reject marketing campaigns that persuade consumers that luxuries are really necessities. The root of the deception relates to the locus of responsibility for creating wealth, who owns the increase, and the proper use of the fruits. The original sin of pride is the most powerful corruption force. We violate servant leader moral principles when we begin to believe it is through our efforts alone that wealth and value are created and "the fruits are mine to do with as I wish." A true moral and leadership deception! Hence, servant leader business principles are a powerful tool for demonstrating love in a 360-degree fashion (employees, customers, the community).

Conclusion

Fair employee treatment is not an optional element for servant leadership. How we treat others is a reflection of our own hearts and its foundational motives. When leaders embrace a self-serving, instrumental approach, employees become means to an end. This is the ultimate dehumanization process. This chapter reinforces the importance of more than a superficial embrace if we are truly to embrace a moral perspective.

SLHRM Leadership Personal Character Reflection: Avoiding Instrumentalism

Servant leaders recognize the danger of adopting worldly standards of analysis that are contrary to moral principles. To my consternation, management frequently uses the term "fat" to describe the inefficient use of human resources. This term reduces flesh, blood, and spirit-possessing employees to instruments of production that are to be discarded or purged based upon the "rational analysis" of management. This is prime example of the dehumanizing influence of rational instrumentalism, a deeply ingrained value system, in which employees are a means of production and "costs" to be managed and minimized. A poignant example of instrumentalism is in Charles Dickens's classic *A Christmas Carol*. The main character, Ebenezer Scrooge, callously rebuffs all requests for charitable contributions and states that the poor should "die to decrease the surplus population." The Ghost of Christmas Present convicts Scrooge when he gives him a glimpse of the starving children he condemned by his callous statement and states that in the eyes of heaven Scrooge is the "hard-hearted" member of the true "surplus" population.

I am not advocating that leaders ignore staffing efficiency, effectiveness, and fiscal stress considerations. However, these decisions require the integration of moral and ethical value assessments founded upon a covenantal relationship. A workplace covenant is the presence of a long-term relationship with an iron clad mutual commitment between employer and employee to promote the best interests of all stakeholders and achieve the mission with excellence. In a workplace covenant, a moral and ethical framework governs all HR decisions in which the value of maintaining the relationship is of prime importance and layoffs and termination are "last resort" options. Clearly, there are instances when fiscal pressures or serious conduct, performance or character deficiencies justify termination, but we approach such decisions with "fear and trembling." We possess a higher calling as servant leaders to remove the judgmental log from our own eye before we can clearly identify the "surplus" population. Removing the "fat" in management decisions is not cosmetic plastic surgery removed by liposuction, but is a decision of profound importance that involves human being employees with souls, feelings, and families. Let us all commit to purge ourselves from worldviews and standards that place barriers to moral employee treatment.

SLHRM Leadership Personal Character Reflection: Kingdom Business Principles

The forging of servant leader character occurs in all aspects of the workplace. If we work for a private sector company, what are the key elements of a moral business? These elements are especially important for those of us who are managers, executives, and owners of businesses. It is important to reflect on several key business principles that help guide servant leaders in business, nonprofit and government organizations. What are the servant leader business principles associated with good character?

One of the key elements is recognizing that the foundation is dignified respect and treatment of all stakeholders (employees, clients, suppliers, etc.). Always remember that moral treatment freely granting dignity to all. However, another important principle is diversity of rewards based upon contributions and performance as broadly defined. Servant leader business and commerce is an ordained activity that embraces an inequality of rewards. The fair distribution of rewards centers on moral motives, means, and ends in a spirit of humility and agape love. If our motives are anything but love, our accomplishments burn in the "fire" of moral standards of excellence. Self-interest and pride corrupts virtue. We must ruthlessly subject our motives to critical self-analysis. Power and success corrupts subtly and incrementally the heart ungrounded in the truth. Define success in moral terms in which profits are a means to support larger and nobler ends.

There is much confusion about the nature of competition. Servant leadership entails excellence, but we do not compete against others in a "fixed sum" manner ("my gain is their loss" and vice versa). Moral competition recognizes that success entails an "expanding pie" of love to cultivate concurrently the growth of servant leader character in ourselves while promoting the wellbeing of others thereby perfecting their faith, gifts, and talents. In essence, we are competing against ourselves as we grow. The competition, however, is a loving and grace-filled exercise in which we realize that we learn as much or more from failure as we do from success. We confuse moral excellence and worldly excellence much too frequently. We must learn that moral winning entails humility.

To be moral, there is a tripartite set of conditions that must be present. The competition must possess a moral root motive based upon a form of love expression, must be conducted in fair and ethical manner (means integrity) and must be directed at a goal that improves the human condition, either spiritually or materially. As such, competition at any level rarely meets the pure standards of morality. Moral competition stimulates innovation, creativity, and learning in both organizations and individuals. Moral competition rejects a destructive "take no prisoners" mentality, but embraces a grace-filled pursuit of excellence that celebrates human dignity.

As the body is composed of many parts of different size and purpose, we all possess a unique marketplace function that requires a variety of resources to accomplish the tasks set before us. The real key is the stewardship issue, that we must honor our unique and diverse resources, gifts, and talents to promote servanthood in word and deed. One of the powerful obstacles is how the fear, pride and the pain and trauma associated with dysfunctional relationships either buries our talents or leads to their expression in immoral or inappropriate means. This is why one of the great job duties of the servant leader is to help others discover the proper nature and use of gifts. For the leader and business owner, one of the prime elements is to exercise his or her creative gifts to produce maximum job opportunities for others to realize their unique abilities and destiny, and therefore job creation is a prime criterion for a servant leader business.

Servant leaders empower others and make themselves dispensable. Servant leadership is the foundation for successful, moral management. It is the path less traveled and requires great courage. We must cease from our own labors, esteem others more greatly than ourselves, and learn to serve the mission first.

Servant business leaders do not manufacture "needs" which are really "desires" based upon lusts. Hence, the goal is to provide products and services that improve the overall human condition. Hence, the scope is broad and includes a full range of goods and services from necessities to recreation. This entails honest and fair marketing principles to reject using fear as the primary promotional strategy, cynically manipulating needs and weaknesses to stimulate demand, persuading consumers that luxuries are necessities, or encouraging excessive levels of spending and consumption. There are powerful warfare elements in business. The ability to generate wealth through our labor blesses all. However, with every good attribute, a counterfeit corrupts and destroys. The root of the deception relates to the locus of responsibility for creating wealth, who owns the increase, and the proper use of the fruits. The original sin of pride is the most powerful corrupting force. We violate moral leadership when we begin to believe that our personal efforts generated wealth thereby enshrining ownership versus stewardship, a true deception.

Understanding the appropriate role of profit is essential from a servant leader character perspective, as profit and wealth is not the end value to provide shareholders and investors with the highest return, but an instrumental means to a greater good. Profit is an important resource used to:

a. Provide high quality living wage jobs that afford for the financial provision of employees and their families
b. To invest in the larger community, improving the quality of life
c. To provide means for helping the poor gain self-sufficiency and dignity through work experience
d. To meet the needs of the larger community through the provision of the specific goods and services provided by the organization
e. Promote sustainable development balanced with environmental stewardship
f. Provide revenue to support church or other faith-based nonprofit activities

Hence, profit maximization should not be the end goal. The goal is to maximize revenue while providing reasonable profit levels. Servant leader businesses accept lower profit levels and provide higher living wages, especially for the working poor while investing in the community through contributions of funds and expertise to various nonprofit and charitable causes. This is equivalent to the admonition of farmers in the Bible to "not glean their fields" to permit the poor the dignity of supporting themselves through work by picking the residual produce. This is clearly a road less traveled, but the rewards are great.

SLHRM Leadership Personal Character Reflection: Emotional/Spiritual Perfectionism

Every day we think thousands of thoughts and make hundreds of small decisions all imbedded within the emotional landscape of our mind. As servant leaders, we must master our inner world in order to be maximally effective in serving others. What does this require? To address this issue, let us reflect on the relationship between emotion, thought, and actions. Thoughts are discrete and identifiable, while emotions are free-floating and not linked to thoughts in a linear fashion. Emotions, positive, negative, or neutral, provide color to our mental world and are necessary elements for servant leader decision making. We cannot completely control our emotions, but we can manage them.

Emotions are a precursor to conscious thought. We feel first, and then "rationally" interpret our emotions. It is not a linear relationship as our initial thoughts influence our subsequent emotions, which in turn influence our thoughts in an ongoing cycle. In essence, it is a complex loop system in which emotions and thoughts are simultaneously both cause and effects. To complicate things even more, we cannot completely control our thoughts either as they arise from the collective emotional unconscious or other forces including the overt and covert subliminal messages from the world around us. So how do we bring thoughts captive? The answer lies in understanding the nature of the spiritual warfare battle. Thoughts, no matter how loathsome, are not moral failures, but temptations. They only become moral failures when they become so powerful that they dominate our thinking or we succumb to the temptation and act out the impulse.

The first principle of avoiding emotional perfectionism is to recognize that negative thoughts and emotions are not moral violations unless we embrace and act on them, either in our mind or in our behavior. Many servant leaders needlessly punish themselves for negative thoughts and feelings and our conscience will add to our misery by taking advantage of our confusion regarding the difference between temptation and moral failure.

A very effective strategy is avoiding repressing negative thoughts. We cannot repress our negative thoughts and emotions, as this only increases their saliency, intensity, and power over us in a latent (delayed) manner. To bring thoughts "captive," we must utilize the 3 R's: to *rebut* the negative thought with truth, to *replace*, not repress, with a moral alternative, and to *rest and reflect* in truthful thoughts. For example, when a negative thought arises such as anger at another person, rebut the temptation to retaliate or punish by choosing to forgive. First, replace the negative thought with prayers or thoughts for restoration; second, rest and reflect on relationship restoration and healing promises; third, seek moral counsel for future action. This provides the needed "cooling" off period for more reasoned, moral decisions.

Another key element is to recognize and accept that negative emotions serve important and necessary functions. Negative emotions are feelings that produce mental discomfort and damaging physiological effects on the body if prolonged and/or intense in nature. Our brains, nervous systems, and bodies operate in a synergistic fashion as each emotion produces a signature physiological response. Negative emotions such as fear, depression, anxiety, and anger are the "dashboard lights" that indicate that something or someone is threatening our security, peace and wellbeing. Negative emotions are an ongoing warning and feedback system. We cannot and would not want to eliminate all negative emotions as they provide important information for problem solving and afford ongoing opportunities for growing in character as we learn to persevere and grow as we overcome the situation that produces the feelings. Negative emotions force us to reach out, and seek solutions. They help us to avoid complacency and are keys for repentance and reflection when we stray off the "straight and narrow path." We cannot repress them, only rebut, replace, and rest in positive alternatives in the midst of the storm.

Chapter 6

Employee Work/Life Balance and Margin Principles

How Many Hours Should Employees Work?

How many hours should employees work? Servant leaders must answer this profound and essential question for themselves and for their employees. The answer is neither a static nor a moving balance, but a shifting and dynamic harmony among our key life domains. These include the following elements:

1. Performing our work with excellence as broadly defined (efficient and effective, mission enhancing, ethical, moral, and treating others by the Golden Rule)
2. Providing sufficient time and energy for our other life domain obligations (family, church, community, etc.)
3. Providing sufficient time for self-care (relationship building, sleep, nutrition, exercise, recreation, etc.)

Returning to our original question, how many hours should employees work? The conventional standard is the forty-hour, five-day workweek. However, is the forty-hour workweek a moral imperative? Clearly it is not when we expand the scope of our focus and discover that the forty-hour workweek is a relatively recent twentieth-century practice. The Judeo-Christian religious tradition embraced the six-day workweek, but did not state a specific number of hours. Today's jobs and occupations vary in their effort and time demands. There are four separate, but interrelated aspects. The first is to answer the underlying motivational reasons for working long hours, the second are those reasons justified, third is the ability work extended hours, and fourth is the cost to family, health and other life domains. The normative question is the most important. Is it morally responsible for us to work longer hours, carefully addressing the factors as noted above?

First, the question of ability relates to such elements as our passion, interest, and love for the work, the degree of intrinsic motivation produced, our degree of control and autonomy related to the quantity, quality, and timing of work, and the degree of fit with our gifts, abilities, and skills. We can work safely and intensively for many hours if we possess great love and passion for our work, our level of intrinsic motivation is high, we possess a significant degree of job autonomy, and there is symmetry between job demands and attributes and our skills, gifts, and abilities (round peg in a square hole!). Our ability to work longer hours without adverse health, relational, and spiritual effects depreciates with lower levels of the factors discussed above. Hence, even a forty-hour workweek can be detrimental if we lack autonomy and job demands exceed our ability and effort levels. Hence, the optimal hours of work will vary by life season. The wisdom of the ages is that when we engage in periods of high time and energy investment, we need to complement with a subsequent season of rest.

One of the factors that both enhances and impedes the achievement of this harmony is the technological innovations of the virtual workplace. Iphones and the associated cellular and computer technology permit employees to work from almost any location and time. Hence, there is a much higher degree of flexibility in work location, hours, and enhanced efficiency levels. However, there is concurrent negative impact as these devices blur the traditional boundaries between work and personal time, tempting employees to be in constant communication, working through breaks, lunch and non-working hours, including vacations. This enables the highly engaged to overwork, while becoming a yoke and chain for those who desire separation and boundaries from work but are forced to respond to work messages. It is imperative that organizations develop a culture that encourages and requires employees to "unplug" themselves from electronic devices to safeguard personal time. SLHRM organizations accomplish this by mandating employee contact occurs during work hours and non-work contacts on a true emergency basis only.

Hence, a major attribute of SLHRM organizations is a conscious recognition and commitment to employee life harmony and wellness. This entails a number of key elements, including a sustainable and reasonable level of work demands and expectations that permit the employee to invest in the full range of life domains. The book *Margin* by Richard Swenson (2004) eloquently illustrates the epidemic of activity overload that afflicts our modern society. Work is one of the major, but by no means, sole or most important, contributors to this pathology. We are an activity- and schedule-driven society. Hence, we become a rest-, balance-, and most importantly a relationship- "challenged" and deficit-ridden society. The values of secular society define success in terms of performance, accomplishment, knowledge, power, money, and prestige versus our intrinsic worth and identity as human beings made in the image of God.

Realistic Performance Standards

One of the hallmarks of SLHRM is setting realistic standards of work performance and effort. Servant leadership recognizes the importance of life harmony and the need for rest and refreshment. Secular companies such as SAS Corporation incorporate life balance into their very fabric by limiting work hours. However, they remain the exception rather than the rule. Why do so many organizations fail to honor this principle? The roots of this mindset are complex. Many servant leaders possess an internalized and false view of their role, assuming a much higher degree of responsibility for success than is realistic. In essence, we become addicted to work and believe that we are the chosen instrument and our labor is the essential element. We internalize these standards both at the individual and at the HR system level through unrealistic "face time" and work effort levels leading to ongoing burnout and disconnection, creating a vicious cycle. One solution, exemplified by mega church pastor Andy Stanley, is the limitation of work hours to 45 per week (Morgan, 2006). The change reduced pressure on the paid staff and produced a higher level of organizational effectiveness through enhanced empowerment of lay volunteers.

As servant leaders, we must work at a pace that does not exhaust our employees or leave them vulnerable to the influence of the blinding effects of pride through work-related "empire-building." We have conditioned ourselves to resist the rest of mind, body, and spirit. We must ruthlessly resist the impulse to equate consistently action and activity with virtue. We need times for quiet reflection and rest.

Servant leaders should serve in the full range of life domains (family, work, faith activities, community, and leisure). There are seasons of our lives in which we need to place more emphasis on one domain or the other. However, we never abandon our responsibility in any of the areas, but shift the relative emphasis based upon the mission priorities. For example, there are times when a great deal of work effort is required to begin a nonprofit organization, and other times work will be at a lower priority due to family caregiving responsibilities. .

Achieving work and life balance is especially acute for women as they shoulder a higher degree of responsibility for child and elder care, hence, limiting their time for work. In essence, many women are now realizing the fallacy that they can work full time and meet the needs of their family and children. That is why more women are opting for part-time work. Understanding our limits is an important element of workplace spiritual intelligence, and the requirements for sacrifice in choosing the best over the good. Servant leader love requires self-sacrifice and denial, and families today must choose between material success/achievement and quality family rearing practices. Raising children properly is the highest calling, and hence a realistic standard of success entails recognizing the limits to time and energy invested in the workplace. The economic value of the homemaker is difficult to quantify, but estimated to be in the range of $112,000 yearly (D'Arcy, 2012). Homemakers make great sacrifices for the wellbeing of the family unit, and we need to support work/life balance practices and acknowledge the contributions and challenges of caregivers.

Compassion Fatigue

When we embrace overwork and activity addiction, a common product is compassion fatigue. One of the signature emotions of compassion fatigue is guilt and condemnation. It is clear that servant leaders should set realistic standards of performance and obtain the rest that we need to serve all of the respective life domains. There are seasons of intense work, when we are out of balance, but only for a limited time, and rest and refreshment should always follow these periods of high activity. One of the important signs of burnout is that there seems to be no end to the demands and no hope of refreshment.

We frequently become victims of our own success. Activity divorced from mission, purpose and calling eventually chokes the joy and peace of our lives. In the workplace, one of the main markers of enlightened leadership is setting boundaries and setting realistic standards of performance. In essence, servant leaders help protect employees by reducing the level of temptation to act on their impulses for overwork. The presence of compassion fatigue demonstrates a need for rest, reflection, and nurturing. We as a society make it difficult to engage in periods of restoration given our worship of activity, results and performance, plus the dysfunctional emphasis on victory at any cost. The seasons of rest are necessary, especially after the hidden stress of "mountaintop" experiences.

There is an ongoing cost of servant leadership devotion. Compassion fatigue gradually extinguishes the motivation and joy received from helping others. When we are in the full clutches of compassion fatigue, there is little to no joy or satisfaction in our job duties. Resentment and annoyance replace a genuine concern for others. The ministry of interruptions becomes very difficult when we lose perspective. Careerism is an ongoing challenge for servant leaders.

The typical organizational culture of face time emphasis of long hours and short-term performance pressures significantly reduces long term commitment. When executives and other management officials support these values, employees internalize the organization's instrumental meta ethic, embracing short-term production and profit over collective servanthood interests. This organizational "spirit" engenders communal "compassion fatigue" thereby attenuating the essential Golden Rule organizational citizenship behaviors (helping those in need) that reduce employee stress. Employees that embrace the organization's dysfunctional values, even though they recognize the pernicious fruits, are unable or unwilling to make the needed changes.

Organizations that are under great stress produce employees that are fearful, fatigued, and risk-aversive. When we lack the energy and time to take care of our own needs, we will walk on past the wounded and needy on our personal road. Compassion fatigue attenuates the precious social reinforcement and support that is essential to enduring trials and tribulations. Employees begin to devour themselves and others. One of the antidotes to this poison is to empower employees to make adjustments in the workplace to cope with the heavy burdens. Managers must tap the latent energy and innovation of the work group to improve efficiency and effectiveness. Employees can work very long hours if they believe in the mission and possess a high degree of autonomy on how to complete the work.

In conclusion, unbridled careerism is an evil, but the challenge for most servant leaders is identifying its presence. When we see the light and embrace our secular work as a ministry and a mission, this realization generates countervailing dangers. The sad reality is that most organizations fail to provide realistic standards of success and performance. When organizations place the utmost importance on short-term goal achievement at any price, there is very little room for the upfront investments in employee balance that realize downstream benefits. Research demonstrates the value of employer efforts to promote work/life balance (Jain & Nair, 2013), but many organizations embrace work/family balance on a superficial basis. SLHRM organizations understand the relationship between work/life balance and employee and community wellbeing. These organizations place employee welfare at the same level of mission and achievement. One heart test of a dedication to life balance is the willingness of an organization to sacrifice short-term financial gains and advantage for long-term employee wellbeing, which positively affects the bottom line.

Embracing Wisdom in Life Harmony

We must seek and be in the company of wisdom. As with all aspects of our servant leader walk, identifying and differentiating wisdom from knowledge is challenging. Knowledge alone is insufficient for moral and ethical decision making. Knowledge is the raw material, while wisdom is the process of applying knowledge to decision making. Many sources of information and knowledge compete for our attention. Wisdom entails an implicit understanding of what is truly of value. The only servant leader standard is that of love in its various forms, *agapao* (unconditional), and *phileo* (brotherly). Unless our motives promote the unconditional wellbeing of others, to encourage and challenge, all of our achievements are suspect and tainted. Hence, one of the highest forms of wisdom is for us to analyze critically the motives for our actions to promote servant leader growth. Our agony and confusion is partly a product of our self-deception regarding our motives for our work and family life behaviors. Why do we strive so mightily to achieve success? There are surface reasons such as societal conformity, and there are deep-seated personality attributes that relate to underlying fears and insecurities that disguise themselves in a myriad array of forms including what psychologists deem cognitive distortions such as perfectionism and narcissism. To achieve peace, we must rebut and replace these underlying false belief systems with servant leader principles.

I would like to lead with a word of personal testimony. My conscious convicts me for my ongoing embrace of worldly standards of excellence. One of the most pernicious enemies is the corruption of our innate desire for recognition and accomplishment. This occurs through adopting ever-shifting worldly standards of success enslaving us to ever-higher levels of effort, success, and performance. Our accomplishments never assuage that disquieting internal voice that we could or should be doing more with greater degrees of effectiveness—a lurking, omnipresent form of doubt.

It is important for us to understand that three factors determine whether our work possesses servant leader merit: (1) are we seeking to achieve moral goals (righteous ends), (2) are we using righteous means, and (3) are we motivated by agape love? If any one of the three conditions is violated, our work is suspect. I have found that in my own life it is better for me to fail than to succeed while pursing the wrong goals, using inappropriate means, than being driven by the wrong motives. If we succeed for the wrong reason, pride will blind us to our true vulnerable state, making us more susceptible to a serious future fall. It is very important for us to receive ongoing guidance from the "wisdom of many counselors," mentors, and accountability partners that help us to continually "test the spirits" underlying our work.

Human perfection is impossible and not the goal. We strive for an ongoing higher level of awareness to change our hearts and motivate our actions by agape servant leader/follower love. This will reduce our level of guilt and work stress dramatically. When we are guided my moral means, motives and ends, we can set a reasonable level of work effort, pace and quality that promotes the best interests of our co-workers, clients, and customers. In essence, we do our "best" within the limits set, and trust for the outcome and the increase.

Key Life Domains and Life Harmony

We then "separate the best from the good," freeing us from the guilt of comparison and meeting our and the world's broken and unreasonable standards. The sad reality is that much of the work stress that afflicts employees is free-will-embraced and self-imposed. We enthusiastically embrace the siren of worldly success, defining luxuries as necessities in terms of power, money, reputation, and prestige. We become prideful, revel in our short-term success, and then become addicted, requiring greater degrees of achievement to produce the "high." We are in effect worshipping enslaving idols that become cruel taskmasters and increasing sources of fear and insecurity. The practice of margin and simplicity is essential to reducing stress and achieving a harmony in the five key life domains of family, work, community, spirituality, and recreation. As such, we must practice an ongoing ordering of time and effort over the five areas based upon careful and ongoing reflection. This requires that we place boundaries around our work, which is the area entailing the greatest time investment. In most cases, this involves sacrificing the fulfillment of our ego needs relating to achieving workplace success so we possess sufficient time and energy to fulfill our roles and obligations in the other life domains. We must devote ongoing quality and quantity time to receive the direction, strength, and energy to meet our obligations in the other areas besides work. This free-will reduction in work effort is another form of dying to the self in which we place the needs of others above our own.

Who needs us? Our families, church, friends, neighbors, community organizations (little league, Scouts, schools) along with the hundreds of daily and seemingly random interactions that provide golden opportunities to reach out. When we are excessively busy, we lack the time, motivation, interest, and energy to give of ourselves freely in the other life domains. In addition, fear in its various forms will increase in power and intensity, further inhibiting our ability to love others. Even in the workplace, we are frequently too busy to support others. Those with the talents, gifts, and abilities to be highly successful face the greatest temptation, especially the employees that are blessed with great energy and drive, the employee who can work 80 hours per week and still feel refreshed, especially in leadership positions. There are two elements to this scenario that produce divided loyalties given conflicting values.

The first is "leading by example." It is important to "practice what we preach" in regard to hard work in terms of work hours and effort levels. However, the leader or organization that deifies the sixty-hour workweek tempts their subordinates to duplicate the same level of effort at great spiritual, personal, and societal costs. Work absorbs the best and the majority of time, energy and mindfulness (living in the present), thereby "robbing" their families, their communities, and community organizations of their desperately needed presence, talents, and love. Most employees lack the long-term physical, mental, and spiritual resiliency to work long hours, producing a pernicious fruit of global physical and mental health and relationship problems. Even if an employee is capable of a seventy-hour workweek, others will suffer because of the life imbalance. This syndrome weakens the family, especially the development of close parental relationships, reducing the child's resistance to the many forms of temptation and counterfeit means for receiving and expressing love, creating ongoing emotional and interpersonal strongholds that burden and oppress. In addition, the cumulative stress of overwork gradually erodes our own foundation, leading to long-term health problems. I have walked this road, reaped the negative spiritual, physical, and mental effects of a perfectionist and legalistic view of work, producing burnout and emotional collapse. I am "on the mend," experiencing a healing by the power of grace. I clearly discerned the need to reduce hours, but I did not listen until my body and spirit forced a retreat. I pray that you do not descend into the pit before being forced to make deep and painful changes!

Family and Worker Friendly Benefits

From a servant leadership perspective, the health and wellbeing of your employees is a foundational element of a moral workplace covenant. Employees are not instruments of production, and progressive organizations monitor employee work conditions and attitudes (burnout, mental and physical illness, family stress, job satisfaction, etc.) to identify proactively dysfunctional management practices and develop long-term solutions.

When the organization embraces "production-first" values, it precludes the development of a balanced approach to employee wellbeing. For example, employees must work through lunch, and commit to "whatever it takes" to complete the job, irrespective of the cost to employees and their families. When "face-time" values dominate, it generates resistance and rebellion, which promotes the development of deceptive protective practices to project an image or the illusion of dedication, high motivation, problem solving, and productivity (process over output). Hence, this self-protective effect desensitizes employees to the pathological realities of organizational life.

The true obstacles to servant leadership are not an external enemy, but our own personal idols and many managers sacrifice family to the "god" of work. This phenomenon is widespread, even in "worker-friendly" organizations. There remain serious policy and practice gaps in most organizations over the balance issue. Studies and personal experience clearly demonstrate that there are dual employment tracks (Elise & Stanislav, 2014). The first is the conventional "fast track" that utilizes the traditional cultural norms of office "face-time" associated with high workplace commitment. The second is the "Mommy" or "Daddy" track that features family and worker-friendly benefits (flexible schedules, flexi-place, leave programs) that frequently stereotype the users as less loyal, motivated, and ultimately less competent. There are clear organizational exceptions (SAS Corporation is one), but they are still in the minority, and there is even great variance within family-friendly organizations by department. A superficial adoption of these worker-friendly practices will only intensify employee cynicism. The key is to neutralize the influence of the implicit face time instrumental cultural values. SLHRM professionals must address and combat excessive departmental workloads and unrealistic performance goals. Servant leaders view the employment relationship as a covenant (an ironclad psychological contract) that balances the needs and interests of the key stakeholders with employee termination as an option of last resort. Servant leaders may not be able to change the culture of the company, but they can provide an oasis of reason and compassion within their "flock" (the subordinates under their organizational authority).

The introduction of family-friendly benefits and a more reasonable work pace frequently generates resistance from management and employees conditioned to a dysfunctional environment, but "tough love" sacrifices and pain is the price of servant leadership. SLHRM professionals must present a cogent and persuasive rationale to both subordinate employees and upper management for adopting worker-friendly benefits. It is important that organizations develop these benefits upon a needs assessment given limited resources. In addition, it is important that all employees benefit, not just a class of employees such as employees with children or elder care needs (Jungin & Wiggins, 2011). It is important not to generate resentment and the formation of a "caste system," disenfranchising younger or single employees. Hence, SLHRM organizations make available worker-friendly benefits such as flextime and flexi-place, and the dollar value of benefits should be roughly equal for all categories of employees. SLHRM organizations reassure employees that when they face work and personal life conflict (family, health, etc.), their needs will be accommodated. Hence, a collective support system will provide an organizational safety net.

SLHRM professionals must make the case to upper management that terminating employees that cannot meet traditional face time expectations would impose excessive short-term costs to the organization including a potential adverse reaction from other employees as well as the associated high costs of hiring a replacement. Most immediate management decisions relative to work/life conflicts are amenable to a variety of alternative options other than termination. There are a variety of relevant short-term strategies that modify the job (e.g., telecommute, hire temporaries) or accommodate the employee's personal situation (e.g., subsidized housing or childcare), or transfer to a less demanding position.

Worker Margin and Organizational Change

A major factor influencing the feasibility of any organizational change effort is the degree of margin within the system. In many cases, employees are operating at maximum capacity, and any management change in the midst of the present crisis will adversely affect performance. All change efforts, even highly beneficial innovations, impose short-term costs, and employees stretched to the breaking point may lack the energy or the motivation to escape the downward spiral. This is where employee empowerment is critical. When employees receive a delegation of authority to solve a problem for themselves, this generates a reservoir of energy and good will. One of the greatest job stressors is a lack of control over the work environment, and a conferral of job autonomy communicates confidence in employee abilities, is a concrete demonstration of trust, and most importantly, provides hope for the future. The long term macro solution is the institutionalization of family-friendly workplace policies. It requires great personal courage and perseverance in combination with a willingness to assume significant personal risk to honor the short- or long-term solutions noted above. We need guidance and maturity in our own walk if we are to advocate a just solution for employees requiring work-life modifications. Given first line management's frequent and understandable suspicion and hostility toward work/life balance policies, how can a work/life balance advocate make a persuasive case, assuming he or she possesses the motivation and courage? One line of reasoning is to make the claim that the stressed employee's situation is the "canary in the coal mine" and an early indicator of a "burned-out" staff. The result will be decreased productivity and higher costs that will adversely influence the long-term success of the organization. The champion manager would also need to present a clear ROI analysis that provides hard data on the benefits of reducing workloads and improving efficiency through employee empowerment and family-friendly policies such as significantly lower turnover as the SAS experience demonstrates (O'Reilly & Pfeffer, 2000). The main impediment to adopting empowerment and family-friendly benefit solutions is that the costs are immediate and the benefits long-term and most organizational cultures emphasize short-term goal attainment.

Threats to Life Margin

Reducing workplace stress is a collective effort between employees and management. For example, many employees accept a job with a long commute, thereby accentuating the pressure of a long workday. The employee thereby increases childcare stress and reduces family time. In an ideal world, the employer would provide high quality onsite or subsidized childcare, but employees accepted the position knowing that there would be no assistance from the organization. As servant leaders, we should make it a conscious policy to reduce unnecessary obstacles and distractions that detract from our family obligations. Employees can reduce workplace stress by:

a. Selecting a position that is compatible with their gifts, passion, and abilities
b. Strive for simplicity by living a modest lifestyle
c. Developing realistic life success and job performance goals
d. Set clear life goals to effectively and efficiently focus our time and avoid distractions (separate the best from the good)
e. Strive for life margin

The true obstacle to SLHRM assessment is not an external enemy, but our own personal idols. Personal life margin is the intentional cultivation of a healthy lifestyle that embraces harmony and balance among the key life domains (family, work, community, church, rest, and recreation). It is the essential reserve of time and physical and psychological energy necessary to support mental, physical, and spiritual wellbeing and promote healthy interpersonal relationships. We cannot reduce margin to a legalistic formula given the complexity of life. There are seasons of intense work followed by rest and family emphasis. What are some of the key principles for remaining "connected to the vine"?

We are frequently our own worst enemy when it comes to life margin. I am a professor, and academics and students are very achievement-oriented, and do not like to lose. Pride inflates the importance of our goals to encourage us to lose our moral compass, leading to compromise in our motives and means. Our drive to succeed can enslave us as we attempt to achieve goals that we falsely believe equate with enduring success. We use the wrong standards and measuring stick to assess success. Servant leader success occurs through the ongoing work of generating loving relationships through character development. Our challenge is to recalibrate our standards of excellence and the goals/ends pursued. As author Richard Swenson (2004) states in his book *Margin*, the most important criterion of success is healthy relationships.

Pride adroitly uses the temptation of accomplishments and recognition to distract each of us from our true mission and purpose. In effect, our moral and spiritual job description is always the most important element. The pride of performance, recognition, and wealth is a powerful drug that manifests diminishing returns, thereby increasing our craving for more attention and recognition. Many leaders are enslaving their lives to the allure of power, wealth, and material comforts over relationships. Very few on their deathbed regret not making more money or missing that promotion; it is the deep pain of lost time and relationships that trouble the soul. Let us commit to place our hearts and minds on the issues of eternal value.

We must make time for the simple but profoundly important elements that are the heartbeat of our lives, which is time spent in loving others. Modern life presents the continual temptation to substitute activity over being, by the need to prove our spiritual mettle by works. Busyness disconnects us from the vine and the life-giving presence. A hectic level of activity promotes identity through accomplishment as we become unable to discern the "best from the good." Our frenetic activity level leaves us vulnerable to compassion fatigue, discouragement and an absence of joy. We become vulnerable to all forms of temptation, given that we lack life balance. Is the root cause of our malady the absence of time, or is it something else?

The key factor is to engage in inner reflection and dialogue to identify our root motive for what we do. When we are at the end of our personal resources this snaps our lethargy and challenges the spirit of self-sufficiency. The absence of a clear life vision distorts our lenses. I understand personally the ongoing frustration and pain of a chronic overload situation. Working mothers have great challenges in this area, and the key is to avoid labeling family member "wants" and luxuries as necessities, forcing women to become "super moms." Our journey in life takes many circuitous paths, and one of the burdens we add is assuming an inordinate degree of responsibility for our family success and safety, especially for single parent families. Being from a single parent home myself, I understand the pain and the fear. We must focus on the essentials. Given the inherent stresses and burdens that single parenting create, the single parent's level of margin is narrower than in a two-parent family. This requires an even more enhanced prioritization process.

Breaking the yokes of oppression includes remedying the absence of margin and simplicity. We must be available for our children. The family is ground zero as dysfunctional families imprison and yoke children with lifetime burdens. The challenge is to build margin so we can engage in vibrant two-way relationships. We must set moral boundaries to cultivate margin and the energy to love others deeply. One key element is to take at least one full day off per week and dedicate this time to rest, recreation, family, and religious pursuits. This entails limiting our work hours, taking time for exercise, sleep, and rest, and eating correctly.

We must separate the best from the good through ongoing reflection. One of the great temptations that we must face is simply adding unessential tasks and duties. If we sweep our house clean, and do not maintain clear boundaries and fill the void that uses activity and accomplishments to fill the "hole in our soul," we will continue to add more clutter. Our role is to perform to the best of our abilities—to put in an honest day's work and be content with our wages. If we take responsibility for success and failure, we are implicitly assuming control over the outcome, promoting a prideful attitude.

A superficial adoption of these worker-friendly practices will only intensify employee cynicism. The key is to neutralize the influence of the implicit instrumental cultural values. However, we must monitor and protect employees from abusive employers who expect employees to work while ill or overzealous, from perfectionist employees who are unable to rest. Servant leader employers should be concerned first for the welfare of their employees and provide the rest that they need to recover.

Specific SLHRM Organizational Practices to Enhance Employee Wellbeing and Reduce Job and Life Stress

From a servant leader worldview standpoint, the organization is shepherd and must protect the wellbeing of employees and customers. Health is the holistic integration of mind, body, and spirit. Servant leader HR organizations proactively identify and remedy threats to employee wellbeing. They embrace the following strategies:

- *Model and practice servant leadership.* When employees are secure in the knowledge that their supervisors support, encourage, hold them accountable, and forgive their mistakes, they possess the security at the core of the spirit to resist dysfunctional stress coping strategies that burden and yoke them and impede organizational mission achievement.
- *Make an authentic and passionate commitment to employee wellbeing.* In essence, it is not a slogan or a superficial marketing claim, but a deeply internalized value that is part of the organization's

core DNA. The commitment to work/life balance is as natural as breathing and embedded in all decision making. Employees will very quickly identify a superficial and manipulative campaign, which produces greater levels of perceived hypocrisy, cynicism, bitterness, apathy, and disengagement. It is better to be honest and promote more instrumental values than to superficially embrace work/life balance for insincere and devious reasons.

- *Leaders and managers must model healthy workplace balance or else employees will discount the message.* Managers must model a commitment that places moral integrity at the center with family needs overriding work. This entails reasonable levels of work effort and hours, sensible performance standards, and spending time with family.
- *Communicate to employees that there will be "seasons" of high work demand, but commit to proactive planning and employee empowerment to reduce the number and intensity of such episodes.* There will be times when extra work effort and hours are necessary to meet challenges, problems, threats, or unusual opportunities. Once the crisis is addressed, managers should return to normal hours, demands, and balanced work hours as quickly as possible.
- *Managers must demonstrate a healthy and sustainable life style (rest, sleep, eating habits, exercise).*
- *Emphasize that promoting employee wellbeing is a major term and condition of a servant leader workplace covenant.* This requires fully integrating a 360-degree commitment to employee wellbeing in all aspects of the organization's culture by integrating wellbeing into the mission, vision, and values. For example, in the values statement appears this phrase "the organization commits to helping employees develop a harmony between faith, family, and work by limiting work hours to no more than 40 per week."
- *Clearly communicate an iron-clad "word and deed" commitment to employee wellbeing with a sustained and integrated communications campaign.* This entails multiple means and methods for communicating that work/life balance is a high priority, including leadership speeches, emphasis at meetings, and prominent articles in promotional materials.
- *Hold all key stakeholders responsible for promoting a healthy work environment and employee wellbeing through the performance management system.* Develop a comprehensive wellbeing benchmark system of SMART performance goals, metrics and standards linked to organizational HR decision making.
- *SLHRM organizations provide meaningful work that reinforces human dignity.* One helpful model in this regard is the Hackman

and Oldham Job Characteristics Model (Fried & Ferris, 1987). Intrinsically motivating work possesses five key elements: job significance, job identity, skill variety, job autonomy, and job feedback.

a. Job significance is the presence of a clear linkage between an employee's job duties and his or her contributions to the mission. There should be a clear connection between the employee's work efforts (process) and products (outcomes) and achievement of key goals. The importance of the work is recognized by the key stakeholders, including internal and external clients/customers and the community as a whole. Job significance provides employees with dignity and respect.

b. Job identity is the condition when employees produce a good or service that bears the imprint of their craftsmanship, a whole work product that bears their "signature." This can be either an individual or a collective recognition. It is akin to the joy and pride of an artist who produces a painting. It reflects their individual and group creative gifts that communicate beauty and truth.

c. A third important element is task and skill variety and growth. Ideally, a job should require a variety of duties that increase the required knowledge, skills, and abilities to facilitate growth and challenge. The result is a qualitative increase in knowledge, skill, and ability levels.

d. A fourth key element is job autonomy in which employees are engaged in meaningful and sustained input and participation over all aspects of their jobs. This includes their performance goals, standards and metrics, work scheduling, pace and effort levels, and performance appraisal, among other key systems.

e. The fifth element is ample performance feedback. Intrinsically motivated employees desire to gauge their success and impact, hence the need for jobs that provide ample performance feedback that is clear, specific, timely, behavioral, actionable (can make changes) and comes from a credible (trusted) source. There are two types of performance feedback. The first type is intrinsic performance feedback, in which the employee directly receives immediate feedback as the job is performed or shortly thereafter. For example, instructors receive feedback from the body language and expression of students on the understanding of concepts taught. The second type of feedback is extrinsic performance information in which the employee receives performance data from supervisors, reports or other metrics in a timely fashion.

- *Engage in a comprehensive employee health and wellness program that promotes employee health wellbeing, joy, and eustress (beneficial stress), and not simply the absence of negative outcomes (disease, injury, accidents, illness, stress).* This entails the following elements:

  a. An integrated workplace hazard monitoring and audit process:

     i. Identify the source and cause of accidents, illness, disease, and negative job stress
     ii. Empower employees to jointly identify, diagnose, and develop solutions for the identified hazards.
     iii. Empower employees to jointly identify, diagnose, and develop means for maintaining and enhancing employee wellbeing.

The table 6.1 is an example of an organizational stress audit (Jex, 1998).

Table 6.1   Master list of stress categories

Role Ambiguity (unclear job duties) Examples

- Employee is unsure about whether they are responsible for both quantity of production and maintenance of equipment
- Unsure about who is responsible for quality control questions when equipment malfunctions

Role Conflict (clashing job duties and job duties not matched to skills and interests) Examples

- High daily production quota reduces time spent in error inspection
- Job entails extensive focus on promoting art as a nonprofit organization development director, but the employee has little interest in art
- Job entails significant degree of mechanical ability that the employee lacks
- The job places more emphasis on improving presentation skills which is a minor part of the job more than interpersonal counseling aspects that are most linked to success
- An employee with a long commute and significant elder care responsibilities must attend meetings in person at the office that could be conducted by phone or computer

Quantitative and Qualitative Role Overload (can't meet work standards) Examples

- A professor who has very high publication requirements in conjunction with a large teaching load
- A research analysis lacks the technical skill and knowledge of advanced statistics required for a project
- Social workers with very high case loads
- A machine operator with no rest breaks for a four hour period
- A manager whose teams is under such short run performance pressures that they lack the time to invest in long term planning to adjust to changing customer preferences

---

Continued

Table 6.1 Continued

- A social worker with a volume of difficult clients cannot take time for a walk or surf the web
- A professor with a high teaching load and year round teaching does not have a block of unstructured time for rest, reflection and planning

Role Responsibility Conflicts (managerial and leadership pressures from supervising, meeting work deadlines, and achieving performance standards) Examples

- A supervisor with an under-performing work team in conjunction with high levels of interpersonal conflict
- Pressure to increase production with a reduction in the overtime budget
- A college recruitment manager who is under constant pressure to fill a quota with no consideration of external factors that may adversely influence demand for education such as employment prospects for graduates

Adverse Physical and Social Working Conditions Examples

- Construction workers in high heat
- Desks that are not ergonomically adjusted for height and weight
- Warehouse worker with back problems caused by ongoing heavy lifting of boxes
- Computer data entry operators that do not allow for sufficient breaks and alternative positions such as standing work stations resulting in excessive levels of sitting (more than four hours daily)
- Isolated night shift clerk at a convenience store
- A police officer that works rotating eight-hour shifts every four weeks disrupting sleep patterns
- A retail store manager's weekly schedule of six twelve hour days
- A sales representative that travels 80 percent of the work week
- Website developer under constant pressure to remain current with changing web site design requirements

Unfair Compensation and Performance Appraisal Measurement Examples

- Police officers in a high crime city that are paid 40 percent below market wages (lack of external equity)
- Supervisor provides higher performance ratings to those in the "in-group" irrespective of their true performance level
- A machinist who is penalized for higher waste rates due to lower quality metal to reduce production costs (penalized for factors beyond control)
- Supervisor fails to express appreciation to the work team members for extended overtime in meeting a project deadline

Interpersonal Conflict and Office Politics Examples

- Employee fails to receive a promotion over a less qualified candidate who has a personal friendship with the supervisor
- Employee receives lower performance appraisal ratings because of his race
- Employees are excessively busy and lack the time and energy to help new employees learn the job
- Employment counselors receive an individual bonus for the number of clients placed decreasing cooperation and information sharing among counselors
- An employee is verbally harassed if they rest when fatigued given the performance pressures

Continued

Table 6.1 Continued

Poor Quality Supervision Examples

- The sales supervisor fails to provide feedback on the employee's presentation delivery weaknesses increasing the employees failure rate
- The supervisor works 60 hours per week and expects staff to do the same reducing work/family balance
- The supervisor complains about minor problems on a contract proposal even though the staff developed the proposal with half of the conventional preparation time
- The supervisor fails to train new employees and provide clear work performance standards
- A social work supervisor fails to allow the work group to celebrate the successes in the presence of heavy workloads
- The supervisor provides favorable job assignments to those he likes, and the most undesirable to the "out of favor" employees

Situational Constraints (lack of key resources)

- Employee lacks complete background information on clients impeding the ability to identify prior preferences
- Teachers must pay for student supplies from personal funds
- Supervisor lacks the authority to empower employees to meet client needs that vary with standard procedure
- Employees must prepare a bid for a road project in 24 hours given the absence of advanced planning

Perceived Control Challenges Due to the Absence of Autonomy

- A teacher cannot change the curriculum to adjust to unique student learning needs
- A computer programmer that cannot influence the number of clients that they support
- The organization fails to consult with employees over production problems that reduce customer satisfaction
- An teacher is not involved in selecting the curriculum

Career Development Challenges Including Inadequate Training and Few Options for Career Growth Examples

- A teacher is not provided with training in distance education techniques for their on-line courses
- The organization fails to provide additional job training to increase the range of skills used on the job

Lack of Employer Covenant Related to Job Security, Workplace Forgiveness, and Transparency Examples

- Employees experience frequent layoffs with no advance warning
- The supervisor penalizes employees for every mistake
- The manager fails to admit weaknesses or apologize for mistakes thereby "chilling" employee motivation to be honest
- The employer encourages employees to use sub-standard materials to reduce costs and elevate sales at the expense of repeat business

Continued

Table 6.1   Continued

Work-Home Pressures Examples

- Employee must drive 30 or more miles to work daily with night meetings
- The absence of on-site and emergency child care requires employees to remain home with sick children
- The absence of elder care support increases home demands with no reduction in work load
- A working mother whose spouse does not share in household duties

Traumatic Job Stress Produced by Unethical Workplace Behavior Examples

- An employee is attacked or threatened by a co-worker or client
- A supervisor who verbally berates a subordinate in public
- A supervisor who makes ongoing suggestive remarks related to the employee's sex life
- A women is denied promotion to management because she is too assertive reinforcing negative gender stereotypes
- Employees engage in theft of company supplies
- Management requires or encourages staff to overbill clients
- Employee discloses contract overpricing to higher management

Adverse Effects of the Absence of Servant Leader Character Elements Examples

- Prolonged high workloads with ongoing criticism of performance demoralizes employees
- An employee lacks confidence in management's credibility
- An employee fails to forgive his supervisor for being passed over for promotion leading to revenge fantasies
- An employee is jealous over the success of a co-worker who they feel has less ability
- Employee become jealous over their absence of success in placing clients in comparison to co-workers even though their clientele are more difficult to place
- Employee is never satisfied with their work or that of others
- A high performing employee fails to recognize the contribution of other team members to her success
- An employee is unable to "laugh at themselves" for job mistakes
- An employee takes work on vacation or fails consistently to use all vacation days
- An employee who fails to discern their tendency to judge others and be critical in public settings thereby increasing conflict
- An employee is angry with themselves and others when the bid is rejected even though it was a very competitive and well-crafted
- Peer group of employees justifies the abuse of sick days as recompense for low pay

The key element is to conduct the stress audit on a yearly basis with integration into mainstream HR and organizational decision making. For example, if the data consistently demonstrates that high workloads are contributing to stress, empower employees with means to increase efficiency and effectiveness to reduce work pressures. In addition, SLHRM organizations commit to staffing levels that do not promote chronic or acute overload. For example, if there are episodic spikes in workload or seasonal elements, proactively increase either temporary or contract hiring. A summary of key SLHRM means to reduce stress appears in table 6.2.

Table 6.2 Organizational practices to reduce job stress

Area	Stress Reduction Practice
Employee Responsibility	The SLHRM organization will encourage employees to seek jobs matched to their skills, temperament, and personality. They reinforce a holistic mind, body and spirit commitment to good mental, physical, and spiritual health through exercise, good nutrition; voluntary religious expression (meditation and prayer) supported by employee assistance and wellness programs and positive program participation incentives. They encourage a commitment to life-long learning and practicing good organizational citizenship behaviors
HR System and Job Design	The SLHRM system should provide valid and reliable selection practices, realistic job previews, and create intrinsically motivating jobs aligned with employee job interests and gifts. Short and long-term employee development is a high priority with generous employee training support. Adequate staffing is provided ensuring that workloads are at manageable levels and that pace of work is sustainable (adequate rest breaks). The organization provides employees with the tools, supplies, and equipment needed to support high performance. There is an unswerving commitment to worker safety and ergonomics. The emphasis is on developing employee strengths, creativity, and providing time for quiet reflection. The organization strives to be a compensation leader with high levels of external and internal pay equity. Performance appraisal systems use multiple sources and methods. The organization embraces the full range of worker friendly benefits including the various forms of dependent care and the flexible workplace. Employees should possess considerable job autonomy and be empowered over key aspects of their work.
Servant Leadership Attributes	Provide employees with a job security reinforcing that layoffs are always a last resort option. Leaders should model a commitment to work/life balance for themselves and their employees by limiting work hours. Managers commit to a moral work environment emphasizing procedural, distributive, and interactional justice and avoid even the appearance of favoritism and ingroups formation. SLHRM leaders seek to understand the needs and feelings of employees through genuine relationship building. Management drives fear from the workplace by encouraging employees to grow and learn through mistakes and failures and openly discuss their own weaknesses and failings thereby promoting two-way transparency. Management sets a clear mission, vision, value, and set of strategic goals for the organization providing a clear moral and performance directional compass. Managers commit to ongoing employee encouragement, communicate a realistic optimism that provides hope, and generates faith in management. The SLHRM manager facilitates the development of employee social support networks and sponsors and encourages opportunities for social interaction among workers.

Time can become another idol that enslaves servant leaders with a yoke of ever-increasing frenetic activity that gradually severs us from the root of our strength, power, and joy. The servant leader development processes entails working individually or in small groups, utilizing planned and spontaneous counseling and advice. This is a discipleship model that requires close personal interaction, and mentoring; in effect, it is a relationship that invests a very precious commodity, time—a major element of Golden Rule love.

Time Management Principles

Another great challenge is to grasp the proper role of time management. Traditional approaches to managing time treat the symptoms rather than the underlying problem. Time management is a rational attempt to balance the many variables and competing interests that are difficult to order. Given the complexity of the relationships and the number of variables, it is a futile exercise. The key is to separate out the "best from the good" and the truly essential from the urgent but not important.

As Pastor John Ortberg (2002) noted, the goal is not balance, but a "well-ordered" life in harmony with our overall mission statement and calling. There will be seasons of intense work with little time off; however, what follows are times of rest in which the "fields lie fallow." Hence, the goal is to receive guidance for separating the "best from the good." This includes allocating adequate time for the key relationships, with spiritual growth and family followed by our needs for self-care (rest, nutrition, exercise). As Pastor Wayne Cordeiro noted (2009), we must "back schedule" to ensure that we fill in those three areas first, then "pencil in" the remaining work schedule. The only means to accomplish this is by developing a deep commitment to life harmony as a moral imperative. A great example is the ministry of Jesus as he centered all of his time and attention with laser-like focus on the central mission attributes of saving the lost. Jesus set boundaries and priorities as evidenced by his statement describing his calling to minister to the lost sheep of Israel, not to the Gentiles (Matthew 15:24). Jesus guarded his time and that of his disciples by withdrawing from the crowds and engaging in solitary prayer (Luke 5:16). We must all commit to the road less traveled when it comes to promoting the wellbeing of our employees. We must not be hearers of the word only, but doers as well.

Spiritual and Religious Friendly Workplace

The spiritual and religious friendly workplace is another key element of a holistic commitment to work/life balance and diversity. Irrespective of our formal beliefs regarding the existence of a divine being, all humans are "hard-wired" to seek transcendence and a greater purpose. Hence, we are all spiritual beings. Let us begin with some of the key elements of the spiritual and religious friendly workplace.

An important self-reflective spiritual discipline is to assess the consistency and integrity between stated policy and practice. Are we officially a spiritual and religious friendly organization? If so, are we both a hearer and a doer? Regrettably, many organizations embrace a form of practical atheism. They possess a shell of spiritual ity, but operate from a practice standpoint with secular management approaches. Organizations frequently become complacent and over-confident in the foundational level of employee spiritual vitality and commitment.

From a spiritual and religious friendly workplace standpoint, all expression and practice should be voluntary and non-coerced. This "free will" orientation ensures that employees will be able to honor their beliefs and conscience. Such an approach encourages genuine spiritual and religious belief and commitment versus coerced activity that promotes hypocrisy. Another major element is a spiritual and religious practice workplace policy that clearly defines permissible activities. For example, what is the policy on evangelism? A related central policy is clearly defining reasonable accommodation strategies for religious beliefs and practices including religious holidays, prayer practices, and leave policy. Another key element is spiritual and religious diversity and discrimination avoidance education of managers and employees. It is important that managers understand the boundaries that protect employees from inappropriate pressure, coercion, and perceptions of favoritism. One approach to adopt is that of respectful pluralism which recognizes the fundamental right of human religious/spiritual expression based on four major principles based on the work of Hicks (2003):

1. All spiritual and religious expression must observe and honor the dignity of all persons and the diversity of views. For example, on an organizational listserve, it would be appropriate to discuss the integration of scriptural servant leadership principles into the workplace, but it would not permit the posting of scriptural passages

condemning homosexuality. As an evangelical, my personal beliefs oppose homosexuality, but I could not use the formal organizational platform or media to promote this view.

2. All religious and spiritual expression is voluntary and noncoercive.

3. There can be no formal establishment of a "state" religion or spiritual practice

4. A forced compartmentalization of religion and spirituality in the workplace disenfranchises those with genuine religious and spiritual beliefs and diminishes the richness and vitality of the human experience at work.

However, for those employees seeking religious and spiritual integration at work, activities such as voluntary prayer/mediation and holy book study time during the workday (breaks, lunch, etc.) and during non-working hours promotes ongoing integration. Other key elements of the spiritual and religious friendly workplace include:

- Promote religious and spiritual events, retreats, seminars, service and volunteer opportunities
- Develop an employee website or bulletin board to promote religious/spiritual activities (not available to the public)
- Draft a policy that permits the appropriate display of spiritual and religious objects in the office and in employee dress while respecting safety and performance standards
- The adoption of a workplace chaplain program either through the creation of a formal full- or part-time position, contracting with a chaplain consulting firm, or securing volunteers from churches
- Develop spiritual and religious mental health counseling programs
- Develop spiritual and religious-based wellness and employee assistance program
- Permit employees to transmit spiritual and religious information on company email or intranet system

These policies and practices will contribute to a more favorable climate for religious and spiritual expression thereby enriching the workplace. However, it is important to monitor the workplace to identify sources of conflict and propose strategies for addressing the problems. If conflict is prolonged and endemic, embrace aggressive intervention to avoid dysfunctional strife that poisons the workplace atmosphere.

Conclusion

As servant leaders, we must embrace a high standard of love-based care and due diligence in protecting the spiritual, mental and physical wellbeing of our employees. When the organization supports employee work and life balance, it embraces a powerful form of faith. It demonstrates a faith, trust, and confidence in employees regarding their motivation, character, creativity, innovation, ability, efficiency, and effectiveness and the ability to complete independently the work with reduced supervision and face time. Second, it reinforces a faith and trust to delay gratification and embrace the long-term benefits of a more supported labor force. It also demonstrates a form of altruism and agape love in that it is willing to accept lower returns for a higher level of wellbeing for employees, which in turn, improves the quality of life for their families, enhances civic capital, and improves the community through the time needed to invest in other life domains. This orientation and belief system requires great courage, trust, and faith. It is not the broad path, but a straight and narrow path that few embrace.

SLHRM Leadership Personal Character Reflection: The Dignity of Work

"For even when we were with you, we gave you this command: Anyone unwilling to work should not eat." (The Bible, 2 Thessalonians 3:10, NRSV)

Work for the servant leader is a central life domain essential for promoting the overall wellbeing of society. Work assumes a redeeming aspect as it represents a central life domain for living and expressing key character attributes, including honesty, justice, conscientiousness, perseverance, and industriousness. Work becomes another window on the orientation of our hearts. A fundamental principle is that all honest labor is dignified. Servant leaders reject sloth, not the absence of a job for those who are unemployed due to economic factors, sickness, or disability. The role of work is central in both secular and religious worldviews, but for different reasons. In the humanistic world view in which man is the measure of all things, work is a means for self-actualization and meeting and expressing one's inner needs and desires. Work then become the primary means for realizing human potential, thereby functioning as the central measure of success and personal self-worth. For many, work is a form of self-worship defining their purpose and identity. It is a seductive, but a spiritually and morally disastrous, deception especially when we define identity and worth on such metrics as success, prestige, and the size of our paycheck. Servant leaders embrace equality of human worth, so the janitor and CEO are due identical levels of dignity and respect. For the servant leader, it is not the education, experience, or status level of a job, but the character and level of obedience of the person that counts. Servant leader character calls us to work with excellence in every endeavor, to do our best and treat others with respect. So irrespective of the treatment we receive by our employers, or the status of our job, servant leaders understand the inherent dignity of each person. The instrumental values of the world will state that if you fail to realize your potential, you are a failure. For example, if I have a Master's degree in Business, but graduated at the peak of a recession and am unable to secure a position commensurate to my education level, but I am working in dignified labor as a janitor, does this reflect a fatal character flaw? Am I demeaned and humiliated given the absence of equivalency between my education and the wage level and status of the job? Is this status a negative reflection on my identity, character, ability, and worth? From the servant leader worldview, when we internalize the values and standards of our superficial success oriented society, we engage in needless self-condemnation and experience shame and guilt given our perceived failures, many of which are beyond our direct control. In essence, our agreement with instrumental worldly values results in our self-imposed alienation. It is a lie that creates much emotional suffering. If the laborer job was the best position we can attain given exogenous factors such as high unemployment and discrimination, or if we choose not to utilize our education given a different understanding of our life calling, or factors such as mental or physical illness preclude us from an equivalent position, from a servant leader world view our occupational status or salary level never equates with self-worth! If we were unable to work another day of paid labor, servant leaders recognize for themselves and others that their identity is not simply a function of a vocation and that we have inherent value simply through being human and made in the image of God.

SLHRM Leadership Personal Character
Reflection: Life's Tests

As an educator and a lifelong learner, I am very comfortable with the notion that our time on earth consists of a series of "tests." We are simultaneously "cramming" and taking exams of one sort or another every day of our existence. There are numerous references that "life is as a series of tests," but this metaphor instills a variety of emotions depending on our own personality, life experiences, and understanding of human nature. For those wracked by test anxiety and the fear of judgment or failure, this concept is frightening, given the identity of the "teacher" and the predicted dire consequences of failure. Conversely, for those who relish life's final exams and take great pleasure from the adrenaline rush, the prideful bravado instills a sense of false confidence that produces recklessness.

There is a sage middle ground that is important to grasp and challenging to place into practice. The greatest danger is for us to use our own wisdom and reasoning and select the tests. It is analogous to having the students write the exam questions based upon imperfect knowledge, limited experience, and scope of understanding. If I can accomplish this task of forgiving someone once at work, and read five self-help books every day for thirty minutes, I am "okay" and passed the test. These types of tests can become a form of anesthetic that temporarily assuages our conscience, but does not address the root causes of our malaise.

From a servant leader perspective, tests are not solely about performance, but about obedience, trust, and character development. I am not justified by what I do or for how many self-developed tests I pass with high grades. Liberty springs from humbly taking the daily tests that life circumstances afford, those "dying to the self" moments that validate our willingness to grow and place the needs of others over our own. The tests that we create are "fixed" to feed our egos. They are means to self-medicate and anesthetize the pain and avoid facing the true root cause of our problems.

I pray for the courage to starve and abandon self-developed tests, and take the love- and fellowship-based obedience exams. When we develop our own tests, we define success, failure, and attempt to predict and control the consequences. All such attempts are vanity and usurp the power of life events to shape us. Our conscience frequently encourages the development and application of self-tests to manipulate and deceive us into believing we are pursuing moral motives. We commit the same errors, both in assessing others and ourselves, when we grade and judge appearances and neglect the inner motives. When we write the exam, develop the answer key, and set the grading standards, this deflects us from the needed perspective and purpose as we confuse the "best with the good" and make mountains out of molehills (and vice versa). Life's tests produce wisdom and learning, while our self-developed tests generate confusion and pride. Servant leaders grade and evaluate using the love standard, which entails achieving the mission and promoting the best interests of others. Truly, we grow in faith when we test ourselves according to moral and ethical standards. One of the most comforting aspects is that there is a test within the test. Even if we fail, if we embrace a teachable spirit, we have passed a very important examination, that of learning to fail with grace as we fall.

Chapter 7

Employee Performance Management Principles

Performance management and performance appraisal is the single most important "window on the soul" SLHRM practice. An appropriate performance appraisal analogy is the tending of a garden. In securing a bountiful harvest, the most difficult work is at the beginning as we toil in clearing the land of rocks, brush, stumps, and trees. Then we must plow, sow, and weed. The harvest comes later. The great daily demand placed on managers through "fire-engine management" reduces the available time for employee development. This creates a vicious cycle as poorly trained and managed employees generate increased downstream problems. The answer is patient, long-term investment in employees. A major solution to the time dilemma is promoting a culture of delegation and empowerment. Hence, supervisors devote less time to micromanagement responsibilities and more time to the value-enhancing goal setting, problem solving, and communication augmenting activities that increase quality, efficiency, and effectiveness. When managers possess more time to plan, they can invest more time and effort in "management by walking around," thereby cultivating relationships.

One of the important elements is to differentiate the performance appraisal process from performance measurement and performance management. See table 7.1 for more detail.

Performance Appraisal Worldview

Let us address the area of performance appraisal first. Is performance appraisal compatible with servant leader values and teachings? Clearly, the concept of accountability is central to the servant leader

Table 7.1 Definition of key performance appraisal terms

Term	Definition
Performance management	An integrated and holistic system for linking the achievement of organizational servanthood and stewardship mission, vision, and values with all structural levels (individual employees, work groups, departments, and the overall organization) utilizing a broad range of methods (surveys, focus groups, archives), sources (employees, supervisors, customers, peers) and measures/metrics (process, outcome, quality, quantity, timeliness, customer service). It entails the complex integration of motivational tools and techniques to produce high quality organizational performance.
Performance measurement	The process of measuring performance at the individual, group, department and organizational levels using a balanced set of methods, sources, standards, and metrics.
Performance metric or measure	A clearly defined and measurable indicator linked to mission achievement (percentage of defect free units).
Performance standard	A metric or measure that contains a target level of performance (achieve an 85 percent customer satisfaction survey rate related to the waiting time for building permits with a standard of three business days for processing).
Performance appraisal/ evaluation	The process of assembling, reviewing, and interpreting a broad range of performance information to produce a valid and reliable assessment (judgment) of the efficacy of employee performance.

worldview. We all must give account of how we live our lives, the truly comprehensive, holistic "performance appraisal" of both our natural and moral job descriptions. For example, a key element of ethical performance appraisal is corroborated information from more than one witnesses or source in the decision-making process, which is absent in most traditional performance appraisal systems. It is critical to devote a sufficient degree of effort and preparation to provide for an accurate rating. Performance appraisal as presently designed and implemented in many organizations violates moral and ethical standards, given that most systems do not emphasize the ethical implications and responsibilities of raters and ratees. Evaluators exercise power over subordinates, influencing work motivation, job satisfaction, and job stress, but even more importantly, the level of employee self-esteem and their job and career success. Most organizations fail to provide the ethical foundation for effective performance appraisal due to an absence of training, quality control, and evaluating the rater on how well he or she administers the performance appraisal process, among others.

It is important to explore the utilitarian and servanthood implications of the various performance management/appraisal approaches. Leadership studies confirm the efficacy of two of the important elements of servant leadership as it relates to performance management and appraisal: encouragement and accountability. Early management research in the famous Ohio State (Stogdill, 1974) and University of Michigan (Likert, 1961) studies, respectively identified two sets of global leadership behaviors, consideration (employee support), and initiating structure (setting goals, providing direction, promoting accountability) and employee orientation (relationship oriented) and production focus (Northouse, 2013). These behaviors are akin to the servant leader virtues of encouragement/exhortation in which we "encourage the discouraged" and the need to challenge others and ourselves through behavioral accountability to moral standards. A major challenge in all management situations is to maintain the "harmonic mean" balance between support, mercy, and responsibility. What is the proper balance in your own managerial decision making? There are no formulas given the complex nature of human motivation and the multiplicity of contextual variables.

Performance Management/Appraisal Motivational Philosophy

Performance management/appraisal systems employ a variety of intrinsic and extrinsic motivational tools. However, the term "extrinsic" and "intrinsic" is a semantic rather than a substantive definition. All motivators entail an intrinsic assignment of worth or value linked to the attainment of a desired end state. Intrinsic rewards necessitate the internalization of values that are self-administered and therefore motivate and guide behavior across a variety of employment contexts. Hence, by definition, they are more reliable and efficient. Motivation is a complex construct amenable solely to indirect measurement, given that it is an internal psychological process. Our behaviors are the product of multiple motives operating at different levels of conscious and unconscious awareness.

From a servant leader standpoint, the erosion of morality begins when self-serving elements influence motives, means, and ends. The locus of motivation (internal or external) does not determine its ethical orientation; rather, it is the nature of the underlying motive. In a workplace setting, an intrinsic motivational approach is more likely to satisfy individual employee and organizational servanthood and stewardship values. The most powerful workplace motivators are employee desires to love their fellow man and promote the Golden Rule with a second powerful motivator being the desire to fulfill our purpose and calling through autonomy and growth in order to promote mastery of their trade or profession. The previously noted Job Characteristics Model of Hackman and Oldham (1976) summarizes the factors that contribute to intrinsic motivational potential (IMP). These include: skill variety, task significance (perceived importance of the job and its link to the mission), task identity (producing a whole piece of work), autonomy and performance feedback or knowledge of results.

SLHRM organizations develop a culture emphasizing that meeting employee needs for transcendence entails a holistic integration of performance at the individual, group, and organizational level. This can only be accomplished by the development of strong and cohesive work teams in which employees are rewarded (monetarily and nonmonetarily) both for their individual job efficacy and for general citizenship behaviors that support team cohesion and effectiveness. There is an inherent recognition that success is a collective team effort in which humility governs work efforts. When we are humble, we recognize that we cannot achieve anything of value fully outside of our relationships with others. There are no self-made men and women, and we all stand on the shoulders of others. This entails development of a performance management system that utilizes a harmonic mean of metrics that measure and reward individual, group, and organizational success, but does not penalize employees for factors beyond their control.

Appraisal Ethics

Servant leaders reserve their harshest criticism for the hypocritical for good reason. When managerial practice diverges from stated policy, the visible contradiction generates disappointment, distrust, and cynicism toward those in authority. It reduces the employee motivation and organizational citizenship behaviors associated with vibrant, productive, and healthy work environments. Employees will not exert the necessary extra effort and creativity to solve problems and make necessary changes when they lack trust in integrity of management. When managers promote the use of the proverbial "tell and sell" approach to performance appraisal (Maier, 1958), employees rightly perceive manipulation and hierarchical command and control values. Another deadly performance appraisal sin is rater bias. The presence of nonperformance factors contaminates appraisal ratings producing a fruit of perceived and genuine unfairness in the rating process and its outcomes, which in turn is linked to tangible outcomes such a lower job satisfaction and higher turnover (Poon, 2004). The various forms of appraisal bias serve as a major fertile source of EEO complaints and court cases involving contested personnel practices linked to performance appraisal. Prime examples include person characteristic bias (race, gender, and age), personal relationship contamination (liking or disliking), and failing to gather a representative sample of performance (Wilson & Jones, 2008). Recent research documents other well-known sources of bias including the corrosive effect of employee and rater impression management and ingratiating measures (Rao, Schmidt, & Murray, 1995; Bolino et al., 2008; Kacmar, Wayne, & Wright, 2009). Employee pandering creates resentment among co-workers disadvantaged by the political strategies. Another finding confirmed by research is the influence of rater affect (liking) of the subordinate (Lefkowitz, 2000). There are a variety of biases produced in the appraisal process generated by rater affect, but interestingly recent research indicates that managers can differentiate and separate personal feelings and emotions from formal ratings providing high performance ratings when warranted (Varma, Pichler, & Srinivas, 2005). This is clearly consistent with SLHRM practices to treat all employees with respect irrespective of personal attitudes.

A detailed overview of the most common rating errors appears in table 7.2. Factors that enhance ethical problems include the absence of 360-degree feedback providing a comprehensive view of the employee's performance along with failing to train and hold managers accountable for the presence of rater errors such as halo, recency, contrast, and the external bias. Training raters and holding the managers accountable for the quality of performance ratings reduces the presence of these biases.

Another key source of discord is the political use of appraisal to punish opponents and reward enemies, thereby eroding trust. Leniency, central tendency, and severity errors can demoralize and demotivate employees given the absence of useful and honest feedback. There is a tendency for both raters and ratees to protect the ego and promote personal and selfish interests over the mission. There are sources of bias from both the employee and rater perspective including the external bias in which the rater blame employees for poor performance and employees blame external forces. Without the presence of servant leader moral character attributes, it is very challenging to near impossible to overcome the ethical and process-related challenges.

Table 7.2   Sources of performance appraisal error

Error Source	
Flawed measures	Contamination: Performance appraisal information process and decision making is influenced by nonperformance related factors: • *Group-based characteristic bias*: race, gender, age, nationality, religion, etc. • *Personal characteristics bias*: influence of affect (liking), physical attractiveness, weight and height • *External factors bias*: Measures do not account for the influence of factors beyond employees control (effect of weather on demand for products) • *Deficiency*: Measures fail to include key aspects of the construct being measured (production metrics that fail to include quality aspects)
Information processing errors	• *External bias*: Outside observers (supervisors, peers or other raters) assign a higher degree of personal responsibility to the employee (lack of effort or ability) for performance problems while discounting external factors. The reverse effect occurs when we assess ourselves with a tendency to externalize responsibility (outside factors, supervisor ineffectiveness or lack of support. • *Assignment of responsibility bias*: When others exhibit problems we are prone to seek accountability and justice (assign the letter of the law), while when we are responsible, we seek mercy and forgiveness. • *Premature conclusion bias*: Reach a firm decision based upon a limited and unrepresentative sample of employee performance and information. • *Fixed decision bias*: An ego-protecting mechanism in which we seek to validate a decision by selective information search and processing. We discount information that conflicts with our views and seek out and use information that confirms our decision. It requires a higher threshold of contradictory information to change our views. • *Negative outcome bias*: We assign a higher rate of influence and importance to negative information and feedback than positive. It requires a higher ratio of positive feedback to override negative outcomes.
Rating errors	• *Halo*: Failure to differentiate between various aspects of job performance. Overall global perceptions override specific assessment of specific job duties. • *Leniency*: Consistently assigns higher ratings regardless of true performance level • *Severity*: Consistently assigns lower ratings regardless of true performance level • *Central Tendency*: Consistently assigns average ratings regardless of true performance level • *Beginning and recency effect*: Excessive weighting of early and recent performance information

Continued

Table 7.2   Continued

Political (Instrumental) Use of Appraisal	• Use performance appraisal as an instrument to influence, persuade, control or intimidate employees
Lack of Rater Training	• The absence of rater training and uniform performance standards contributes to appraisal system unreliability as managers employ a different set of metrics for rating employee performance
Overreliance on Pay and Other Extrinsic Measures	• An absence of a balanced reward portfolio undervalues intrinsic motivational approaches thereby contributing to the "mercenary" syndrome of answering to the call of the highest bidder and increasing turnover to unacceptable levels
An Overconfidence in the System Design versus Process	• An overemphasis on the mechanics of appraisal versus the quality of the rater and ratee relationship process.

Source: Tversky & Kahneman, 1974; Feldman, 1981; Bernardin & Beatty, 1984; Murphy & Cleveland, 1995; Hodgkinson, 2003; Lakshman, 2008.

When managers fail to provide accurate ratings, it creates a climate of deception with wide-ranging negative consequences. Leniency and/or ambiguous feedback inhibit the identification and correction of performance deficiencies and problems. This rewards incompetence and penalizes good faith employees by eroding recognition for performance excellence. Leniency denies employees a truthful assessment thereby promoting a form of self-deception. For those employees that are performing at or above standards, it dilutes the significance of their recognition. This reduces organizational trust levels, inhibiting employee and organizational learning, growth and accountability. In contrast, rating harshness or severity demoralizes and denies credit to employees, a form of management theft that creates discouragement.

The underlying values emphasized by many performance appraisal systems are utilitarian in nature, rewarding employees for individual performance. Hence, employees quite naturally engage in self-serving and narcissistic behaviors, thereby reducing organizational citizenship and loyalty. These systems reward mercenary self-serving behavior on the part of supervisors and employees alike instead of the altruistic, mission enhancement values needed to promote organizational loyalty. Another problem is the absence of employee input from both raters and ratees thereby depreciating the quality and utility of the system, thus depressing system acceptance and the motivation to use it effectively. Objective indicators of lack of acceptance include skewed rating distributions such as leniency and central tendency along with perfunctory performance feedback.

Factors that Contribute to Unethical Performance Appraisal

It is vitally important to recognize and address the "root-cause" character barriers to effective performance appraisal. One major temptation is to use the power of performance appraisal as a "command and control" and political influence instrument. A second major temptation is the influence of our character weaknesses tempting us to manipulate ratings given fear, envy, and insecurity when a subordinate "outshines" the rater. Conversely, the "fear of man" produces the inability to provide negative feedback and constructively manage the emotions produced by conflict. Finally, there is the sister strongholds of "people pleasing" and the addiction to positive feedback through affirmation anxiety. From a character foundation standpoint, the antidote is a servant leader courage in which the motives of the heart emphasize mission achievement and promoting the best interests of employees. The underpinning is cultivating trust in management based on the servant leader character traits of love, transparency, humility, forgiveness, encouragement, challenge, and conscientiousness.

Critics of performance appraisal present compelling critiques, but it is misleading to promote the belief that all performance appraisals are futile, given their complexity and the many sources of bias (Bowman, 1999). Traditional methods of conducting performance appraisals are more likely to manifest the various categories of evaluation error given the absence of multiple sources/methods and quality control. See table 7.2 for the various sources of error.

Solutions to Performance Appraisal Problems

Given this litany of problems, what are some of the key servanthood solutions (see table 7.3)? Performance appraisal systems embedded within a larger system of performance management can be effective in spite of the obstacles if managers are dedicated to relationship building and utilizing multiple source of input and involve employees in the appraisal process. The first is the character issue. An effective performance appraisal environment requires a learning organization in which mistakes and poor performance are opportunities for problem solving and learning. Until employees are comfortable discussing and taking responsibility for mistakes, self-protective and self-promotional motivational effects will override all others. In order to implement this

Table 7.3 Key elements of effective performance appraisal systems

1. Ongoing clear, specific, behavioral, and timely performance feedback from a credible source
2. Employee participation in all aspects of the performance appraisal system (developing goals and standards, self-evaluation, two-way communication and problem solving in the appraisal interview)
3. Clear, specific and detailed performance documentation based upon first-hand information such as a performance diary
4. A holistic and integrated set of individual, group and organizational performance measures grounded upon a detailed and updated job analysis. Include metrics that assess quantity, quality, timeliness, and customer satisfaction. Another key area is a balance of subjective and objective performance measures as not all components of the job are quantifiable or measurable. For subjective elements (traits such as initiative) provide specific behavioral definitions and require documentation.
5. Clear performance (SMART) goals and standards that measure and reward organizational values, work process/behavior, and performance (outcomes).
6. Rater and ratee system support and training addressing the following subjects:
   a. rating errors and how to avoid them
   b. goal setting process (SMART goals)
   c. Multi-source, 360-degree appraisals (clients, peers, subordinates, other managers) Most employees report a deficit of specific, behavioral, and timely performance feedback. A fundamental principle of effective system design is multiple methods and measures. Any single metric contains error (contamination) and does not fully encompass the desired outcomes (deficiency). As such, organizations should employ a variety of quality, quantity, and timeliness measures focusing on work process and outcomes.
   d. Contextual factors outside the employee's direct control are taken into consideration
7. A systematic assessment of the appraisal systems effectiveness in terms of:
   a. Process compliance: adhering to system procedures, quality of feedback
   b. Psychometric assessment: identify rating bias (race, gender, age) and rating errors (halo, leniency, severity)
   c. Assess employee attitudes toward the system
   d. Impact on behaviors (turnover, absenteeism, retention, etc.) and productivity
8. Hold managers accountable on how well they manage the appraisal process, "rate the rater" on their own performance appraisal
9. A fair appeals process. The key is to develop a balance between individual and organizational performance. Organizations should not punish employees for factors beyond their control, but it is important to instill a sense of corporate responsibility to reduce the "free-rider" effect.
10. A major challenge is linking individual performance to overall organizational performance in a valid fashion. Performance appraisal systems must address issues related to the nature of teamwork. As occurs in many situations, there are short and long-term aspects for both the performance and interpersonal dimension, some of which work at cross-purposes with each other. Again, the foundational values determine the organization's direction. Another issue is selecting team members for interpersonal skills and teamwork "fit" and the means available to assess the ongoing interpersonal dynamics.

Source: Roberts & Pavlak, 1996.

learning organization, management must be transparent, forgiving, encouraging, empowering, and challenging (setting and maintaining standards). The mission and truth promotion goals of performance appraisal must take precedence. Sadly, these attributes are lacking in many organizations. The second solution is combining the past, present, and future into an ongoing process. Performance appraisal must promote learning from past performance, but not be controlled by past failures or successes. An emphasis on the future inspires employees and motivates them with a compelling vision providing hope and fulfillment. Ideally, employees believe that management respects and values their past and present performance, but is not satisfied like a proud parent given their confidence in the employee's future growth potential. The "present" focus of an appraisal system is important to ensure that managers and employees are communicating on a daily coaching and mentoring basis. Effective performance appraisal is a process of ongoing employee-manager communication founded upon trust. The key process factor is employee voice, or the presence of employee participation in all aspects of the appraisal system (goals, standards, evaluation, and the performance appraisal interview), clear, specific, and challenging goals and standards, and ongoing specific, behavioral, and timely performance feedback. These important management servanthood and stewardship competencies are essential elements of managerial style, and explain why there is such variance within and between performance appraisal raters and systems. A manager practicing these voice attributes will be successful irrespective of the technical soundness of the system. For other important factors (see table 7.3 for more detail).

SLHRM managers are wise to honor and practice these principles. Effective performance appraisal entails a very significant investment of organizational and SLHRM energy.

Who Is Responsible for Employee Poor Performance?

As servant leaders, it is very important to possess a balanced view of how to define and respond to performance problems. Hence, one key element is to reflect on the overall dynamics of assigning responsibility for organizational performance problems. The TQM work of Deming (1986) illustrated the tendency to blame individual employees and assign an excessive share of the responsibility for performance and ethical problems. Deming believed that the locus of responsibility resides with ineffective management systems, not individual employee contributions. The psychological process surrounding the assignment of responsibility for poor performance is termed attribution theory in psychology and is widely used in organizational research (Taggar & Neubert, 2004). A capsule version of this very powerful descriptor of human behavior is that a supervisor, when reviewing a poorly performing employee, is more likely to blame the employee by relating it to the worker's lack of ability, motivation or character (internalizing the responsibility) rather than external causes such as poor selection, training, support, resources or supervision. Why is this case? One reason is that supervisors quite naturally desire to protect their own egos and reputations thereby discounting other external explanations including their own contributions through ineffective supervision. The result is a disagreement between manager and employee on the root cause and solution to the performance problem and ongoing conflict and distrust. This same phenomenon occurs at the executive level as well. Deming stated that organizations frequently "scapegoat" employees for organizational performance problems outside of their control and caused by poor management. Hence, employees and managers differ in how they view performance problems. The truth is frequently in between. How can we address these differences? First, learn to seek information that challenges your initial feelings and evaluations by attempting to disprove them. Take the approach that the employee "is innocent until proven guilty." Examine your behavior closely to ensure that you are not creating a climate where your attitudes create self-fulfilling prophecies in your employees. Attempt to increase your understanding of alternative views by "putting yourself in your employee's shoes."

My question for the reader relates to who is responsible for your organization's poor performance? A servant leader approach is to instill a collective level of responsibility for poor performance without scapegoating. This entails a higher level of transparency than most organizations provide. When organizations fail to embrace a balanced approach, it promotes a Darwinian "survival of the fittest" environment with many discarded, broken, and wounded bodies, given an instrumental view of employees.

Another frequent research finding on a factor that contribute to poor performance is high levels of employee dissatisfaction with the quality and frequency of performance feedback given the absence of rater time, observational opportunities, and a lack of manager self-awareness regarding their communication styles and orientation (Bernardin & Beatty, 1984). For example, what a manager defines as "detailed and behavioral performance feedback," employees perceive as a general personality attack. Research clearly reflects one of the enduring findings in performance appraisal research is a consistent discrepancy between employees and managers over the specificity, sign (positive or negative), frequency, and utility of performance feedback (Ilgen, Fisher, & Taylor, 1979). There are constellations of factors that contribute to differential performance appraisal perceptions. One key element is the absence of systematic performance feedback quality control policies that hold managers accountable for feedback quantity, quality, and integrity. One of the major causal factors underlying performance perception discrepancies between employee and rater is ambiguous feedback, which itself is a contributing factor to incompetence across all life endeavors. Driving ability self-perceptions clearly demonstrate this phenomenon. The average motorist perceives himself to be a safe and skilled driver, while concurrently reporting that a high percentage of other drivers are incompetent. Most motorists receive little direct feedback on their driving behavior and skills, and the slight amount of feedback becomes discounted given the ego-protecting attribution bias that externalizes responsibility (blame the other person or external circumstances). One of our servant leader obligations is to communicate truth to our subordinates. Encouragement, correction, and accountably are three pillars of a servanthood performance management process. Unfortunately, there are many obstacles to loving employees in a fashion promoting their best interests.

One great challenge of SLHRM performance appraisal is when newly hired or promoted employees produce work of uneven quality, and we are under intense performance pressures to improve the bottom line. The challenge relates to the high level of program accountability and a reduced margin for error in allowing employees to learn from their mistakes. We need to exercise patience for employees in the new situation and provide a clean slate to avoid unfair advantage or disadvantage. In these type of scenarios, employees warrant closer supervision. There are valid and invalid reasons for close supervision Invalid reasons include the desire to maintain coercive control and power over employees to maximize personal advancement and/or gain and insecurity over subordinates' achievement levels (outshine the supervisor). Examples of valid reasons include directing inexperienced employees and supervising consistently poor performers that are not making adequate progress.

Hence, experience demonstrates that most performance problems entail a complex combination of causal factors, including management/leadership system weaknesses and deficiencies (e.g., absence of formal SMART performance goals), individual and group employee attitude and behavioral problems (e.g., low levels of commitment and high levels of defensiveness), and unique contextual factors (e.g., intense performance pressures). When managers and employees personalize the situation and fail to practice humility and teachability, they attenuate their ability to solve the problem in a collegial manner.

From a SLHRM perspective, the ideal is to view our relationship with our employees as a covenant—a mutual long-term relationship. A foundational principle in covenantal problem solving is to engage in critical self-reflection before we start to define the problem and generate solutions. In other words, servant leaders assume ownership and responsibility for the problem. What can I do to solve this situation in a moral fashion? This entails assigning accountability to both parties, but in a nonjudgmental fashion. Irrespective of how accountability for the performance problems would be ideally, apportioned, servant leaders assume the moral perspective and identify their contributions to the problem before assigning responsibility to others.

Managers require external data to validate self-perceptions regarding their management styles and micromanaging. Subordinate evaluations and ongoing employee communication are two important tools for uncovering employee views. A key factor relates to institutional accountability. When there is no feedback from the important stakeholder groups, it clearly limits the efficacy of the performance measurement system. Organizational members possess opinions on their

Table 7.4 Performance counseling techniques

1. *Establish trust based on humility*: Supervisors should express their concern over the problem and the necessity of addressing the issues jointly. They should communicate a sincere willingness to solve the problem and provide the foundation for the employee to prosper. Supervisors need to acknowledge the presence of relationship conflict and accept responsibility as a manager for some aspects of the situation.
2. Clearly describe the nature of the problem (what, when, how) and its consequences in a clear, calm and nonjudgmental fashion.
3. *Discuss problem context*: The supervisor should provide background information on the depth and breadth of the problem's contextual performance issues (factors that are beyond the employee's control) and the organizational pressures that the manager faces.
4. *Employee input*: It is important for employees to provide their view on the cause and solution to the problem and what the manager needs to continue to do and stop doing.
5. *Empower*: Jointly develop a solution to the problem and empower employees to set goals and craft solutions.
6. *Produce an action plan to implement the solution*: Develop a specific action plan with SMART performance goals and standards.
7. *Regular communication*: Schedule regular follow-up meetings to discuss progress and any means for assisting the employee.

leaders, but they are frequently reluctant to provide honest feedback given their natural tendency to defer to authority figures given fear of adverse consequences. Effective performance management systems encourage and educate all the key stakeholders on how to provide appropriate feedback. SLHRM organizations adopt a standardized performance counseling formula summarized in table 7.4.

SLHRM organizations embrace a patient but firm approach to performance counseling that honors employee dignity while affixing joint responsibility for problem solving.

Performance Management/Appraisal Stress Coping

There are many character, career management and negotiation learning points associated with employee responses to stressful superior-subordinate relationships in the areas of performance management. As servant leader employees and managers, we need to develop a career management toolkit of coping and adaptive strategies (Cartwright & Cooper, 1997). Coping strategies provide internal psychological adaptations to the stressful situation. We may have little to no control regarding the external situation, but we can influence how we respond in terms of our thoughts and the associated emotions. These trials become fertile areas for character growth through patience, persistence, and reframing problems into opportunities. One strategy is to recognize that we grow in patience when we serve "unjust masters" with excellence. The second dimension relates to what stress researchers term "adaptive responses" that entail changing the external environment through a physical or interpersonal intervention such as engaging in a principled negotiation strategy. From an adaptation perspective, strive to identify the interests of your supervisor and strive to serve him or her more effectively. A third dimension for thought is the development of institutional safeguards such as anti-bullying policies to reduce the frequency of dysfunctional work relationships. Servant leaders proactively reduce performance appraisal stress through a variety of organizational practices.

Forced Distribution Systems

One of great debates in performance appraisal relates to the pro and cons of forced distributions systems, or grading on a curve. Critics claim that forced distribution systems elevate rating inaccuracy, reduce managerial flexibility, and generate employee perceptions of unfairness given conflicts with employee self-evaluations (Stewart,

Gruys, & Storm, 2010). Performance appraisal research confirms the presence of the self-esteem bias, as most employees rate their performance well above average and forced distribution systems conflict with employee self-images thereby generating negative job attitudes including unfairness and lower work motivation levels (Meyer, 1980). The reliance on comparative performance standards accentuates employee insecurity and depreciates teamwork and cooperation. When the focus is comparative, it encourages employees to become prideful and complacent when anointed "superior," insecure and fearful if they fail to "measure-up" and reduces motivation to improve given complacency with high ratings and discouragement with low placements on the rating scale. When the focus is on meeting benchmarked standards of objective quality, there is less "scapegoating" of individual employee performance and more emphasis on management and employee joint responsibility for problem solving. The impetus for performance appraisal distortion accentuates with the adoption of a forced distribution compensation and promotion system, as managers must "game" the ratings to provide key employees with desired rewards. This also contributes to "in-group" and "out-group" rating behavior as managers attempt to reward "star" employees at the expense of their "B" employees given the limitations on the number of workers eligible for merit or bonus awards. This erodes appraisal system trust and acceptance thereby contributing to perceived and actual management hypocrisy. However, there is widespread dissatisfaction with forced distribution systems but in spite of the weaknesses, it is used quite frequently given that it reduces the evaluation burden, as it is easier to assess relative performance, especially at the "tails" of the normal curve. In many workplaces, all of the employees are truly exceptional thereby forcing managers to make inflated and "artificial" distinctions that demoralize and create conflict.

Developmental versus Administrative Uses of Performance Appraisal

Another key debate in performance appraisal is how to balance the foundational performance appraisal purposes of employee development and administrative decision making (Bernardin & Beatty, 1984). Some researchers argue that appraisals are more accurate and useful for improving performance if they are diagnostic and not linked to pay or other administrative outcomes. Opponents argue that employees will not take the process seriously unless there is a bottomline outcome. Where managers make mistakes in linking performance appraisal and compensation is focusing exclusively on monetary rewards as this is dysfunctional for several reasons including the classic case of goal displacement in which monetary rewards focus employee attention and effort on the measured behaviors (quantity of output) at the expense of equally important, but unrewarded, job duties (such as maintenance). In addition, it is important to reject embracing the Theory X view that employees are motivated by money alone and not the intrinsic satisfaction that occurs from a job well done, and the failure to recognize the utility of nonmonetary rewards such as recognition and time off. Another demotivating factor is the "bait and switch" routine in which organizations make midyear "corrections" on performance pay formulas thereby reneging on promised rewards. Other characteristics that reduce employee trust is the linkage of the appraisal rating and compensation system without employee input into the performance standards and an absence of clear communication and employee understanding regarding how managers make performance decisions. Performance appraisal information is most accurate and comprehensive when used to developmentally coach and mentor employees. Using performance appraisal ratings for administrative decisions inflates ratings as managers seek to reduce rater-ratee conflict and maintain workplace harmony. It also reduces the breadth, depth, and accuracy of performance feedback given concerns that honest feedback may adversely influence employee job standing. One solution is for the first level supervisor to present an overall summary of employee performance to a panel of senior managers who make the final administrative decisions. This removes the direct responsibility from supervisors, enabling them to assume the role of coach, providing performance feedback. There is an inherent conflict between the administrative and development applications of performance appraisal systems. For example, when managers use appraisal ratings for compensation and promotion decisions, there is an unfortunate natural tendency to reduce the quality and quantity of performance feedback to reduce employee anxiety and manager discomfort. Hence, if an adverse action such as a layoff occurs, the absence of balanced feedback accentuates the "surprise" effect. Over the long run, this cycle erodes the two-way communication needed for effective performance management. Organizations sometimes embrace performance appraisal "religion" right before layoffs. The underlying motive is to protect the company from a legal liability from wrongful discharge and discrimination lawsuits. The unfortunate consequence of the instrumental use of performance appraisal is the erosion of employee trust and the reduction in the motivational value of performance appraisal.

Performance Appraisal and SLHRM Character

The performance management process reveals servant leader character. Performance management is a "window on the heart" personnel practice that greatly influences employee trust. HR servant leadership performance management requires great *agapao* (the Greek verb form of agape) love, or the ability to promote the best interests of employees irrespective of our personal feelings and relationship history. Servant leader character begins with an understanding that we possess both a moral and employer job description. Our moral job description is ultimately the most important. A major SLHRM job element is promoting both job descriptions through character development. Should SLHRM organizations invest the time and effort for character development in the presence of high workloads? The answer is clearly an emphatic "yes" as unless the organization makes character investments, both individually and corporately, the foundation crumbles. Performance management is the desired system for managing employee performance, as traditional command and control and "tell and sell" performance appraisal systems are contrary to servant leader principles (see table 7.5).

Promoting a character-based foundation for the appraisal process is a joint effort between manager and employee. Each possesses critical duties and obligations to promote servanthood and stewardship interests. An excellent point to contemplate is the nature and influence of "tough love." A key element of our journey as a servant leader is the delicate balance between encouragement and accountability. We tend to align ourselves to one approach or the other depending on our personality, gifts, and life experiences. The proper balance requires an unselfish devotion to loving the other person, irrespective of their reaction to our decisions. The only way to get this right is ongoing trial and error in conjunction with ongoing reflection given all the complex variables associated with human motivation (we deceive ourselves and others regarding our motives).

Managers must assume a role of humility recognizing that effective evaluation/assessment requires great skill given the complexity of variables and potential for deception. This entails an ongoing personal commitment to engaging in moral reflection in making decisions to promote the best interests of others. Emphasize the importance of loving employees by delicately balancing encouragement, support,

Table 7.5 Differentiation between traditional performance appraisal and performance management

Appraisal Issue	Traditional Performance Appraisal	Performance Management
Single Source Performance Appraisal	Single source witness: Relies solely on supervisor interpretation of performance information. A key factor is the balance between process measures and outcome measures. For example, should the organization penalize an excellent salesperson for factors beyond his or her control, and conversely, should a poor salesperson receive rewards for high level of sales in a boom market in which almost anyone can sell? If not, how can the reward system be adjusted?	Utilizes multiple sources (witnesses): self-evaluation, peers, clients, other supervisors
Reliability of Single Source Information	Low levels of reliability given the prevalence of criterion deficiency and contamination with single source appraisals.	Higher reliability given multiple sources and method. Biased sources more likely to be exposed as outliers.
Purpose of assessment and the assigning of responsibility for performance problems	Judgment and legalism: Traditional performance appraisal attempts to assign the proper degree of employee responsibility for his or her level of performance. Judgment requires a degree of knowledge and character integrity that exceeds the intellectual and moral capacity of most managers. Supervisors judge on the surface, focusing on the superficial aspects and possess a tendency to overestimate individual employee responsibility and underestimate system factors beyond employee control. Most managers fail to first assume personal accountability for their contributions to employee performance problems and fail to recognize the many external factors that influence performance.	Learning and development: Focus is to improve organizational performance by recognizing the collective, systems based accountability for performance, a balance of individual, group, and organizational accountability. The focus is on long-term growth and development. The focal point is not assigning responsibility and "blaming," but to solve problems and enhance growth at all levels. Performance management is more effective because it requires management and employees assume joint responsibility for performance problems, and second, to seek the contextual factors that are beyond employee or organizational control that adversely influence performance.

Sources of Error	More error sources given the reliance on a single decision maker. Tempts managers to act upon self-serving interests and impulses (reward friends, punish enemies, take credit for the contributions of others) contributing to inaccurate evaluations (dishonest scales) reducing employee trust and confidence. The end result is a form of employee theft given the withholding of valid praise and correction contributing to self and organizational deception/hypocrisy inhibiting character and competency growth and development. If we love our employees, we will provide the proper level of praise and correction.	Fewer error sources given the multiple sources of information and higher quality control standards associated with the performance measurement process. Information and sources are audited and verified with a consensual, group based decision model that reduces both the opportunity and temptation to act upon selfish motives given the higher degree of transparency.
Feedback Frequency	Traditional performance appraisal provides perverse incentives to avoid providing daily corrective feedback and praise. It provides a false sense of security that once or twice a year appraisals can provide the needed correction or reinforcement. The research literature clearly demonstrates a consistent discrepancy between employees and managers over the quality and frequency of performance feedback. One of the most serious obstacles to appraisal system effectiveness is the constellation of factors that contribute to differential perceptions.	Performance management encourages ongoing communication and learning that facilitates timely discussion of problems by reducing status differences.
Competition and Comparison	Traditional performance appraisal systems that employ a comparative perspective (a forced distribution or grading on a curve) reduces teamwork and increases dysfunctional competition, creates a prideful orientation in the winners, and creates envy and jealousy in the "losers." The goal is to cooperate and learn from each other.	Performance management systems are more likely to employ objective standards of performance that place no quota on outstanding performers. This enhances cooperation, teamwork and altruism as employees are rewarded for helping others.

and accountability. Another key element is assuming responsibility for performance problems (remove the log in the eye) by identifying personal contributions to the situation and factors beyond the employee's control that influence the situation. Managers need to assume a teachable and humble spirit.

From the employee perspective, employees must engage in servant followership. As is the case with managers, effective evaluation requires ongoing reflection and self-analysis given the complexity of variables and potential for deception. Emphasize the importance of loving other employees (and the manager) by delicately balancing encouragement, support, and accountability. Assume responsibility for performance problems by identifying personal contributions to the situation. Identify factors beyond the employee's control that influence the situation. In summary, assume a teachable and humble spirit, provide respect to your employer, and work diligently. Another vital attribute is promoting employees to management positions with careful screening and preparation. A helpful practice is developing separate performance evaluations for management potential, as technical skill excellence does not equate with excellence in management.

In addition to the character elements, employee involvement in all aspects of the appraisal system design, development, and administration is foundational for success including self-appraisal. One of the key elements of gaining employee acceptance of the appraisal process, is that the criteria and decision rules that govern the plan's administration are clear, specific, accepted and administered in a fair and transparent fashion. Violating these conditions enhances employee resistance behaviors. Other key elements are ongoing clear, specific, timely, and behavioral performance feedback along with clear, specific, challenging performance goals and standards jointly developed by managers and employees. In addition, a key is to develop multi-source appraisals (peers, clients, other managers). Negative experience with peer appraisal is common, however, as it requires a high degree of trust and low levels of competition for these systems to work. They can be invaluable, however, as peers frequently possess the most complete knowledge of employee job performance.

Comprehensive managerial and employee appraisal training is a key factor in promoting appraisal system character. Most managers lack training on the long-term benefits of an effective performance appraisal system. There is a quid pro quo of support, training, and time in return for managerial investment in rating employees. SLHRM organizations provide extensive performance management training to support newly promoted managers and provide ongoing continuing education in performance management skills development. Failing to devote sufficient resources to management training, development, and accountability produces a pernicious fruit. The organization often promotes employees on technical skill and job performance and frequently commits the cardinal "sin" of assuming management competency. Management should institute a formal management development plan, provide coaching and mentorship, and institute a subordinate appraisal system. If performance management skills do fail to improve, another option is to demote the employee to a team leader and institute a form of a self-directed work team management. Effective performance appraisal training is not performed in isolation, but is embedded in the larger supervisory or management skills training programs of best-practice organizations including FedEx. Well-crafted administrative procedures and forms are a necessary, but not a sufficient condition for effective performance appraisal systems. The reason is that performance appraisal entails two of the most complex processes, interpersonal relations and information processing. These skills are not inherited but are learned behaviors shaped by personality and life experiences. They include:

- Character- and values-based appraisal and the sources and consequences of errors
- Tools and techniques for involving and empowering employees
- Active listening skills
- Providing feedback and counseling techniques
- Performance documentation tools (diaries)
- Goal and standard setting techniques
- Appraisal quality control measures
- Audited performance measures/metrics
- Hold managers accountable through their own performance appraisals regarding their effectiveness in developing and evaluating employees
- Provide subordinate appraisal of managerial effectiveness.
- Assess the presence of rater bias (psychometric analysis)
- Measurement of employee perceptions regarding distributive and procedural justice implications of performance appraisal (surveys, focus groups)
- Appeals process
- Contextual factors are taken into consideration

Effective performance feedback systems are in reality two-way communication systems with mutual responsibilities. As great as the ongoing need for managers to receive training on performance feedback delivery techniques, the impetus for the training employees as receivers on how to respond and process performance feedback is even greater (Schawbel, 2014). The goal is instill an ethos of receiver responsibility for learning, irrespective of how well or poorly the performance feedback is delivered, its level of accuracy and relevancy, and the credibility of the source (Stone & Heen, 2014). Much of the reluctance and fear associated with the performance feedback delivery process on the part of the sender can be mitigated by training receivers to monitor their body language and tone of voice as they receive performance feedback and provide their response in a nondefensive and nonaggressive fashion. When both the sender and receiver are trained, this increases both the quantity and quality of communication strengthening relationships and problem solving.

The performance management/appraisal process requires the highest levels of managerial and employee integrity. This process is in a continual state of flux given its complexity and the opportunities for self-deception. Let us commit to the high calling and the road less traveled.

Volunteer Management Performance Measurement

In addition to full-time employees, performance management/appraisal systems are critical for the effective management of volunteers. How the organization approaches the volunteer management process is another servant leader truth test. Nonprofit organizations possessing the most effective volunteer programs are high commitment in nature recognizing that the search for transcendence and meaning is a prime motivational factor. Hence, meaningful volunteerism entails a "count the cost" investment of time, energy, and passion. The harvest is great and the laborers are still too few, hence the need to promote sustainable volunteer workloads. This is why effective volunteer performance management programs entail a systematic commitment to succession planning to produce the next generation of disciples.

In an ideal performance management system for volunteers, the same principles that apply to full-time employees relate to volunteers as well. Volunteers are provided with clear job descriptions with specific performance standards and metrics, receive a comprehensive orientation to the organization and the position, receive ongoing formal and formal training linked to individual strengths and weaknesses and position requirements, obtain regular and ongoing performance feedback, participate in setting performance goals and standards, receive regular performance appraisals including self-evaluation of performance and evaluating their supervisor, peers, and staff, and receive ample recognition with rewards and advancement linked to performance. Volunteers should receive both formal and informal recognition and awards and other statements of appreciation. Ideally, there is a volunteer management coordinator managing the recruitment and retention of volunteers constructing individual development plans for each volunteer. Another key factor is to ensure that the benefits of volunteers/programs exceed the cost. It is critical to actively consult with line and staff personnel to place volunteers in areas of need that do not impose excessive supervisory costs in terms of time and effort. These principles are very demanding, but SLHRM organizations recognize the tremendous blessings and value produced by motivated, passionate, and well trained volunteers. There also needs to be systematic evaluation of the volunteer program effectiveness and return on investment.

Conclusion

The performance measurement and appraisal process provides great organizational character tests. In essence, the policies and practices of the organization reflect the organization's worldview and moral values. The formal organizational structure of policies and procedures is a reflection of our collective view of human nature. A foundation and structure of servant leader policies and practices is a necessary, but still not a sufficient condition. The next question relates to the integrity of implementation. The worst incarnation of leadership practice is a façade of grace and servanthood that masks the instrumental and self-serving utilitarian and Darwinian heart. This hypocrisy shipwrecks faith and trust.

SLHRM Leadership Personal Character Reflection: Doing Our Best

The workplace is competitive, even "cutthroat," by its very nature. As servant leaders, we are called to compete, but against what and whom? One key to uncovering the truth is grasping the nature of excellence, but how does the servant leader define it? Servant leader excellence entails four factors, obedience to ethical and moral precepts, the presence of love based motives (the desire of the heart), giving our best efforts regardless of the circumstances, and to practice transparency and learn from our mistakes. Hence, these are personalized accountability standards assessing how well we use our individual abilities, gifts, talents, and opportunities. Servant leaders do not arbitrarily compare themselves or compare others and grade on a curve! This is both comforting and disconcerting given the implications. Let us take the issue of giving our best efforts.

What does it mean to do our best? The term "best" entails a combination of effort and outcome. The definition of the "best" entails several factors including ability and gift level, level of effort and the amount of time devoted to a task. To complicate matters, what defines maximum effort varies by external conditions and extenuating factors (illness, fatigue, etc.) introducing a great degree of variability in defining our best. Our maximum performance under conditions of great stress is frequently lower than when performed under ideal conditions. A frequently overlooked element in defining our best is the need to adjust efforts based upon a strategic prioritization, to separate the "best from the good." Our best must always equate with agreement with moral priorities and plans. The first element is whether we should be engaging in the task or job in the first place. One of the great impediments to servant leader growth is our temptation to promote self-serving interests over the common good. We can exert maximum effort only in a limited set of circumstances, duties, and time duration. What is best performance over a short period, those maximum effort times of burning the candle at both ends, is a recipe for burnout if "best" efforts do not include adequate time for family, community, church, rest, and relaxation. The desire to do our best absent a clearly prioritized mission statement increases our vulnerability to a legalistic works mentality that enslaves us with unreasonable performance standards and skewed effort levels producing a spirit of perfectionism. At work, what our "best" entails should never include sacrificing our family, our health, or our community obligations unless it is an absolute emergency and critical to mission achievement with significant implications for the wellbeing of others. Time and energy are precious resources, and the discerning of what is "best" requires a clear understanding and harmony of life priorities. In most cases, we are devoting our maximum effort in the wrong areas and driven by selfish motives. Let us commit to defining our best in servant leader terms, not ours.

SLHRM Leadership Personal Character Reflection: Ethical and Moral Boundaries

The battle over time is one of the great life struggles. Our addiction to activity impedes developing a more nuanced understanding of life purpose and calling. Time can become an idol when our schedules become more important than loving others. Human beings employ an almost infinite array of strategies and objects to experience meaning. All of these strategies become idols (activity, money, power, prestige, relationships) when they replace love as our first allegiance as they temporarily satisfy but ultimately fail to fill the void in our heart and spirit. All of our idols become sources of fear and insecurity given their inability to provide us with the unconditional love that is essential for our security and growth. Why is this relevant? Even as servant leaders, we can lose sight of the true "compass point" purpose. As we spend great amounts of time and effort working for others, we lose sight of the critical factor, to be in relationship with others. The Bible (John 15:5) likens our situations to branches connected to the vine; with the severing of that vital link, we lose our life-giving sustenance.

One of the things I teach students is the need to balance our lives between work, family, and leisure. In reality, life is too complicated, there are too many variables, and the system interconnections are impossibly complicated for rational calculation. When we attempt to balance on fully human terms, we budget time for discrete tasks making us more vulnerable to disruptions impeding our ability to find peace, rest and enjoy the present. The life of Jesus Christ demonstrated the importance of the well-ordered and harmonious life as Pastor John Ortberg stresses in the book *The Life You've Always Wanted* (2002). A well-ordered life does not attempt to achieve a static equilibrium, but a dynamic harmony recognizing the need for seasons requiring varying investment levels in work, family, church and the community depending on life circumstances as guided by life priorities. Servant leaders set priorities, but also demonstrate the ability to improvise, to be sensitive to what we term the "ministry of interruptions." The most important parts of our day are frequently unplanned and unanticipated, and we must make a conscious choice to act upon these opportunities. A rigid "checklist" approach to time management elevates stress and increases our resistance to answering these calls. The other major element of the well-ordered life is division into seasons. There are times when our lives are unbalanced given the importance of key life demands linked to our life priorities. Servant leaders will at times endure sleepless nights, labor for long hours, expose themselves to danger, and sacrifice their personal interests for the wellbeing for others. They also recognize that there are times to rest and refresh. We need to practice emotional and physical awareness to identify the absence of harmonic order in our lives. The universe will keep on running with or without me!

Many servant leaders become prideful, thinking they are immune from the consequences of an absence of life balance, but this is a dangerous illusion. This zeal to service is clearly a strength but gradually evolves into a destructive pattern with loss of perspective. Energy and passion channeled and focused in the right direction becomes a laser in the hands of the servant leader, but the energy dissipates and is not effective without strategic and moral direction. Busyness overwhelms servant leaders, as we are unable to separate the best from the many good things that can distract us. Seek servant leader priorities and cease from your own labors.

Chapter 8

Employee Staffing Principles

The nature and quality of the staffing process is another key element of SLHRM. The staffing process is another "window on the soul" test of SLHRM integrity. As a HR professional or manager, take the time to reflect on the factors contributing to the success of the selection process. Personnel selection is not an exact science for either employee or the organization, hence a combination of trial and error, and experience being an important teacher. As Jim Collins (2001) notes in *Good to Great*, the key staffing factor is "getting the right people on the bus." This entails hiring employees who passionately embrace the mission, vision, and values of the organization possessing the appropriate combination of character and competency for a long-term relationship. Hence, the goal is to select employees that possess the ability to fill multiple roles over the course of their organizational membership. This does not preclude hiring for specific positions, but recognizing that a flexible, organic approach to selection cultivates both employee growth and organizational effectiveness. It is important to reinforce that from a SLHRM perspective, the employment relationship is a covenant. This entails establishing a set of mutually recognized and observed obligations and benefits that govern and order workplace interactions, terms and conditions. In essence, the employment relationship is one of the most important life roles. Managers are "shepherds of the flock" possessing a humbling and fearful level of accountability. The staffing process establishes a foundation for the communication and demonstration of the organization's values.

The Employee Recruitment Process

Let us begin with the recruitment process. The foundation is to apply the Golden Rule standard from the applicant perspective treating candidates with the greatest respect. This entails placing yourself in the role of an applicant and asking, "Would I want to work for this organization after experiencing our recruitment process?" The best practice standards begin with providing clear and accurate information on organizational mission, vision, values, job requirements, work conditions, advancement opportunities, and job security. In essence a 360-degree realistic job preview that addresses the strengths and weaknesses of the job and the organization. This enables applicants to engage in self-selection if their skills and interests do not match the organization and job characteristics. A second major element is to provide extensive training for HR and line managers on the relevant recruitment techniques. It is important to involve existing employees in the recruitment process for several reasons. First, the organization's employees should be your most passionate and persuasive advocates. When current employees truly believe in the mission, are part of an extended family of colleagues, their enthusiasm and authenticity persuades job applicants on the organization's desirability. Consider employees to be deputized recruiters equipped with formal and informal thirty-second to five-minute elevator speeches that paint beautiful portraits of the organization's mission. Second, your employees will provide essential information on candidate quality and fit. Hence, it is important to train employees on the protocol for formally recruiting employees including their elevator speech. It is vitally important to provide applicants with an opportunity to meet supervisors and current employees. In essence, the goal is for all applicants to reflect favorably on their experiences and be an advocate for the organization irrespective of the final hiring decision.

Recruitment and Selection "Rules of Thumb" and Best Practices

One major principle is that candidates should generate within the search committee an excitement and confidence in their abilities. If there is lukewarm support or a general malaise or unease, it is important to honor the discernment and conduct additional research. As such, the preferred course of action may be to bypass the candidate. Many organizations have rued the day of hiring a lukewarm candidate that became a problem employee. We should only hire an applicant when it is clear that the person exceeds the minimum selection criteria and there is a degree of excitement about their candidacy.

Another important principle is to use "superstar hiring" with great caution (Groysberg, Nanda, & Nohria, 2004). It is a great temptation to hire the top performers from other organizations. Sports are a good example of the associated pitfalls. When teams hire the "big names," they fail to recognize that success is a team effort with a dedicated infrastructure that supports high performers. Performance often is lower and organizations are disappointed but the result is predictable given the inattention to the larger system factors that contribute to effective performance. Success in one setting does not ensure success in another, given the complex contextual factors that contribute to effectiveness.

Another important hiring process practice is to communicate the dollar value of benefits to job candidates in the form of a benefits inventory listing individual benefits and their collective values. When employees receive benefits-cost data, they are more appreciative and understanding of the organization's investment in employee wellbeing and develop a more favorable perception of employers.

An additional key principle in the selection process is to cultivate in word and deed that the organization is an "employer of choice" with a reputation for integrity and a dynamic work environment. As is the case with individual employees, our good name and reputation is invaluable. When our organization possesses a status as a desirable and trustworthy work environment, this produces great advantages in attracting applicants. However, humility is the operative word as it takes many years to develop a good name, but it only requires a few critical incidents of failure to tarnish the years of good work. It is much more difficult to restore a tarnished image than it is to maintain an existing good reputation. "Word of mouth" recruiting is the organization's best friend or worst nightmare.

Another important lesson is to ensure that the organization treats all contingent labor and volunteers with dignity and respect, with a significant investment professionalizing the contingent and volunteer recruitment, retention, and development process. The treatment of contingent and volunteers is another "window on the soul." If poor treatment exists, it is another source of information causing applicants to view the organization skeptically. In today's labor market, "just-in-time" service delivery and production methods mandate greater labor flexibility, but we must ensure that the organization views all volunteer and contingent workers with respect and not as disposable commodities. One important factor is to recognize that the absence of stability is a stressor for most workers. This entails adequate training and development investment, high levels of supervisor communication, feedback, support and encouragement, and relevant empowerment opportunities.

Another key principle is to not only screen for competency and character, but also examine the applicant's mission fit. It is important that organizations within the selection process communicate clearly their mission, vision, and values and develop valid and reliable assessment methods. This usually entails assessing the candidate's understanding and commitment to the mission during the interview process. Many organizations face a dilemma relative to training and human capital development. Training resources are scarce, but one countervailing element to low salaries is employee training. If the organization provides generous training options, this practice enhances recruitment and retention. This is a tangible means for saying to employees we care for you, you are important, and that the organization links management and employees together in a common cause. For some organizations, the root motive may be self-interested and utilitarian, but for the SLHRM organization the motive is the Golden Rule and loving your employees. However, these employees are still likely to leave the organization after a relatively short period. Hence, should we invest in employees that may leave the organization before recouping the cost of the investment? On a global basis, from both a principal and utilitarian basis, the benefits exceed the costs. When the organization gains an identity as a quality "farm system" that develops talent valued by other employers, employees will sacrifice short-term financial gain for the experience of working in your organization. Hence, it is a moral arrangement that provides a steady stream of qualified applicants.

Another key best practice standard entails providing clear and accurate information on organizational mission, vision, values, job requirements, working conditions, advancement opportunities, and job security. The best means for providing a clear portrait of the organization is a 360-degree realistic job preview that addresses the strengths and weaknesses of both the job and the organization. This enables applicants to engage in informed self-selection to match their skills and interests to the nature of the job and other key organizational characteristics.

A key element is to provide extensive training for HR and line managers on best-practice recruitment and staffing techniques. One of the foundational needs is to instruct managers on valid and reliable interviewing techniques. This includes educating managers on the many errors that bias the information search and analysis process. One of the key weaknesses is making premature candidate assessments based upon incomplete information, biases and stereotypes, and other common attributional errors. It is important to teach assessors that without a conscious effort to evaluate the results of the entire interview, interviewers reach premature closure within the first five minutes. Hence, it is important to instruct managers on how to develop and administer a standardized interview protocol with behaviorally based questions clearly linked to the essential duties and competencies. This requires developing a list of questions with a standardized scoring system with multiple assessors in a panel interview format.

A final important element is to ensure that in the interview process there are opportunities to meet a variety of supervisors and current employees. However, it is also important to reject the temptation to increase the length and depth of the interview process to unreasonable levels. Some organizations are requiring five or more interview iterations, which places excessive stress on applicants.

SLHRM organizations recognize that a job is not merely a means for earning money to meet basic life needs, but an extension of our calling to use our talents and gifts for the greater good. Clearly not every job is a lifetime commitment and destination, but irrespective of whether the position is full-time, part-time, permanent, or contingent, in or out of the applicant's area of interest, or a long term or a temporary position, the organization should approach the recruitment and staffing process with honor and respect. It begins with a user-friendly application procedure with a sophisticated HR applicant management information system that provides multiple application avenues and sources from in person to online applications and other Web-based social media avenues such as Facebook, LinkedIn, and Twitter. SLHRM organizations that are desirable places to work will have little difficultly in filling most positions even without formal recruiting given the power of reputation and "word of mouth" endorsements. Research demonstrates that referrals can be one of the most effective recruitment sources (Zottoli & Wanous, 2000; Keeling, McGoldrick, & Sadhu, 2013; Obukhova & Lan, 2013).

Another user-friendly element is the ability to submit a single resume for multiple positions with a convenient and simplified Web-based employment application process with reasonable information demands and requirements. It is important to ask the applicant to provide only the essential job-related information to minimize the time and effort required. For larger organizations, one-stop recruiting centers enhance applicant convenience. If the process is Web-based, providing ongoing candidate access to application status is another helpful convenience factor. Another key element is timely and dignified personal notification of employment decisions, positive or negative. It is both frustrating and demeaning for candidates never to receive a formal notification of their job status, or a very perfunctory, bureaucratic, or insulting rejection letter or email. At a minimum, the organization should warmly thank applicants for their interest and their investment of time and energy in the application process with an email. All interviewed candidates should receive a timely letter or phone call expressing appreciation for their time and effort.

Evaluating the Effectiveness of the Recruitment Program

Finally, it is important to implement a comprehensive assessment of the effectiveness of the recruitment process with a balanced set of recruitment metrics. They will include surveying or interviewing job applicants on the quality of the recruitment and selection process, both those that were selected and those that were rejected. In addition, it is important to assess such factors as the yield and quality metrics for various recruitment sources (see table 8.1). For example, it is important to track the cost per applicant and the cost per hire by recruitment source. In this fashion, the organization can track ROI for the various recruitment methods. In addition to costs, best practice organizations track the quality of hires per recruitment source through such metrics as hiring, retention, and promotion rates. The goal is to be a wise steward of the limited recruiting resources. In the example in table 8.1, there is great variability in the cost per qualified applicant generated, with the most cost-effective being newspapers and the most expensive intern programs, but from an efficiency standpoint intern programs are much more accurate.

SLHRM Recruitment and Selection Approaches from the Applicant Perspective

SLHRM organizations embrace the Golden Rule standard and view the recruitment and selection process from the applicant perspective. This includes providing accurate information on the details on the screening (resumes, applications, ratings of training and experience) methods and the steps in selection process beginning with interviews. The organization should provide a clear overview of the number and length of interviews, the identity and location of the interviewers (HR, supervisors, peer employees, etc.), the general content and type of questions (behavioral, situational, etc.), and the general nature of

Table 8.1 Sample evaluation of recruitment program for police officer

Recruitment Strategy	Col A Applicants	Col B Minimally Qualified	Col C B/A Efficiency Hit Rate %	Col D Budget	Col E D/B Cost Per Ap
1. Local Newspaper	950	50	5.3%	$1,000	$20
2. Professional Newsletter	75	45	60%	$500	$11.11
3. Walk-ins	600	15	2.5%	$0	$0.0
4. On-Campus Recruiting	50	30	60%	$3,000	$100
5. Community Groups	45	20	45%	$500	$25
6. Intern Programs	10	10	100%	$40,000	$4,000
7. Social Media	250	35	14%	$3,000	$66.67
8. Referrals/ Friends/ Relatives	100	30	30%	0	$0.00

	Col F Hired	Col G F/A % Hired	Col H F/B Hiring Efficiency	Col I 2 Year Retention Rate	Col J 2 Year Prom. Rate
1. Local Newspaper	5	.5%	10%	70%	10%
2. Professional Newsletter	34	45.3%	75%	85%	12%
3. Walk-ins	2	.3%	13%	65%	8%
4. On-Campus Recruiting	18	36%	60%	90%	15%
5. Community Groups	7	15.5%	35%	70%	9%
6. Intern Programs	9	90%	90%	95%	17%
7. Social Media	4	1.6%	11%	70%	10%
8. Referrals/ Friends/ Relatives	12	12%	40%	80%	12%

the scoring process. If tests are used, describe their general purpose, content and length and provide a general description of the type of tests involved including IQ, work sampling, assessment centers, aptitude, achievement, personality tests such as Myers-Briggs or the DISC, and ethics tests. Finally indicate whether there will be background checks (criminal and/or credit and financial history) and references required.

Applicants and the organization alike should practice transparency and humility in all interactions. From the applicant perspective, seek out positions compatible with your endowed passion, gifts, and natural abilities. This entails conducting research and asking questions on organizational mission, vision, values, job requirements, work conditions, advancement opportunities, and job security. Transparency and honesty at the applicant stage reduces future employee turnover, internal employee job stress, and externalized dysfunctional stress adversely affecting co-workers.

The appropriate matching of applicant abilities and interests with job requirements releases the creative energies enhancing performance and serving as a source of support, encouragement, and expertise for other employees. In essence, a higher level of servanthood and stewardship effectiveness! Placing applicants in positions compatible with their gifts and abilities generates a great synergy.

As per the applicant perspective, the applicant should provide productive, honest, and constructive feedback on the organization's recruitment and selection process. It is an ethical practice as well for a job candidate to reject an interview or other screening steps if they possess no intention of pursuing further employment.

A key element in the selection process is the balance between gifts, abilities, and character. Much of the current literature emphasizes fitting jobs to employee abilities and interests to reflect applicant strengths and passion. The theory is that employees will prosper and be exponentially more effective if placed in the areas that match their abilities and interests (Digeorgio, 2004). As such, this entails a much more flexible and organic selection process given the more flexible job design and organizational structure. However, a focus on gifts, skills, and abilities is incomplete.

From the applicant perspective, today's labor market is the most competitive in decades. Recent data from the US Bureau of Labor Statistics indicates that there are 2.7 applicants per job opening in November of 2013 compared to only 1.5 per vacancy in 2007 (Bureau of Labor Statistics, 2014). These odds are daunting in themselves, but they understate the level of competition for the desirable living wage jobs. A *New York Times* article on the teaching job market at the height of the 2010 recession detailed numerous disheartening scenarios with outrageous and depressing applicant-to-position-opening ratios of 3,620 positions for 8 openings, a ratio of 450 to 1 (Hu, 2010). Given this reality, what is the logical and appropriate response to the applicant facing such numbers? One of the key survival strategies is to recognize that the battle is lost or won in our mind and how we respond to the stressful situation. The first survival strategy is to commit to an attitude of hope. Without hope, we lose the ability to resist the negative voices in the internal dialogue of the mind. The fruit is an understandable discouragement given the logical conclusion that the job market mountain is steep, dangerous, and impassable. Hope is the foundational response that keeps those in other dire circumstances moving forward. The vast majority of job seekers will find a position within time, if one refuses to weary in their efforts.

A second important principle is to develop a realistic definition of success during the job search. If applicants expect a job offer after the first few interviews, we lay the foundation for disappointment which will gradually metastasizes into skepticism, cynicism, bitterness, anger, and despair with repeated rejections. A baseball analogy is helpful here. An excellent hitter is successful only 3 of 10 times. In the job market, the success ratio is frequently much less. Hence, we need to develop a realistic definition of success that includes personal satisfaction for the important life and character lessons learned during the job search process. For example, we need to celebrate and reward ourselves for our good faith efforts and learning to persist as we "pound the literal or cyberspace pavement."

Third, it is critical to reject equating personal worth, value, and identity with the success of the job search. Believing that what we earn and produce defines our significance, dignity, and purpose is the ultimate form of "identify theft." It is very tempting to equate each rejected resume and unsuccessful interview as a commentary and a repudiation of who we are as a person. This frame of mind will allow arbitrary employer decisions to control and manipulate your emotions. The proper response is to recognize that we possess inherent and eternal dignity, meaning, and worth irrespective of our employment condition.

The Role of Employee Character in the Selection Process

The "house" of excellence in skill and ability must rest upon a foundation of moral character. SLHRM organizations should be assessing servant leader character behaviorally. Irrespective of the level of employee ability, weakness of character erodes the foundation and when the wind and rain comes, the house falls. In regards to character, we reverse the formula and should focus more effort on identifying and remedying our character weaknesses that we all possess. We must approach character issues assiduously for several reasons. The first is that our character strengths can gradually become weaknesses with time and the influence of factors such as pride. The second is that appearances are deceiving, both for others and in regards to self-understanding as impure motives are frequently the catalyst for righteous actions and conflict.

How should the selection process incorporate the assessment of character issues? One key component of character is that our motives for seeking a position reinforce motives to serve the broader public and community interests and are of course moral and ethical. Servant leaders should institute formal selection practices that shed light on applicant motives. Second, we should seek discernment as we interact with job candidates to reveal clues regarding their underlying motivations. Our intuition and spiritual discernment is the foundation for further job candidate probing. We must be judicious and wise in using explicit servant leader character assessment as a criterion for evaluating candidates. The key is to define clearly character in job-related and behavioral terms. For example, forgiveness is foundational character attribute essential for promoting creativity and innovation in the workplace. If leaders severely punish employees for errors, this creates a climate of fear conditioning employees to think and behave in a self-protective fashion thereby minimizing the risk taking essential for ingenuity and resourcefulness. For example, asking candidates a situational question on how they would manage an employee who placed great efforts into a new project, but failed to meet client expectations, produces good insight on their character in this area. Other means to assess character include standardized tests related to character and ethics (Dalton & Metzger, 1993; Behling, 1998; Gross-Schaefer et al., 2000).

What are the major servant leader character attributes and their relationship to key job attitudes and outcomes? The table 8.2 presents a summary.

The six character attributes above are foundational elements, but are not exhaustive of the full range of character traits. Unless we hire men and women of character, we will sabotage our efforts for servanthood and stewardship. As a SLHRM professional or manager, take the time to reflect on the success of the selection process. Hence, without introspection, we cannot discern the important character attributes of the candidates.

Table 8.2 Selected servant leader character attributes and the work-related attitudinal, behavioral, and performance outcomes

Servant Leader Character Attribute	Selection Measures
Love: Promoting the best interests of others	Situational interview questions that assess the candidates understanding of the importance and nature of love. For example, have the candidate respond to a scenario of how to resolve conflict with difficult employees in a moral fashion.
Humility: Recognizing our strengths, weaknesses, and limitations	Provide situational interview questions on how the employee honors and recognizes employees for their excellent work. Secondly, have them provide an example of when they failed in an endeavor and what they learned from the process.
Forgiveness: Forgiving others and ourselves for mistakes, failures, and offenses	Use situational interview question to uncover how applicants view failure in themselves and others and provide a specific employee failure scenario and ask for their response on how the situation should be managed.
Transparency: A commitment to open and honest communication of strengths and weaknesses	Provide situational interview questions that ask the candidate how they learn from mistakes and failure and how they help others learn from their mistakes and failures of themselves and others.
Hope and perseverance: The ability to sustain a course of action irrespective of the obstacles	Ask the candidate to provide specific examples of how they overcame adversity in challenging work situations and how they encourage others during the times of trial.
Compassion: A commitment to understand the emotions, needs and problems of others	Ask the candidate their approach to performance management and how they maintain long-term productivity. In addition, ask a situational interview question on their strategies for understanding the needs and problems of others.

Southwest Airlines is a "best-practice" example of blending value, character, and competency elements into the selection process. McGee-Cooper and Trammell (2010) summarized the key elements of their success, identifying the following factors:

1. Select based upon favorable attitudes toward teamwork and a commitment to service over self-interests.
2. Emphasize the needs of employees first to demonstrate the authenticity of employee commitment.

3. Promote from within.
4. Employ ongoing methods and options for employee communication and input.
5. Ongoing celebrations of achievements and expression of employee appreciation.
6. Cultivate and embrace diversity.
7. Promote volunteerism.

The integration of character into the process increases the challenge, but SLHRM integrity entails the equal weighting of character and competency.

Employment Discrimination Avoidance

One of the key moral areas related to the staffing process is ending employment discrimination. Clearly, there is a clear and compelling ethical and moral justification for eliminating biased treatment unrelated to job qualifications or character. A "letter and spirit" understanding of servant leadership clearly rejects discrimination as a serious sin of pride. All humans are created equal and discrimination wounds and scars both parties as it strips each of human dignity imprisoning in the guise of false identities. It blinds the "superior" group or race with delusions of superiority while paradoxically haunting their conscious with insecurity and fear regarding the truth of equality, the anxiety about losing their favored status, and fears of eventual rebellion, retribution, and revenge. The "inferior" group is scarred by the identity that they are inherently flawed, tempting them to respond with bitterness, despair, anger, discouragement and fear. This produces individual and collective suffering at the physical, psychological, and spiritual levels. From a utilitarian standpoint, discrimination is a form of social tax producing high costs through the underutilization of human potential and the deforming of the human spirit that produces dysfunctions including, crime, welfare dependency, and negative mental and physical health care outcomes, among others. In addition to these direct costs, we incur huge opportunity costs given the lower tax revenue and societal productivity. Embracing diversity is a servant leader value, and irrespective of the moral justification, the utilitarian rationale alone requires a vigorous endorsement. The reality is that the demographics of the labor market are changing with a much higher percentage of women and minorities (Bureau of Labor

Statistics, 2013). From a SLHRM standpoint, a diverse labor pool is not only ethical and moral, it makes perfect business sense through more efficient and effective service delivery and higher quality decision making.

SLHRM organizations embrace ethical and moral selection practices. A key element of ethical and moral selection relate to Equal Employment Opportunity considerations. Equal employment case law has codified the Equal Employment Opportunity Commission's (EEOC) 1978 Uniform Guidelines on Employee Selection. The EEOC deems if the overall impact of the global selection process produces a selection rate of 80 percent or less than the dominant group, the organization must review its component selection methods to identify areas in which protected groups are disadvantaged. Hence, any selection instrument that influences the employment status of an external or internal applicant becomes a "test." Interviews, performance application forms, résumé screening, and educational requirements are all considered "tests" under the law and are subject to findings of adverse impact using the 80 percent rule. Intent is irrelevant in adverse impact cases. The prevailing legal criterion is the presence of disparate impact on protected groups. This legal standard was adapted given the inability of individual level equal employment case law to address the aggregate impact of societal (and more impersonal) forms of discrimination.

Another area for confusion relating to Title VII of the Civil Rights Act and subsequent case law and legislation permits employers to set qualifications for a position based upon any criteria or criterion as long as it does not violate employment law or other public policy statutes. So, hypothetically (to use an outrageous example), a restaurant owner could require an undergraduate degree for a dishwasher position. There is no regulation against silly, foolish, unwise, or poor HR policy or practice. Equal employment opportunity law only enters the equation when the educational requirement manifests an adverse impact on protected groups (race, gender, etc.). A smaller percentage of African Americans possess an undergraduate degree than do Caucasians. Hence, it is likely that African Americans would be screened out by the education requirement at a higher rate, thereby triggering a finding of adverse impact using the 4/5 (80%) rule. For example, if 20 percent of whites are hired, the 4/5 rule states that a hiring percentage of less than 16 percent for African Americans triggers a presumption of adverse impact. Once adverse impact is demonstrated, the employer must then prove two points: (1) that there is no other screening device that can be substituted for the educational requirement that does not discriminate, and (2) that the educational requirement is a valid (accurate) predictor of success on the job. Let us illustrate this point with a specific example. How would the EEOC view a restaurant that set a college degree requirement for their dishwashers given the owner's desire to have a highly educated workforce? However, education is not a necessary skill set and would not be a valid predictor of success as a dishwasher given the largely motor and manual skill set required. Interestingly, the employer would be vulnerable to an EEO lawsuit only if education generated an adverse impact on protected groups. If there was no difference in hiring rates between African Americans and whites when using this educational requirement, there are no actionable legal grounds to challenge this criterion even though it is an example of an ineffective and inefficient HR practice.

Conclusion

As we conclude this chapter and reflect upon the key learning points, it is important to recognize that the staffing process tests the character and motivation of SLHRM organizations. It is critical that the organization promotes the dignity of all applicants through Golden Rule HR processes. The foundational goal is to attract and retain the employees that are best suited to the organizational mission and promote an organizational culture of performance excellence and high moral character.

SLHRM Leadership Personal Character Reflection: Courage and Overcoming Fear, Facing the Giants

Where are the giants in your life that impede the expansion of your physical, spiritual, and emotional territory? I was greatly blessed by the film "Facing the Giants" about a losing football coach who used biblical principles to bring revival in himself, thereby providing the spark for a transformation that ignited his family, the football program, the school, and an entire community. One of the "fear-busting" principles he employed was to redefine what "victory" entails. In order to attack the giants, the first step is to identify the enemy. Their real adversary was not an absence of talent, as they possessed the gifts and abilities to achieve their life purpose. Nor was it a low level of motivation as every player wanted desperately to win. The root cause was their belief that losing made them "losers" thereby agreeing with the success-oriented worldview that accomplishments (the wins and losses of life) are the foundation of our identity.

This false belief created giants of fear that grew more powerful with each loss generating enslaving self-fulfilling prophecies of discouragement yoking the players and coaches with a slow growing cancer of negative self-image. The coach discovered the servant leader principle that we achieve victory not through a winning record, but the slow cultivation of moral character as we endure and grow through trials and tribulations. He redefined the definition of team success by adopting the principle that we are stewards of our God-given gifts and abilities and that we honor God by giving our best efforts in pursuit of team goals regardless of the circumstances and the ultimate outcomes. Hence, this is a revolutionary concept that we are not responsible for the outcome, only our best efforts. "Winning" is realizing the collective potential of the team as each member dedicates himself to developing their talents to support the communal efforts of the squad.

Winning occurs when we exert every ounce of our energy in a moral fashion, playing by the rules of the game. As the coach stated, when we win we give thanks to God, and when we lose we still praise him. Atheists and agnostics ridicule the notion of prayer before football games, but they miss the essential principle that God uses all circumstances to shape our character. Winning challenges us as we are tempted to worship our "greatness," while losing tempts us to yield to despair, shame, condemnation, and hopelessness denying the power of the experience to teach us great character lessons. Hence, both winning and losing in a football game promote character growth to realize the unique purpose for each individual player and coach. Servant leaders are able to use both winning and losing to reveal the hidden motives of the human heart and promote self-knowledge, learning, and discovery. The coach discovered that great power occurs when we truly embrace a faith in the power of learning during adversity. Let us all agree to "face the giants" in our lives recognizing that victory occurs by facing our fears and learning from the circumstances as they unfold.

SLHRM Leadership Personal Character Reflection: Courage and Overcoming Fear, Enjoy the Ride!

There are foundational moments in life in which we are asked to complete a task that is clearly beyond our strength, natural gifts, and comfort zone. When that time comes, whom will you serve? Will I act in faith and move forward or will I run as fast as I can in the opposite direction? Irrespective of our decision, we will experience a range of emotions, from excitement, joy, and anticipation, to fear, anxiety, and dread. The key element is how we respond. The analogy that resonates is that of a roller-coaster. Life is a mandatory roller-coaster ride and we can either enjoy the ride, or go "kicking and screaming." We choose how we respond to the situation, either with faith and confidence, with what psychologists term eustress (positive emotions), or with stress (negative or damaging emotions). When the university president graciously offered me the Interim Dean position, it was like a giant scary roller-coaster, with sheer mountain steep climbs and deep canyon chasm dips. It had those warning signs that all with heart and back conditions should get out of line now! The emotions are boiling, and in the midst of the internal dialogue a loud voice is screaming, "you are going to die," or at least fail and throw up!

However, the truth is that those who love roller-coasters and those that fear them are experiencing the same physiological responses, but with radically different emotional interpretations. To the person who loves roller-coasters, it is an adventure and an ecstasy producing a wonderful adrenaline rush. To those who would choose to fear, it is a form of torment and torture. We make the choice. Servant leaders will complete the good work in one form or another. Stress or eustress, death or life. We make these little choices every day. Our fear steals the joy of eustress, or turn eustress into stress. It is another act of deception, designed to steal, kill, and destroy our destiny. We must struggle with the "fear of fear" syndrome which deceives us into labeling and transforming natural eustress childlike wonder and excitement into stress by our fear of failure. Conversely, when we embrace a healthy understanding that we learn from our mistakes, we can change our stress into eustress. When faith and fear are equal, you are still in faith when you stand your ground and move forward. Our emotions deceive us. You will complete the roller-coaster ride and eventually learn to enjoy it! In addition, even if you do run away, exercise self-patience, forgive yourself, and get back into the game!

This principle was illustrated by my own roller-coaster rides with the fear of public speaking (a fear worse than death for many). About fifteen years ago, I had a major presentation to the Provost with a colleague. It was an important meeting, but my anxiety over the speaking situation increased significantly given that I had a petty rivalry with my colleague that increased my level of performance anxiety. I prepared well, but for some reason in the middle of my presentation, I looked into the eyes of the Provost and lost my place. I could not regain my composure. What stress! My worst fear as a public speaker came true, the deer in the headlight syndrome! What shame and suffering! The Provost had the other colleague do the follow-up presentation the next day to the Board. I felt humiliated with permanent damage, or so I thought. However, life as I knew it did not end!

I gradually recovered with time and reflecting on my religious foundation of forgiveness. The reality was that even though I "vomited on the roller-coaster," life went on and I learned valuable lessons. My colleague was supportive, and we reconciled. I repented for my jealousy. My boss still had confidence in me, my promotion and tenure went through, and students still took my classes. I learned a great degree of humility from this situation. The memory of this event occasionally enters my consciousness, but I have learned to respond with confidence and transform my stress into eustress. Below are seven principles in your battle against stress:

1. *Face your fears with courage.* Courage is not the absence of fear, but persisting in its presence. Moving forward in spite of how we feel is a necessary faith requirement, which, in turn, facilities the cultivation of eustress emotions. When we face our fears and persist in their presence, it gradually reduces the emotional intensity as our confidence grows.
2. *Embrace trust and humility and reject pride and perfectionism.* Even though from an authority standpoint we are responsible for the outcome as a servant leader, we must not confuse assuming authority with internalizing and allowing failure to erode our self-worth and personal identity. Hence, we learn that failure is not the "end of the world" and we learn to fail with grace. Our role is to obey by getting back on the roller-coaster!
3. *Reject emotional reasoning or decision making by feelings. You may feel like a "loser," but your true identity is not based upon performance, but in the inherent dignity of being a member of the human race with a unique purpose and calling.* In personal conflict situations with others, the solution is to always respond in love, and reject personalizing the situation. It is important to recognize that our battle is not with the person, but the emotions and interests that are influencing and controlling the person. Those forces want to dominate you as well using your emotions as the means to

increase the level of pain and suffering. Learn to love your enemies and serve just and unjust masters.

4. *Our moral job description is the most important element.* As servant leaders, we need to serve with love until we are released to a new assignment. In other words, do not get out of line of the roller-coaster! Resist the temptation to flee challenging situations. Stand still, and walk through your fears!

5. *Practice Grace.* When others or institutions fail us, make the choice to reject unforgiveness and bitterness. We are all "works in progress" that need forgiveness and grace like water for parched fields. Let others get on their roller-coaster again!

6. *Reject complacency.* In your battles, you are not alone. Your fears will try and steal the victory and say that you lack the strength to reboard the roller-coaster. That is a lie! With the power of humility and patience, you will pass the test!

One other way of viewing this situation is to borrow the Nike slogan, and "Just Do It." When we experience fear while moving forward, we are not "faking it." Courage by definition is stepping forward in the presence of fear. By rejecting the lie of our emotions and physiology, we are practicing a high form of courage! We are honoring servant leader courage by believing by faith for a good outcome. It is not what we feel, but what we do and obey that controls our destiny. Hence, by moving forward, we are learning to undo the lies of the cycle of fear no matter how slowly we make progress. When you agree in your mind to try (even before you do), in spite of all the obstacles and fears, you are "doing it." When you take that first step, however clumsy or with shaking knees, you are "doing it." If you fall, you are "doing it." When you fall and get up, you are "doing it." When you move forward and make mistakes, you are "doing it." If you get discouraged and retreat, but plan to try again, you are "doing it." Even when we fail and we give up, but have a hope of reengaging, we are "doing it."

In breaking free from the fear strongholds, intent is the key. If it is *not* my intent to flee, and I do it anyway, it is the passion within that controls me. It does not void our responsibility, but it provides the foundation for self-forgiveness, repentance, and hope. The key is to achieve agreement between your mind and heart to defeat fear. If in our heart we would rather stay in slavery, then we are agreeing with our fears in a covenant of disobedience and giving birth to a more serious form of bondage. If we desire freedom, but are unable to break free, the weakness of the flesh (passion) is less severe than that of the will and heart. The great example of this in Milton's epic poem *Paradise Lost* in which Satan defiantly boasts that it is better to rule in hell than serve in heaven. I hope and pray that you will win the battle against stress in your life and experience peace.

Chapter 9

Employee Training and Development Principles

SLHRM entails making disciples. Hence, a foundational element of leadership DNA is developing subordinates, thereby promoting the fulfillment of their purpose and calling. Several key character elements are at the center of this approach. The first is humility in which we step back and equip our subordinates for a greater degree of success than our own, thereby promoting the needs of the mission and others first. Hence, we assume an attitude in which we esteem others more greatly than ourselves, and bear each other's burdens in love. In essence, the leader is learning how to love employees from an altruistic perspective. This entails providing discipline and corrective feedback in a fashion that provides hope and encouragement. Hence, the leader needs to communicate clearly his or her appreciation and that they are pleased, but not satisfied, with the employee's performance given their great potential. SLHRM organizations develop leaders that make themselves dispensable, while empowering others. They help others unbury talents and use them appropriately.

The Cultivation of Employee Job Performance and Character Strengths

One of the key objectives of a training and development program is cultivating areas of strength. The 1981 movie *Chariots of Fire* illustrates this very well. When we are in our ability, gift, and calling "zone," time stands still and work becomes a form of worship, joy, and play. When we are working in our gift zone, it becomes a transcendent spiritual experience. When we are in a position utilizing our gifts, the wind is at our back! This reinforces the SLHRM principle that it is much easier to increase our performance in an area of strength from good to excellent than raise an area of weakness from a "D" to a "C" (Digeorgio, 2004).

One of the great obstacles to SLHRM character growth in both our personal lives and the job development domain is a pride-based personal rights focus. Our political, social, and economic system glorifies individual rights, thereby inculcating the self-obsessive, atomistic orientation that contributes to elevating the gratification and protection of the ego as the central pursuit of human development (à la Maslow's self-actualization). Hence, SLHRM organizations strive to create a workplace environment in which employees transcend narcissism and cultivate a high level of spiritual and emotional intelligence to promote employee development and mission accomplishment. One of the great challenges is instilling a servant leader and follower character to serve all with equal levels of excellence. Yes, it helps to have a sense of humor as we are tested and our rough edges smoothed by the difficult "sandpaper" people that make this objective challenging. It is easy to help train those who are pleasant and like us, but unconditional love is cultivated by choosing to act graciously toward those who mistreat, dislike, or attack us, especially when such treatment of us is unjustified. As servant leaders, we must embrace turning the other cheek. Enduring unjust criticism does not always lead to a favorable outcome, but these types of experiences greatly enhance our humility, patience, and overall character.

At one time or another, we will question our choice of career. We may believe that a higher power providentially guided us to our current position, but question whether we are to remain. This is a common pattern after the initial euphoria and/or the challenge associated with the position erodes. This situation is similar to the tests we face as new servant leaders in which we burn with a great emotional energy but endure a gradual dissipation of the emotions. We must then rise to the challenge of choosing to love others in a deeper and more mature way. The joy of career development is discovering what we are and what we are not! One of the worst positions in life is to assume the role of an actor filling an unwanted role.

SLHRM Career Development Principles

Effective career development and training program development entail the possession of a level of humility and transparency deriving from a clear confidence that our identity and inherent worth as human beings comes not from our performance, gifts, or abilities, but the quality of our character. This enables us to place our performance and character strengths in perspective recognizing that excellence is our present and future goal, while perfection is an aspirational goal never fully completed in this life. Hence, we grow through transparent reflection, honestly assessing our strengths and weaknesses, and assuming full responsibility for our moral and character flaws and failures. I have learned this truth on my own life walk. Transparency enables us to demonstrate humility in a tangible fashion. How can we be humble when we fail to be ourselves, with weaknesses and flaws? The practice of transparency is very difficult given our fleshly impulse to hide our faults and to project to others our complete control of our lives and the situation. The absence of transparency increases guilt and fear leading to shame when reality does not match the fiction. Transparency is the action side of humility and produces great fruits. We soon learn that operating under the mantle of grace and forgiveness stimulates the healthy pursuit of excellence while minimizing perfectionism. These are difficult, but essential, lessons to learn. Below is a list of key point career servant leader development principles.

1. *Servant leader development requires intense effort and sacrifice, and we must first ensure the integrity, spiritual legitimacy, and viability of the mission in order for our request of employee sacrifice to be justified.* Does the ROI of the organization justify the opportunity costs at the spiritual and temporal levels? In other words, there must be an assessment as to whether the organization promotes viable interests (the substance test). In other words, is the organization's ethos (mission, vision, values, the motives, means, and ends) promoting the greater good? Many organizations are compatible with servant leader objectives, but is this organization the correct match for the employee? It is akin to separating the best from the good. This requires ongoing reflection.

2. *Count the cost!* Once the viability of the organization meets scrutiny, the next question relates to whether or not the leader perceives a symmetry between his or her gifts, abilities and calling and the current and future position requirements. Are the candidates willing to invest all their energies in developing their skills at this crucial stage? Is the candidate willing to devote great time, energy (sweat and tears) into their servant leadership development? Developing into a servant leader is like becoming a parent, it is a twenty-four-hour job! Are you willing to pay the price?

3. *Can you make disciples?* Even though intense effort is required at the beginning, we labor in vain unless the mission, vision, and values are "contagious." We will eventually "burn out" and weary in our well doing if we fail to reproduce ourselves. Thus, does our service in this organization pass the passion test? Does working in this organization generate excitement and strong emotions to create successors?

4. *Can you humble yourself and collaborate?* The leader's true beliefs emerge in his or her approach to collaboration. If agape love is the foundation, the servant leader cares little to none from their personal perspective who receives the credit, only that the mission is completed. When there is conflict and competition within and between work units, only a genuine commitment to collaboration can overcome the obstacles. When there is resistance and conflict, this is an indicator of potential character deficiencies (the presence of pride and self-interest) in addition to conflicts of legitimate collective interests and needs. The individual capacity question is important. Given the breadth and depth of the knowledge, skills and competencies required to develop a servant leader, we must approach the task with "fear and trembling" recognizing that we will need spiritual strength and the favor and the support of wise and skilled mentors and role models for the discipleship development process.

5. *Leadership and management development must be systematic entailing mentorship and sponsorship.* Leadership growth requires sustained coaching and feedback. As an organization grows, the nature of the leadership roles also changes. The job requirements of the founder are very different from the leadership of an established organization. As a founder, the size and scope of the organization allows for personal involvement in all aspects of organizational development. As the organization grows in size, the chief executive must empower and delegate management responsibilities while increasing emphasis on long-term strategic growth. It is important to cultivate both mentors and sponsors to provide the requisite levels of support and success. A mentor provides the personalized professional and character development advice, while a sponsor is an individual of higher status with power and influence who can become a champion for the employee. These factors are especially important for women managers to break through the glass ceiling (Tolar, 2012; Ibarra, Carter, & Silva, 2010).

6. *Succession planning is a key element of leadership development, but most organizations lack the expertise, time, and resources to*

implement the required practices effectively. Organizations are lost in the wilderness of "fire-engine" management and the tyranny of the urgent to the neglect of what Covey, Merrill, and Merrill (1994) and their time management system indicate are the critical type 2 long-term planning issues for future success. Without investing sufficient resources in the "high upfront cost but great downstream benefit" management techniques such as strategic planning and succession planning, discipleship making occurs erratically.

7. *The principle of promoting employees to management and leadership positions because of their technical competence and success is very common error.* The organizational landscape is strewn with leaders and managers promoted without either the natural aptitude or the appropriate training to the detriment of their own success and wellbeing. Research clearly demonstrates that the leader's emotional intelligence skills, his or her interpersonal, communication and stress management skills, explain a great deal of the variance in leadership success (Goleman, 1998). Organizations do leaders and those they serve a great disservice by not carefully selecting, developing and supporting leaders.

Leadership development is not for the faint of heart and spirit! In the following section, we address the great challenge of character development.

Character Development Principles

The key is to approach character development from both a deontological (consistency of principles) and a teleological (a greater good, utilitarian) perspective. The foundation for character growth is a relentless "testing" of the integrity of motives, means, and ends. This ongoing analysis will serve as the foundation for the necessary legal, ethical, and moral test. All three levels must meet the standards. From a servant leadership standpoint, it all begins with a foundation of humility, mission clarity, and importance, serving others first and empowering employees. A behavior from a SLHRM value perspective is immoral if motivated by self-aggrandizement and glorification including satisfying the ego needs for recognition, power, and achievement, enhancing one's image, or obtaining favorable treatment to promote personal versus mission based outcomes. In addition, they are all unethical if they impede the mission in some fashion or attenuate trust. The absence of servant leadership traits (love, courage, humility, empathy, compassion, forgiveness, and altruism, among others) reduces the capacity to commit to the mission, understand the true needs of others, and to grasp the root causes of problems and their solutions. Poor leadership spanning the wide spectrum from micromanagement to laissez-faire abdication impedes organizational effectiveness and increases the presence of dysfunctional behaviors such as higher levels of dysfunctional competition, conflict, and personal attacks through demonizing opponents along with reduced organizational cohesiveness and problem solving capacity given the absence of commitment and interest in the mission. The higher levels of conflict inhibit recruiting and retaining high quality employees.

In an ideal world of management and leadership selection, development and evaluation, the "toxic manager" would be identified and either rehabilitated or removed. Unfortunately, our HR management practices are imperfect, and poorly selected, trained, and evaluated managers are plentiful. Part of "Business Savvy 101" is learning how to manage a dysfunctional boss. As servant leaders, we have the obligation to love the "extra grace required" people placed in our lives. Another attribute of poor management is the generation of "in" and "out" groups as reflected in leader-member exchange theory (Northouse, 2013). Career progress (or lack thereof) is influenced by the quality of experience during the first year. It is important to take external action when managerial incompetence threatens employee career progress. Classification as a "poor" employee makes it is very difficult to overcome the negative stereotypes even with improving employee performance. In essence, employees retain an unseen weight that impedes their career progress (Burns & Otte, 1999; Abu Elanain, 2014). Placing the employee in the out-group generally entails the employment of a less empowering leadership approach (Northouse, 2013). Hence, it is critical from an SLHRM organizational standpoint to identify the presence of in-groups and out-groups and reduce their influence by better management training in conjunction with such quality control measures as subordinate evaluations linked to the supervisor's appraisal. It is important that employees secure wise counsel when confronted with this situation in order to determine how to respond from endurance, voice, to exit.

SLHRM Training and Development Principles

One of the key metrics related to engagement and servant followership is the level of peer support. In many jobs and occupations, the majority of learning occurs through on-the-job training (OJT). Depending on the job, up to 90 percent of all training occurs on an informal basis (Snell & Bohlander, 2013). Best practice organizations recognize that a major component of servant followership is employees taking the time to help others. SLHRM organizations recognize and reward good citizenship. One of the most serious costs from disengaged, discouraged, overwhelmed, and/or cynical employees is the loss of the "Good Samaritan" employee who generously helps others as compassion fatigue sets in and the workplace becomes more Darwinian in nature.

Below are reflections on best practice training and development programs.

1. *Employee development is a responsibility for every organizational member.* In order to serve with excellence and meet our potential, we must embrace a lifelong commitment to learning. These elements include:

   a. *Embracing a humble and teachable spirit.* This entails identifying our strengths, weaknesses and recognizing our limits. We must actively seek feedback and guidance from others. It requires great strength and humility to seek out negative performance and character feedback. It entails even greater levels of humility to receive and process the information in a nondefensive manner.

   b. *Helping others (peers, supervisor, and clients) on the job is a critical duty as research demonstrates that much organizational training/learning occurs through informal on-the-job-training.* Servant leaders and followers are unconditionally committed to supporting and encouraging friend or foe, even if it personally disadvantages or inconveniences. Servant leaders need to embrace the ministry of interruptions. The biblical accounts of the leadership of Jesus indicate that he was never too busy to help those in need. We must provide our assistance and performance feedback in an honest, considerate, loving and supportive spirit. This entails providing specific, behavioral, timely, and nonjudgmental feedback. The cumulative fruit of this Golden Rule commitment is a workplace of joy minimizing employee stress and emphasizing excellence is a major leadership job requirement.

2. *Drive fear out of the workplace.* Emphasize that servant leadership development and learning *requires* making mistakes. Ruthlessly

eliminate perfectionism and replace it with a devotion to the healthy pursuit of excellence that recognizes the inevitability of failure, personal trial, struggle, and blunders and their value in learning and character growth.

3. *Training and development programs should be designed and administered according to adult learning theory principles:*

   a. Provide numerous opportunities to apply directly key learning objectives in a non-judgmental and non-threatening manner.
   b. Provide timely and specific performance feedback to improve performance
   c. Develop a curriculum that is compatible with the learning style preferences of the audience. This entails a learning style diagnostic assessment to identify the specific types of learners including visual, aural, reading/writing, and kinesthetic (Zapalska & Brozik, 2006). With the identification of learning styles, it is important to develop a curriculum that actively engages student learning according to Bloom's Taxonomy, in which the leader creates, evaluates, analyzes, applies, understands, and remembers (Halawi, Pires, & McCarthy, 2009).
   d. Training and development programs are designed to reinforce key organizational values and should not only increase technical proficiency, but link the subject of learning to the larger mission, vision, and values.

4. *Management and HR practices should reinforce the application and integration of learning objectives:*

   a. Managers and employees should be jointly responsible for training implementation and integration, with accountability reflected in the performance appraisal process.

5. *Organizations should provide adequate financial and logistical support for training:*

   a. The American Society for Training & Development reported in 2012 that the average organization spent 3.1 percent of the payroll budget on training (ASTD, 2012). Regrettably, many organizations invest less than the average amount which is objectively low.
   b. Provide employees with an individual development plan (IDP) that provides a comprehensive diagnostic of present and future

performance strengths and weaknesses (gaps) along with a short- and long-term action plan of training objectives.

  c. Provide employees with an individual learning account (ILA), a yearly sum of funds that the employee can invest in training and development activities.

6. *Organizations must support their employees training and educational efforts by providing release time from regular job duties to reduce employee stress levels.* Without some release time, the everyday pressure reduces the time and energy for application, reflection, and learning.

7. *Personal Career Development Strategies:*

  a. Engage in systematic personal self-assessment (know thyself) by inventorying:

    i. Personal character and performance strengths and weaknesses
    ii. Passions, areas of gifting, likes and dislikes
    iii. Personality attributes (the Big Five of openness, conscientiousness, extraversion, agreeableness, and neuroticism) and disposition through diagnostic assessments such as the Myers-Briggs (MBTI) (Bahreinian, Ahi, & Soltani, 2012).
    iv. Predisposition toward dependence on authority figures

  b. Establish mentors and sponsors, ideally inside or outside the organization, network with other managers, and volunteer for projects to demonstrate job skills

  c. Enhance employee efficacy (confidence) perceptions regarding the objective of the training (Luthans & Peterson, 2002). Employee efficacy is a major factor in employee motivation and persistence in learning given the psychological confidence that we can cope with the demands of the new situation. It is important that employees believe that management supports them and can be trusted.

8. *Organizations should monitor supervisory behavior to combat what is termed in-groups and out-groups.*

  a. Managers assign employees into long-term "in-group" and "out-group" categories based upon job performance early in the employee's career. In many instances these category assignments are made on incomplete, unrepresentative or misleading information

b. The classification into the out-group changes the management mode used. Out-group employees are more likely to be micromanaged using traditional hierarchical authority and receive less empowerment and developmental opportunities along with fewer opportunities to develop and display talents (Northouse, 2013). In-group employees receive higher levels of encouragement and empowerment. Subordinate career advancement is adversely influenced when your boss is in the "out-group" by reducing supervisor "upward influence." This situation results in lower levels of resource support (financial, personnel, and information) and power (Kanter, 1979). The manager's relationship problems with other organizational stakeholders frequently "spills over" to employees.

Another best-practice recommendation for leadership development is to implement an on-line knowledge utilization and sharing system (Widén-Wulff & Suomi, 2007). The key is to record and communicate internal institutional knowledge and external best-practice programs and research. These systems are searchable by subject area and enhance the effectiveness of training and development as well as general management problem solving. It is essential to preserve institutional memory and knowledge from departing members while promoting innovation. They can also contribute to the desired balance between in-house and external training. Internal training capacity is essential for long-term success, and external training provides the supplemental and synergistic innovation and creativity needed to support major changes.

Most organizations have moved to some form of e-learning or virtual learning. These systems can be highly effective and cost efficient. They provide an "on-demand," as needed, asynchronous learning environment. Many of the programs are completely self-directed, provide immediate corrective feedback, and operate at a pace compatible with trainee motivation and ability levels. However, the e-learning domain possesses definite limits. One issue is that there are significant differences in computer literacy levels impeding the effectiveness of e-learning programs. In addition, there are individual learning style differences contributing to preferences for a "high-touch" traditional approach. Ideally, there needs to be an assessment of learning styles.

E-learning is even more important given the growth in virtual organizations and the flexible workplace (Green & Roberts, 2010). The virtual workplace entails a hybrid approach of webcasts plus residency type experiences. Training programs for the virtual workplace are extremely important given the need to enhance group cohesiveness. As per the elements of virtual workplace teaching, one foundational element is group conflict and processing skills. Given that virtual groups possess fewer opportunities for in-person socialization and bonding, it is critical to learn how to interact with team members that are largely unknown from a personal level. The foundational element is to provide occasions for bonding while inculcating the conflict management skills that enable groups to function cohesively. Another key area is performance management skills given the need to empower and hold others accountable. Virtual teams rely less on "face time" and more on empowerment and hence require self-directed work team training to address such issues as conflict management, setting performance goals, and motivational approaches.

Training Program Evaluation

A key best-practice recommendation is to engage in systematic evaluation of training and development program effectiveness, providing ongoing feedback on the success of the training program from the key stakeholder perspectives including employees, all levels of management (entry level, midlevel, and executives), and clients. It is important to document and communicate training success to instill confidence in the efficacy and relevancy of training. Without early success, discouraged employees and managers lose hope. In terms of a training program assessment framework, the Kirkpatrick's evaluation model is well developed and regarded, and provides a good foundation (Roberts, 2010; Tan & Newman, 2013). Let us take the example of supervisor performance appraisal training. The Fitzpatrick's five levels of analysis begin with assessing attitudes. Did the participants perceive value in the performance appraisal training? This is usually assessed by attitude and satisfaction surveys. The second level is learning. Was there a measurable change in best practice evaluation techniques as measured by traditional exams and role playing exercises? The third level relates to behavior. Did the training change behavior in the desired format? For example, did managers hold more frequent performance counseling meetings, and engage employees with higher levels of participation through increased use of self-evaluations? It is important to gather information from the perspective of the manager's subordinates to measure the effectiveness of training efforts. Hence, the organization conducts subordinate surveys of managerial behavior in the desired change areas such as more frequent informal performance feedback. The fourth level is changes in performance. Did employee productivity increase after the introduction of the performance appraisal training? The final level is ROI. Did the monetary and other resources invested in the training program produce an acceptable rate of return? This is the most difficult and complex assessment given the multiplicity of variables and the associated measurement difficulties.

Needs Assessment

The final foundational element of a comprehensive training and development program is a needs assessment. There are different levels of analysis, from the individual to the macro. At the macro level, it is important to link training needs with a SWOT (strength, weakness, opportunity, and threat) analysis to ascertain the interface between macro mission interests and strategic needs. One of the dangers with the training process is to fail to link training to long-term system issues such as changes in service delivery patterns that require higher levels of computer skills.

Conclusion

In summary, training and development is a key factor in a SLHRM organization's success. Training and development requires the embrace of a long-term perspective in which employees and leaders work synergistically for the common good. It is another "path less traveled." SLHRM organizations invest in employees to ensure their long-term growth and development not only as employees, but in all life domains.

SLHRM Leadership Personal Character Reflection: Overcoming Fear

One of the most destructive workplace emotions is dysfunctional fear. Natural fear is a valuable and necessary element to alert us to danger and respond appropriately to a threatening situation. Dysfunctional fear is a pernicious counterfeit and is the antithesis to faith. Dysfunctional fear causes us to exaggerate the risks and engage in distorted thinking patterns that predict negative to catastrophic outcomes through "magnification," "fortune telling" and pessimistic "what-if" thinking. The result is paralysis of will as dysfunctional fear controls our motives, thoughts, emotions, and workplace behavior. Dysfunctional fear afflicts individual employees, work groups, and organizations as a whole through the explicit or implicit values that govern workplace behavior.

A workplace dominated by fear exhibits a variety of symptoms depending on its origin. There is fear of failure, fear of success, fear of man, and a many variants in between. Fear manifests itself in a continuum of effort and motivation levels. For example, fear of failure at the one end manifests minimization of effort, apathy, disengagement, and lack of motivation for those who are fearful of even trying. On the other pole is perfectionism and workaholism in which performance is the foundation of self-identity and failure results in shame and condemnation based labels of negative self-esteem such as "loser" and "failure." Other behavioral manifestations of fear include compassion fatigue, absence of creativity and innovation, disengagement, and bullying behaviors, among others. I would like to share with you a basic principle that breaks the yoke and stronghold of fear at the individual level. If we are able to conquer the stronghold of fear in our own lives, we are equipped for organizational battle. First, there are several key principles that we must grasp:

- *Love is the complete antidote for the poison of dysfunctional fear. Love is a choice, a conscious decision to promote the best interest of others by placing their needs over our own.* Since love is a choice, it reflects another key principle, that in order to love, we must possess the freedom to chart our own life course. In order for us to grow and mature in love, we must exercise our free will faculties by making decisions on whose interests to pursue, our selfish needs or to promote the welfare of others. *It matters not what we physiologically or emotionally experience when we are in fearful situations as these are the temptations of fright.* Leaders of belief and faith trust and move forward in spite of what they feel or experience in the form of obstacles.
- *We defeat ourselves by the belief that we must be "fearless" from a physiological or feelings standpoint, a form of emotional perfectionism that cripples faith.* This is another lie and creates what psychologists label an "emotional reasoning" state in which we assume that reality matches how we feel. Emotions are deceptive. Our healing occurs when we gradually learn to trust the truth over the exaggerations of our fears.

SLHRM Leadership Personal Character Reflection: Fear and Bravery, Victory over Public Speaking Fear

One of the great obstacles to servant leader growth is the presence of fear to steal our confidence in our abilities and gifts. In essence, the fear causes us either to bury our talents or to apply them inappropriately. Public speaking is one of the most common and greatest fears. Speaking skills are essential to servant leadership, and performance anxiety/fear is a natural emotional state given our desire to impress others. I have had my own trials and tribulations with public speaking for many years. The goal of this section is not to provide specific tools for improving our public speaking skills, but guidance on how to view public speaking from a values-based perspective. A recent incident helped uncover the fallacious belief systems that are the foundation of public speaking fear. One of my colleagues casually noted that I have gained confidence in public speaking situations over the last two years in my role as Interim Dean. On the surface, this is a positive comment and development. However, in the realm of the mind, our insecurities will gravitate toward a negative interpretation.

My insecurities through the influence of pride, perfectionism, and the fear of man (judgment) attempted to darken my perception. What was the issue? My pride was hurt because the problem that I wanted hidden (being visibly nervous) was noticeable in the first place. What is at work here? The first is the legacy of shame produced by our weaknesses and the need to hide them from others. The mind still believes the lie that noticeable public speaking nervousness is a failure and shameful and that others will view me as weak, not worthy, foolish, and unreliable. When my colleague stated that I was more comfortable in speaking, this highlighted the fear that others noticed my speaking nervousness in the first place (the baseline fear) which the conscious condemns, producing shame. The temptation is to "run and hide" given that public speaking fear remains and complete deliverance is a work in progress. If we are not careful, the mind locks into a vicious cycle of obsessive self-conscious thoughts regarding our feelings, producing fear and anxiety and feeding the cycle of shame and torment.

However, I recognize the flaws in this line of reasoning. The key is to challenge and rebut these fallacious thought patterns. First, remember that our public speaking performance is not the basis for our identity or worth. Perfectionism equates identity with success and therefore promotes an unrealistic goal of 100 percent victory in our eyes and that of others. It also reflects a lack of gratitude for the skills that we possess and that public speaking anxiety is beneficial as it increases our performance and reduces the complacency that over-confidence produces. Hidden pride is one of the pillars of our public speaking fears. We want to look in control and take credit for the effectiveness of the message; hence, we become overconfident in success, and excessively responsible for inevitable flaws and weaknesses.

Second, our conscious exaggerates the severity and consequences of our public speaking weaknesses through magnification and "what-if" thinking (predicting catastrophe) while minimizing and devaluing our strengths. The reality is that we will continue to grow and improve as a speaker if we remain patient, vigilant, and assume responsibility for our growth. We need to look at the past, present, and future recognizing we are long-term works in progress requiring grace and patience.

Also, examine the evidence. I have confronted these issues before and made great progress recognizing that we will grow in spite of and because of our weaknesses, sins, fears, and failures. Recognize that public speaking perfection is an illusion and to use this situation to be more transparent and helping others learn from our challenges. When we respond in love and patience, we will always be victorious, as love never fails.

Our insecure mind state discounts the presence and depth of our gifts leading either to a "bury them" mentality or to use the gifts in limited and "safe" zones. We need to make a key decision. What is more important, how I look and feel to myself and others, or moving forward to realize our servant leader calling and purpose? We do not have to be perfect in our public speaking. We should rejoice in incremental, one-step progress, recognizing that becoming more comfortable requires a season for growth, and it is critical to reject black-and-white thinking viewing the presence of anxiety as a failure or weakness.

When fear-based pride knocks related to presentations, open the door and stand with the truth that when we embrace courage, we achieve great character growth. Recognize that you are making great progress irrespective of the emotions, thoughts, and feelings. These pride and fear based strongholds are very resistant until we humble ourselves. Know that arguing with our conscience is futile. When someone says that you look nervous in a presentation situation, this does not mean that you are not effective, as our insecurities want us to exaggerate the importance and impact of weaknesses.

Another revelation relates to the influence of engrained fear, which is the wounded, scarred, and fearful part of our soul. Our job is to reject listening to our "old man" nature. It is not our true self. The old nature promotes "fear of man" through judgment and punishment. We must resist listening to the inner voices of gloom and doom, the public speaking "false prophets." When we embrace a courageous perspective, we will not fear what man (including our own critical inner voices) says.

Ironically, I used one of my own devotionals addressed to my students to reinforce growth related to public speaking fears. A key element is: Are we willing to persist in the presence of our anxieties even when we do fail, look foolish, fall, and appear nervous while speaking? This happens in reality only rarely, but our conscious uses our tendency to focus on the negative and exclude the positive against us. Do I have the courage to persist in spite of my fears in order to achieve the mission and meet the needs of others? Am I willing to fall off the bike and get on again? A personal story clearly illustrates this point.

As a teenager, I loved hockey and had the opportunity to play on the high school team. Growing up in Pittsburgh during the sixties, there were no skating rinks and I did not start to skate until I was sixteen. To play hockey, you must obviously skate well. However, I had a problem. I was unwilling to pay the price to learn how to skate with the required degree of excellence. Why? I was more fearful of falling and getting hurt and looking foolish in front of others than of the benefits produced by pushing myself to gain mastery, which requires the occasional tumble. As such, I never mastered skating well enough to play hockey.

Thankfully, I am not making that mistake again with my public speaking. Are we willing to pay the price, fall, and get hurt on occasion?

Chapter 10

Employee Compensation Management Principles

Compensation System Worldview

Compensation is a foundational component of the SLHRM system. As servant leaders, our stewardship of money is a window on our spiritual state and character. The compensation process reveals important worldview elements that manifest profound implications for HR practices. One of the most pernicious pathologies is defining self-worth and identity according to our job accomplishments and the most tangible indicators of "value," our salary. The other element that contributes to our enslavement is rampant materialism, which encourages the belief that happiness is a function of what we own and consume. Second, the goal as servant leaders is not happiness, which is transitory and influenced by highly variable factors, but deep spiritual joy, generated solely by a harmony of life domains, an island of peace in the trials and tribulations of our lives. If we embrace the subtle but powerful deception that materialism and accomplishments are the key to happiness and joy, we are at the mercy of a multitude of elements beyond our control. When accomplishments and pay levels determine our value, we worship enslaving idols of the heart that imprison us with pride, fear, and insecurity.

Each compensation system embraces an implicit and an explicit view of human nature, a motivational approach that focuses on satisfying selected needs and values. Using the framework of Douglas McGregor, Theory X organizations assume that money is the best motivator, an extrinsic approach; but relying primarily on monetary compensation is a double-edged sword (McGregor, 1960). A reliance on monetary compensation is effective in the short term, but generates many perverse consequences over time. A balanced compensation portfolio consisting of monetary and nonmonetary elements is an attribute of management best practice (Jackson & Schuler, 2006). For many jobs, employees are primarily motivated intrinsically and performance enhancement programs using extrinsic approaches such as pay can decrease motivation and performance (Deckop, 1995; Deckop & Cirka, 2000; Markova & Ford, 2011). A theory that provides excellent guidance on the mixed influence of compensation is equity theory (Pynes, 2013). Equity theory accurately describes our reasoning and value assessment process of how we compare our inputs to a job (effort, performance level, qualifications) with the outcomes or the returns (pay levels, promotion, recognition) received. If these ratios are out of balance, the employee attempts to restore equity by adjusting inputs such as reducing work effort. If employee efforts fail to restore balance, workers experience increasing levels of stress and frustration. When organizations invest little effort in nonmonetary forms of compensation that reinforce intrinsic motivation, it creates greater levels of compensation dissatisfaction. This decoupling of pay with performance occurs in many settings, especially with professional, highly educated occupations. For example, the intrinsic nature of the work is the primary motivator for social service workers and teachers (Borzaga & Tortia, 2006; Bassi & Fave, 2012). A competitive and reasonable level of compensation is a necessary factor, but should not be the primary motivational approach.

An important element in developing an effective salary policy is integrating employee hearts both spiritually and psychologically into the mission and ethos of the organization. A recruiting strategy based on being a compensation leader may attract high performers, but many of them will possess a mercenary attitude and leave the organization for the next high bidder unless they embrace the mission. A critical decision that an organization must make is whether they will deploy a "star" approach predicated on the productivity of a small number of talented employees or a broader, team-based development process of solid "B" players. Part of the answer relates to the nature of the service or product and its relationship to individual performance. From a SLHRM standpoint, cultivating a team orientation is the mandated approach. This embrace of the team perspective receives strong endorsement from the research literature, which demonstrates that star hiring usually fails given that the supporting team infrastructure does not move with the employee, and the new support system is not as effective (Groysberg, Nanda, & Nohria, 2004).

What is the servant leader worldview on compensation? The table 10.1 provides a summary of servant leadership's elements, along

Table 10.1 Key SLHRM worldview compensation elements

Element	Servant Leader Worldview	Labor Market View	Humanistic
Main mission-related objective of compensation	a. To promote human dignity b. To enable man to express his innate gifts, abilities and skills in the fulfillment of his or her purpose and calling c. Express the Golden Rule by the example of a fair and just compensation system. d. To provide employees with a means to meet basic maintenance needs (food, clothing, shelter, health care, etc.) e. To recognize and reward competency of performance and character.	a. To fairly compensate employees for the monetary value of their labor as determined by labor supply and demand and worker human capital attributes (experience, skill level, competency, performance). The key goal is to promote a labor supply and demand balance to avoid labor market distortions and to attract the appropriate quality and quantity of labor given market conditions.	a. To promote human dignity in a foundational social relationship domain. b. To provide employees with a means for supporting their basic maintenance needs (food, clothing, shelter, health care, etc.) c. To recognize and reward competency of performance and character.
Main values emphasized	a. *Agapao* love expression, or promoting the wellbeing of others b. A balance of internal, external and individual equity: pay based on qualifications, merit and contributions (good and faithful servant) c. Fairness: the use of "honest weights and measures" in measuring the performance and employee contributions	a. Market equity and balance between the cost and productivity of labor b. Employees are viewed instrumental units of production, a depersonalization of human beings	a. Supports self-actualization by meeting higher order needs b. Provides for individual growth and development
Employer obligations	a. A high level of moral and spiritual accountability for employee treatment. Provide a just-wage to support employee growth and development	a. Adhere to market principles and legal guidelines b. When reduced to a market "machine" decision making process, disguises moral and personal accountability	a. Provide a just-wage to support employee growth and development
Worker attitudes toward compensation unfairness	a. Work with excellence even for unfair superiors b. Attempt to influence employers through respectful voice mechanisms to develop a just compensation system c. Realize character development through enduring trials and tribulations	a. Quit and seek new employer if dissatisfied with salary levels, terms and condition of employment, or employee treatment b. Seek restitution through the court system for egregious violations	a. Seek new employment if dissatisfied with salary levels, terms and condition of employment, or employee treatment b. Attempt to negotiate a more equitable compensation system

with a comparison of two other worldviews—that of the labor market and of humanism. Clearly, all three perspectives share common elements, but only servant leadership emphasizes the intrinsic dignity of the individual and views work as a means for Golden Rule—love contributing to employee spiritual, physical, and emotional wellbeing and growth. There is an innate dignity in all honest labor.

Wage System Fairness

A key point is an unswerving commitment to wage system fairness. Servant leaders are autonomous moral agents who cannot claim that we are labor market technicians locked in a machine-like system. Reducing compensation to a market machine process disguises our moral and personal accountability. From a servant leader perspective, we must embrace and promote all forms of compensation equity as noted in the points that follow (Pynes, 2013).

- *Internal equity*: A logical internal hierarchy of job classifications linked to a logical and fair ordering of knowledge, skills, abilities, qualifications, and other human capital characteristics (positions requiring higher skills receive higher compensation).
- *External equity*: Pay is market competitive.
- *Individual or merit equity*: Pay levels are fair relative to individual performance and skill level (value added to production and service delivery).
- *Employee need equity (Living Wage)*: Pay a wage that supports human dignity and quality relationships.

As with other aspects of servant leadership, compensation equity requires an ongoing intentional commitment to paying employees according to their contributions.

Debate over the Living Wage

What occurs if the market equitable wage is below a decent standard of living? Does the employer possess any larger servanthood obligations to address unmet employee needs? Our discussions to date have addressed the pros and cons of including employee need as a factor in individual employer compensation decisions. We miss the larger "lay of the land" if we ignore moral and ethical obligations as well as the larger market and public policy concerns. This issue will be a matter of ongoing debate as the following section addresses.

One of the most heated compensation debates relates to individual need equity, or the living wage. What are the pro and con arguments? Figart (2001) provides a very cogent summary. The main argument against the living wage is that it distorts the effective and efficient operation of labor markets (Figart, 2001). A free labor market entails wages linked to productivity rates, the value labor adds to the production process, worker skill levels, and labor demand. Wage payments above the market equilibrium level distort the relation between the marginal value of labor and aggregate wage levels thereby inflating production costs. The result is lower demand for labor and the substitution of capital for labor attenuating overall job creation and economic growth. The result is an overall depreciated societal standard of living, higher taxation levels to support expensive social safety net programs, lower investment in job creating industries, an increase in governmental dependency, and lower individual economic and moral self-sufficiency. In effect, the living wage hurts the low-wage worker, the very population that the law attempts to serve (Figart, 2001).

In contrast to the conservative economic views, the Catholic Church's teaching on social justice provides a strong moral and conceptual foundation for the living wage (Figart, 2001). The Catholic Church is the primary Christian institutional advocate as represented in a more than one-hundred-year tradition of encyclicals on living wage policy (Zigarelli, 1993). Capitalist labor market theory atomizes workers and falsely assumes that promoting the self-interests of individual employers and employees cumulatively is in the best interests of society. This view is a distortion of the communal and social interconnections of labor to the larger health and wellbeing of the community and society as whole. Hence, capitalist labor market theory dehumanizes workers and impedes the ability of workers to support their needs in a dignified manner. The capitalist labor market increases wage and income inequities between skilled and unskilled labor, results in outsourcing of labor, substitution of technology for labor, reduces living wage jobs for minorities, results in decline of cities, and promotes outsourcing of public sector jobs (Figart, 2001).

We cannot have a just and healthy society if a large segment of the population is burdened by preventable poverty. In order to fully understand the debate, one must understand the philosophical basis of the just wage movement. The foundational principle underlying the living wage movement is that dignified human labor is essential for body, mind, and spiritual health. The justification derives from a variety of worldviews, including the religious rationale for the living wage. The Judeo-Christian Bible commands employers to treat fairly both the poor and the laborer. Treating workers fairly glorifies God and enables these workers to raise their families in a fashion that promotes healthy spiritual, physical, and mental development. Hence, we have a more just, moral, and prosperous civil society. Social justice theory states that the ultimate goal of the economy is to meet the material needs of employees to support a good and moral life. Hence, employers possess a moral obligation to provide wage rates that help employees meet their basic needs given that the right of private property is subordinate to human needs. If employers are unable to pay a living wage, society should supplement the salaries of workers with a variety of means including the negative income tax, childcare, and food subsidies, among others.

Proponents posit that paying workers a living wage enables workers to support the basic needs of their family thereby promoting a just, moral, and prosperous civil society. Employers who pay less than a living wage receive subsidies through societal cost shifting onto families through working longer hours, the need to work two or more jobs, less time for family needs, poorer quality child rearing, and the associated adverse mental and physical health outcomes with the higher levels of stress (Figart, 2001). Another major source of subsidy is the government through food stamps, welfare, Medicaid, and housing assistance, among other programs. Finally, churches and nonprofit organizations, both faith and secular, absorb costs and indirectly subsidize low-wage employers through food banks, housing programs, and other forms of assistance. Living wage supporters in the United States cite decreasing social mobility and increasing income inequality due to the increase in one-parent families (in which the parent is usually a woman), the depreciation of the value of the minimum wage, the reduction in unskilled manufacturing jobs, lack of national health insurance, and the globalization of labor markets as key factor justifications (Figart, 2001; Economic Policy Institute, 2011). The substitution of capital for labor, lower levels of construction employment, and international competition and the globalization of markets reduce the pool of living wage jobs, forcing more workers into the service economy (Figart, 2001).The result is a dramatic increase in jobs that pay below poverty wages with a concurrent erosion of the quality of life for millions of low-wage and skilled workers and their families. The pernicious combination of lower governmental spending in social services given higher deficits in combination with the increased demands and stagnating revenues of the nonprofit and church sector decrease the effectiveness of the social safety net. Hence, these sources of church support are unable to meet the needs of the millions of low-wage workers with its present level of resource support given that only 5 percent or less of Christians tithe (Barna Group, 2013).

The living wage generates much controversy, with a considerable contention over the specific definition of basic needs. How can we differentiate necessities from needs, wants, and luxuries? The definition does vary somewhat by culture, but social scientists have developed well-validated measures of life quality, including access to basic health care, adequate nutrition, and safe and affordable housing, among other key areas (Malik, 2013; Gross National Happiness, 2014). How would you view your compensation policy if the prevailing wage were inadequate to rent a basic apartment or provide health care for your family as it is in many developing nations?

From a research standpoint, the independent research on the living wage issue has demonstrated little negative impact on employment levels and municipal budgets (Chapman & Thompson, 2006). Another follow-up question relates to the efficiency/effectiveness of labor markets. Clearly, we operate in a hybrid system with significant government regulation, much of it directed at what economists term market failure. A labor market may operate efficiently, but impose significant externalities upon society (low-wage employers receive indirect subsidies given that they fail to provide health benefits). In addition, markets often internalize other forms of inefficiency including forms of gender discrimination in which predominately female dominated occupations such as personal care–giving receive lower wages than comparable male professions (Pynes, 2013). This is a very complex issue requiring a delicate balance to preserve the powerful positive incentives of free markets while reducing the impact of their imperfections.

Finally, should employers voluntarily provide a higher rate of compensation than the market requires? To be a leader in compensation recognizes the value added by employees. This is certainly easier when the organization is profitable or fiscally secure. A second important question relates to whether family size or the number of dependents should be a factor in wage levels. Compensating employees at differential wages based on family need raises many issues of internal equity. However, there are no legal prohibitions against considering family need in terms of compensation unless there is an intended or unintended discriminatory impact. We (as a society) must address both individual and systematic factors that contribute to a high degree of stress on our lower income workers. We have micro and macro obligations as servant leaders.

If the labor market human capital elements do not justify a living wage, the SLHRM organization should make every effort to enhance employee human capital skills and performance to either increase employee productivity to justify higher wage or strive to place the employee with a new employer that can utilize his or her talents and meet living wage requirements. Even though employers may realize a loss on their investment in the short term, the cumulative and aggregate benefit of such a practice will be to enhance the reputation of the employer, increasing the quality and quantity of the applicant pool to replace those who left.

Numerous public policy interventions can assist low-wage workers and their families including the earned income tax credit (Hamilton, 2010), tax credits/subsidies for hiring low-income workers (Hamersma, 2003), higher levels of student aid (Golonka & Matus-Grossman, 2001), and tax credits for job training (Lydon & Walker, 2005). Another important area relates to governmental regulation, including elevating the minimum wage that has eroded in purchasing power significantly over the last forty years (Addison, Blackburn, & Cotti, 2013). This area is by definition a political question relating to the balancing of key economic, religious, and social values. Our response, both as individual employers and a society, is an important element of servant leader social responsibility.

In conclusion, this discussion addresses very critical compensation and public policy issues. There are several levels of analysis, with the most proximate at the level of the individual employer and the balance of stewardship and servanthood values. From a stewardship standpoint, employers should provide a compensation system that is internally equitable in relation to job skill requirements and employee merit performance levels and externally or labor market competitive.

Elements of Servant Leadership Compensation

Compensation is a foundational element of SLHRM management. Servant leader compensation requires an unyielding commitment to speaking truth into the lives of employees. We clearly need moral courage for this lofty task. Commit to a "best-practice" compensation system that develops employee character and trust. This begins with "honest weights and measures" through fair, valid and reliable performance metrics and standards.

A foundational best practice principle is to develop a valid and reliable performance measurement and appraisal system with ongoing employee involvement. A valid performance measurement system reduces errors from key sources including contamination (the presence of nonperformance factors such as race bias), deficiency (measures lack key elements of performance such as quality of service), and imbalance or the inappropriate weighting of performance factors (quantity is much higher than quality). Another key balance element is that the system should promote a balance between monetary and nonmonetary rewards and motivators developed with ongoing employee input. Servant leaders encourage and recognize others. A final balance factor is to promote a comprehensive equilibrium of performance measures linked to individual, group, and organizational process (behavior) and outcome metrics.

Servant leader human resource systems embrace employee empowerment in all HR systems. To enhance the fairness and effectiveness of the compensation system, employees should play a major role in developing the compensation system policies, procedures, decision rules and criteria. This demonstrates trust in employees while enhancing employee acceptance, commitment, and motivational effectiveness. However, given that we live in a morally imperfect world, there is need for additional employee safeguards through a viable and independent appeals procedure. Another key element is to promote transparency of compensation system information and the decision making process which facilitates trust and the empowerment process. A final element is a "user-friendly" compensation system that is Web-based and accessible by employees.

Best Practice Principles and Their Violation: The Sears Case

Another pillar of the SLHRM compensation system is to recognize and reward employees for character growth and development. Explicitly use the system to promote servant followership and leadership. A case that illustrates the antithesis of the SLHRM approach was that embraced by Sears and illustrated in a Harvard Business Review case study (Paine & Santoro, 2003). The Sears scenario illustrates many of the key temptations that organizations face in serving their customers, clients, and members. It is very easy to rationalize and embrace a self-serving and expedient orientation. In this case, Sears instituted a new compensation system that replaced a flat compensation rate for various types of car repairs with a commission system that lowered employee reimbursement rates per repair or maintenance item. Hence, it generated powerful incentives for unnecessary and inflated car repairs, increasing conflict and stress between service advisors and the mechanics that completed the work. It also reduced employee autonomy and compensation. Sears paid a very high price in loss of customer trust in addition to tempting its employees to violate their obligation to protect the interests of consumers (Paine & Santoro, 2003). Key lessons from the case include:

- *The absence of explicit moral values that promote a covenant-based, long-term, relationship between the organization, its employees and its customers through honesty, high service quality, customer safety, and employee wellbeing is a recipe for ongoing moral and ethical temptation and violations.* The crisis revealed the chief executive's instrumental leadership philosophy that selected the expedient path of short-term profits over the welfare of his employees and customers. The case also demonstrated the absence of leadership transparency and accountability given his resistance to voluntarily assuming responsibility for the system's deleterious influence on employees and customers. This contributed to organizational inertia (unwillingness to solve the root problem) and the externalization of blame for the associated ethical and performance problems.
- *The absence of employee input in designing the compensation system enhanced employee dissatisfaction given reduced employee acceptance and system fairness perceptions.* The end result was an erosion of trust, based upon the belief that the company's foundational motive was to increase employee workload and sales volume while reducing employee pay, a classic assembly line "speed-up" scenario. This system demonstrated a dearth of trust in employees.
- *The absence of balanced performance measures that reward employees for quality, quantity, timeliness, and customer satisfaction contributes to dysfunctions such as goal displacement (quantity over quality, accuracy, and honesty) contaminating the entire performance management process.* This resulted in the adoption of a quota system that encouraged unnecessary work.
- *Unfair compensation systems frequently increase employee competition and generate conflicts of interest.* In this instance, service advisors emphasized volume and profit while mechanics committed to high quality (Paine & Santoro, 2003). The motivational forces in the Sears system created incentives that impeded teamwork and honest communication between mechanics and service advisors. In effect, they were working at cross-purposes in terms of promoting quality as both possessed incentives to inflate and exaggerate service problems to increase sales.
- *An absence of balanced rewards as the compensation system failed to employ nonmonetary forms of incentives including recognition and*

award programs. The system embraced a Theory X motivational philosophy assuming that mechanics possessed little or no desire to achieve higher order needs (growth, recognition, accomplishment). In effect, the system reduced the discretion and autonomy of both service advisors and mechanics eroding the intrinsic motivational potential of their jobs.

- *An absence of auditing and quality control procedures to guard against unnecessary service work exacerbated the financial incentives to cheat.* In an ideal SLHRM system, employees of character will reject unethical compensation systems given the internal moral compass, but clearly external means for ensuring ethical conduct have their place as well.

This system motivated employees to maximize repair work with no regard for quality or honesty, resulting in governmental investigation and adverse company publicity (Paine & Santoro, 2003). Relevant remedial suggestions follow:

1. Emphasize a clear and seamless linkage and value congruence between the organizational mission and vision values and compensation system motivational approaches in which the focus is on serving the customer while providing fair compensation rates.
2. Develop the compensation system in partnership with the employees.
3. Promote transparency of financial and performance information.
4. Hold employees accountable for ethical conduct (honesty, accuracy, customer service, no overage, staying within estimates).
5. Promote pay equity by instituting a base salary at a market-competitive wage level in order to reduce employee status differences and comparison envy/pride.
6. Embrace generous human capital investment (mechanic certification and cross-training) policies and practices that demonstrate faith and trust in employees.
7. Develop a balanced scorecard set of performance standards (quality, quantity, timeliness, and customer satisfaction) and link to the compensation system.
8. Create a balanced compensation system that rewards employees at different levels (individual, work group, store, and company) to reinforce the relationship between employee performance and organizational performance. Evaluate and reward only those factors under the employee's control and minimize the "free-rider" syndrome.

9. Institute a profit sharing system at the store and the company level to increase the relationship between employee individual and group effort and performance.

These principles are key elements of a SLHRM compensation systems and overcoming the "knowing" and "doing" gap by identifying and overcoming the obstacles to implementing moral and ethical policies.
Other key learning points:

- *The serious ethical and/or performance problems chronicled in this case placed tremendous pressure on employees and customers. Executives and managers possess a deontological (ethical) obligation to protect employee interests and integrity.* When the organization violates its fiduciary obligations, employees must make difficult decisions to address the cognitive and affective ethical dissonance that a guilty conscience creates. Organizational dynamics frequently place significant barriers to a righteous organizational response. A major factor that influences an employee's course of action is the degree of employee loyalty to the organization (See the work of Hirschman, 1970). When loyalty is low, employees are more likely to embrace either active or passive exit. Active exit is leaving the organization, while passive exit entails a "checking-out" at work as the employee psychologically disengages thereby reducing job effort and performing at a minimum level. When loyalty is high, the employee is more likely to attempt voice, or an active process of intervention to change the organization. Employee voice is effective when the following three conditions are present (Hirschman, 1970):

  - There exists an effective means to express employee discontent (union, grievance process, suggestion system, employee surveys, town meetings, receptive managers, etc.)
  - The organization possesses the time and resources to change direction
  - The organization possesses self-interested reasons (loss of sales, customers, or institutional memory) to take seriously employee attempts at voice and exit

- Organizational loyalty is a function of trust and reflects a cumulative form of psychic capital. This loyalty can work in both directions regarding ethics. For example, employees may overlook or rationalize away misgivings based upon their confidence in the intentions of the organization (psychological trust). In other words, they are excessively liberal in giving the organization the benefit of the doubt. For voice to be credible there needs to be a legitimate perceived threat of exit (Hirschman, 1970). When employees possess few employment options, or employees readily replaced, voice is muted. The same thing occurs at the customer level if new clients readily replace customers or clients who are dissatisfied and no longer patronize the business.

- *As servant leaders, it our duty to actively seek employee voice and hold ourselves accountable irrespective of the bargaining power held by employees.* The best-practice organizations possess many formal and informal policies and practices including 360-degree feedback systems, employee empowerment, and suggestion systems, among others to increase employee input thereby promoting the organization's long-term wellbeing and interests. When companies embrace employee voice, a bountiful crop of goodwill is harvested thereby enhancing organizational problem solving and learning.

- *Many organizations, unfortunately, are not sincere in their desire to increase employee input. These organizations recognize the utilitarian benefits of embracing employee voice (the letter), but are unwilling to share power when it adversely affects their short-term selfish interests (power, profits, reputation, etc.).* These organizations institute pseudo participation, or the conscious intent to manipulate employees by superficially soliciting employee input with no intention of utilizing the information for management decision making. This takes various guises from gathering information through surveys, interview and focus groups and not providing and acting upon the results to disingenuously commissioning problem solving teams and never seriously considering the recommendations. The end result is a bitter fruit of employee disillusionment and cynicism that erodes employee trust.

- *The Sears case reinforced the importance of managerial upward influence. As servant leaders, we are entrusted with our "flock" of employees.* Leadership is a great responsibility, and we should not aspire to management positions unless we are willing to make the ultimate sacrifice to protect the health, safety, and wellbeing of those under our authority. When faced with an unethical management policy that adversely affects the welfare of our employees, we must exercise due diligence by exercising upward voice, implement the necessary management adjustments within our scope of authority to protect our employees, or consider resigning from our position if the organization persists in the egregious management policy despite our protestations.

The Sears case illustrates many of the conundrums of management. How does a company that was a leader in developing management systems to maximize customer satisfaction in its retail division develop a compensation system that was antithetical to its foundational cultural values and practices? How does an organization diverge from the straight and narrow path and "morph" into a consumer predator? Was Sears' leadership consciously aware of the unethical elements of the plan? What can we learn from the Sears case in terms of how to safeguard the organization's integrity? These issues are clearly critical given the servant leaders obligation to protect the organization's employees from unnecessary temptation and conflicts of interest. Money leads people astray in three major avenues. The first is in traditional materialism. We strive to build the "American Dream" through honest hard work, but end up worshiping wealth. A second path is pure greed entailing the use unethical or criminal means. At the other end of the spectrum is the entitlement and comparison mentality trapping both the working poor and executive with an identity of victimization and dependency with unmet compensation demands.

There are situations necessitating the use of compensation policies to reward employees for honoring their commitments. The danger occurs with an ingrained entitlement mentality. Encouraging obedience through compensation as a form of operant conditioning reduces intrinsic motivation and the associated behavior when the awards cease. For example, rewarding employees for no unscheduled absences is valuable, but only when coupled with a high level of performance. The goal here is to link attendance with performance as well. In determining the reason for absenteeism, management must be very careful to avoid overly intrusive questions and "armchair" psychological assistance or projecting motives and reasons. Employees with good faith absences may experience guilt or shame if management emphasizes the costs to the workplace of their absence thereby encouraging presenteeism, or working while ill. A nuanced approach is sensitive to both system and individual differences. Management must address the cumulative effects of the incentive system and its impact on employee motives. A short-term focus on rewards will provide the appropriate incentives, but management must then engage in the longer term and more challenging task of instilling a servant followership mindset in which employees are committed to excellence as a basic value orientation. Persuading employees that management can be trusted and concerned for the wellbeing of employees is a central focus. As servant leaders, we are to protect the less mature employees by reducing or eliminating the temptation trigger points to the maximum extent feasible. Many absence reduction programs include unintended incentives for employees to game the system and misrepresent the reason for missing work to collect the bonus. As such, we are encouraging the less mature and ethical employees to violate their conscience (assuming it is activated in this case). As servant leaders we grow by both facing and avoiding temptation, but keep in mind that we were never meant to endure ongoing temptation without respite and relief as our resistance margin is gradually eroded.

Conclusion

In summary, the principles of SLHRM compensation exceed traditional minimum standards of legal compliance and extend to the moral imperatives of a just wage system. We need to be both hearers and doers providing employees with fair and attractive wages that provide for employee needs and ensure high levels of retention and performance. The goal is to promote the dignity and wellbeing of our employees and their families as well as benefit the greater community.

SLHRM Leadership Personal Character Reflection:
Rising Above Circumstances

For we walk by faith, not by sight.

The Bible, 2 Corinthians 5:7, NRSV

Many servant leaders are circumstance-focused, evaluating their situation in the workplace based upon the naturalistic evidence provided by the senses. This "walking by sight" isolates us from growth opportunities. One of the "signature" elements of servant leadership as demonstrated by our military men and women throughout history is the ability to rise above the obstacles. By its nature, life presents many painful external situations that we cannot change, but we do possess the ability to transform our reactions. This is a fertile area for servant leader growth by embracing learning from life situations that contribute to character development (dying to the self).

Many leaders mistakenly say "First change my circumstances and how I feel, and then I will believe or obey." A clear moral and spiritual law is that we must have faith in following the moral and ethical path, in spite of our circumstances and the evidence of the senses. In essence, we choose to follow and believe the moral and ethical response in spite of how the intellect assesses the situation. Once we act on faith, either our circumstances change or we will grow in our ability to cope and transcend the situation. In certain cases, we learn to endure the pain and suffering, preparing us for future trials and service.

A related point is the importance of maintaining our commitment to excellence in helping others in the midst of the storm of trial. When we willingly and unselfishly share our time, talents, resources, and encouragement when we are suffering, a powerful act of faith and trust does not go unnoticed by others. Most people follow the selfish and self-defeating principle focusing on our personal needs in adversity rather than on being a blessing to others. Agree with servant leader principles rather than our senses, and great character growth and peace grows.

SLHRM Leadership Personal Character Reflection: Tempting Others to Sin

One of the most humbling aspects of leadership is to recognize that as shepherds of the flock, we possess a great responsibility not to discourage our employees and tempt them to react in anger. Many managers are oblivious to the fundamental servant leader worldview understanding of leadership that assigns great moral accountability for being the source of temptation. How do managers tempt employees? The answer to that question requires more than a dissertation solely devoted to the subject, but I will endeavor to introduce several fundamental principles. First, we tempt our employees to anger when we fail to provide the necessary encouragement and recognition. In essence, we "steal" the intrinsic heart rewards that are essential for stimulating ongoing motivation and the promotion of hope in difficult circumstances. Most employees report a drought of job-related feedback disheartening their resolve and eroding their commitment by the lack of acknowledgment. When we fail to recognize good performance, we are using dishonest scales and stealing from employees! Servant leadership calls us to encourage and support others with the comfort that we receive. In addition, we are failing to use what research deems the most effective motivator, honest and heartfelt praise and encouragement!

Second, we tempt our employees when we fail to provide the necessary discipline to correct poor performance and improve behavior. Servant leaders discipline because of the foundational love for the employee; undisciplined employees, like uncorrected children, will operate in a spiritual vacuum, testing the boundaries until they are broken in spirit and body.

Third, we tempt employees to anger and bitterness when we develop in-groups and out-groups in the workplace with unequal treatment not based upon character and performance, but upon the manager's arbitrary likes and dislikes. We must be no respecter of persons and treat all according to their character and faith.

Fourth, we tempt employees to higher levels of distrust and cynicism when there is a gap between policy and practice. The absence of consistency between words and deeds shipwrecks the faith of many employees. If we promote empowerment in policy, but in practice only support employee decisions that validate or rubber stamp a preordained management decision, we promote organizational hypocrisy.

As servant leaders, we must continually test both our motives and actions to avoid even the appearance of impropriety. If any of these temptations are present, we must change course and address the root cause issues to regain employee trust. It becomes a long road back, because it takes much more time and effort to regain trust once it is lost. Being a "hearer and a doer" is the path less traveled, but well worth the cost given the bounty of trust produced from righteous treatment!

Chapter 11

Final Reflections

The SLHRM organization and leader can never lose sight of the fact that the moral ethos is the collective sum of the implementation of the policies and practices of human resource management as reflected in individual and group decision making. The SLHRM culture rests upon a worldview and the associated attitudes and behaviors that construct the edifice of HR policies and practices. Hence, there is always ethical, moral, and spiritual accountability for our HR systems. No matter how formalized, routinized, and bureaucratized, human free will decision making is at the heart of ethical and moral accountability. Hence, a SLHRM organization begins and ends with leaders who embrace character growth and integrity through self-knowledge. Growth in SLHRM is a lifelong and intermittently painful individual and collective growth process. We can all relate to the central role of trial and tribulation in the shaping and restoration of the heart. A "mountaintop" experience inspires given the breadth and depth of vision, but the close quarter warfare involved in the servant leader maturation process is waged on a daily basis in the dense undergrowth of the spiritual jungle with limited lines of sight. We must rely on our moral compass for direction, strength, and wisdom, to resist the hidden dangers of ambush by the idols of this world that seek to rule our hearts. We must resist the root cause of our great enemies of discouragement and despair, as there are specific actions we must undertake while relying on others to do the rest. The development of such a balance is a major challenge of our walk as servant leaders. When we assume an excessive degree of responsibility for the outcomes related to the HR system, this produces insecurity and fear. When we fail to pursue the harmonic balance, we shirk our free-will responsibilities and fail to grow in faith. Achieving the harmonic mean is an ongoing life challenge.

Commitment to SLHRM excellence, the need for achievement, and the desire for recognition are all desirable attributes if they are under the dominion of our moral compass, but cruel taskmasters when the focus is the egocentric promotion of selfish ends. We must ask the painful and profound question, what is our treasure and who are we really serving? The reality is that servant leaders are no different from others chained to traditional notions of success that distort our shape, mission, and purpose. For some of us, work becomes the idol of worship as we labor for an iconic, self-made, image of success in lieu of the realities of serving others. The result is a form of moral integrity but a sterile, ritualistic, and legalistic version. If we do not embrace the larger moral vision, we repeat a cycle of angst, stress, and pain for the rest of our lives and we will have that "Groundhog Day" surrealism until we surrender our idols.

In conclusion, one of the great paradoxes of servant leadership is that the foundational principles of SLHRM are simple to grasp and communicate, but extremely challenging to practice. It is easy to label oneself a servant leader, but immensely challenging to live as one. We must struggle against three powerful enemies: the inherently self-centered human motives to seek pleasure and avoid pain, the temptations produced by the worldly idols of success and affirmation, and the presence of spiritual evil.

This profound truth reinforces the challenges of SLHRM in the workplace, the path less traveled. SLHRM organizations have the high privilege and daunting responsibility of instructing employees and other key stakeholder students in the character and competency elements of servant leadership. We stress that competence without moral character is a silent colony of termites undermining the pillars of our witness leading to an inevitable structural collapse. We instruct employees on the twin towers of accountability and encouragement that define Golden Rule love in the workplace. Knowledge of servant leader principles is necessary, but knowledge alone does not protect us from a gradual erosion of fervor and dedication to serving others.

A SLHRM prodigal is a manager who knows the truth, but has abandoned his or her first love of serving others for four major reasons: the path of expediency in realizing the temptations of obtaining worldly riches (power, fame, promotion, recognition, etc.); succumbing to burnout and fatigue from the bone weariness inherent in "well doing" without adequate rest and boundaries; the "fear of man" in which we place the approval of others over moral principle; and the blinding influence of pride that extinguishes the light of humility and transparency. The SLHRM prodigal is in dangerous waters as the greatest moral failure is to know the truth and embrace it, but fail to practice and live it out. There is a higher standard of accountability and negative consequences if we espouse the truth but choose not to practice the principles.

How do you know if you are a SLHRM prodigal? One indicator is the disquiet in our souls as our conscience convicts us. Success born of impure motives or means will always leave a sour taste after the initial sweetness of success subsides. Another indicator is the attitudinal, behavioral, and performance feedback received from peer employees and subordinates. When there is a significant discrepancy between words and actions, policy and practice, and a hearing and doing gap, employee engagement, passion, and commitment suffers as trust erodes.

What is the solution when one is lost in the wilderness of the SLHRM prodigal? The first strategy is prevention, entailing a ruthless and ongoing commitment to identifying and testing the integrity of our motives and actions. We must identify the root cause of our actions. A journal is an effective means for identifying long-term patterns and changes in our behavior. Second, embrace an ongoing commitment to 360-degree appraisal through an accountability partner and mentor who will speak truth into your life. Finally, embrace subordinate and peer appraisals that provide candid feedback on how others perceive our actions.

Conclusion

The goal of this book is to provide reflections and a starting point for ongoing growth in servant leadership in the area of human resources. If we commit to loving our employees as ourselves, we begin with a strong foundation for long-term success. It is my hope that the readers will commit to the paths less traveled and shine brightly in an increasingly dark organizational environment.

References

Abu Elanain, H. M. (2014). Leader-member exchange and intent to turnover. *Management Research Review, 37*(2), 110–129.

Addison, J. T., Blackburn, M. L., & Cotti, C. D. (2013). Minimum wage increases in a recessionary environment. *Labour Economics, 23,* 30–39.

Argyris, C. & Schön, D. (1974). *Theory in practice: Increasing professional effectiveness.* San Francisco, CA: Jossey-Bass.

Arthur, J. B., & Huntley, C. L. (2005). Ramping up the organizational learning curve: Assessing the impact of deliberate learning on organizational performance under gainsharing. *Academy of Management Journal, 48*(6), 1159–1170.

ASTD (2012, December 6). $156 billion spent on training and development [Web log post]. Retrieved from http://www.astd.org/Publications/Blogs/ASTD-Blog/2012/12/156-Billion-Spent-on-Training-and-Development.

Babakus, E., Yavas, U., & Ashill, N. J. (2011). Service worker burnout and turnover intentions: Roles of person-job fit, servant leadership, and customer orientation. *Services Marketing Quarterly, 32*(1), 17–31.

Bahreinian, M., Ahi, M., & Soltani, F. (2012). The relationship between personality type and leadership style of managers: A case study. *Mustang Journal of Business and Ethics, 3,* 94–111.

Barbuto, J. E., & Wheeler, D. W. (2006). Scale development and construct clarification of servant leadership. *Group & Organization Management, 31,* 300–326.

Barna Group (2013, April 12). *American donor trends.* Retrieved from https://www.barna.org/barna-update/culture/606-american-donor-trends#.UuggZRBOnIU.

Barsade, S. G., & O'Neill, O. A. (in press). What's love got to do with it? A longitudinal study of the culture of companionate love and employee and client outcomes in the long-term care setting. *Administrative Sciences Quarterly.*

Bassi, M., & Fave, A. D. (2012). Optimal experience among teachers: New insights into the work paradox. *The Journal of Psychology, 146*(5), 533–557.

Behling, O. (1998). Employee selection: Will intelligence and conscientiousness do the job? *The Academy of Management Executive, 12*(1), 77–86.

Bekker, C. (2010). A modest history of the concept of service as leadership in four religious traditions. In D. van Dierendonck & K. Patterson (Eds.), *Servant leadership: Developments in theory and research* (pp. 55–66). New York: Palgrave Macmillan.

Bernardin, H. J, & Beatty, R. W. (1984). *Performance appraisal: Assessing human behavior at work.* Boston, MA: Kent Publishing Company.

Beugre, C. D., & Baron, R. A. (2001). Perceptions of systemic justice: The effects of distributive, procedural, and interactional justice. *Journal of Applied Social Psychology, 31*(2), 324–339.

Black, G. L. (2010). Correlational analysis of servant leadership and school climate. *Catholic Education: A Journal of Inquiry & Practice, 13*(4), 437–466.

Blanchard, K., & Hodges, P. (2005). *Lead like Jesus.* Nashville, TN: Thomas Nelson.

Bolino, M. C., Kacmar, K. M., Turnley, W. H., & Glistrap, J. B. (2008). A multi-level review of impression management motives and behaviors. *Journal of Management, 34*(6), 1080–1109.

Bolles, R. N. (2013). *What color is your parachute? A practical manual for job-hunters and career-changers.* Berkeley, CA: Ten Speed.

Bolman, L. G., & Deal, T. E. (2003). *Reframing organizations: Artistry, choice, and leadership.* San Francisco, CA: Jossey-Bass.

Bonacum, L., & Allen, N. (2007, October 10). CCH survey finds most employees call in "sick" for reasons other than illness [Press release]. *Commerce Clearing House.* Retrieved from http://www.cch.com/press/news/2007/20071010h.asp.

Boone, L. W., & Makhani, S. (2012). Five necessary attitudes of a servant leader. *Review of Business, 33*(1), 83–96.

Borzaga, C., & Tortia, E. (2006). Worker motivations, job satisfaction, and loyalty in public and nonprofit social services. *Nonprofit and Voluntary Sector Quarterly, 35*(2), 225–248.

Bowman, J. S. (1999). Performance appraisal: Verisimilitude trumps veracity. *Public Personnel Management, 28*(4), 557–576.

Boyce, A. S., Ryan, A. M., Imus, A. L., & Morgeson, F. P. (2007). "Temporary worker, permanent loser?" A model of the stigmatization of temporary workers, *Journal of Management, 33*(1), 5–29.

Brandes, P., Castro, S. L., James, M. S. L., Martinez, A. D., Matherly, T. A., Ferris, G. R., & Hochwarter, W. A. (2008). The interactive effects of job insecurity and organizational cynicism on work effort following a layoff. *Journal of Leadership & Organizational Studies, 14*(3), 233–247.

Bureau of Labor Statistics (2013, December). *Labor force projections to 2022: The labor force participation rate continues to fall.* Retrieved from http://www.bls.gov/opub/mlr/2013/article/labor-force-projections-to-2022-the-labor-force-participation-rate-continues-to-fall.htm.

———(2014, January 17). *Job openings and labor turnover survey: Highlights.* Retrieved from http://www.bls.gov/web/jolts/jlt_labstatgraphs.pdf.

Burns, J. Z., & Otte, F. L. (1999). Implications of leader-member exchange theory and research for human resource development research. *Human Resource Development Quarterly, 10*(3), 225–248.

Cartwright, S, & Cooper, C. L. (1997). *Managing workplace stress.* Thousand Oaks, CA: Sage.

Cerit, Y. (2009). The effects of servant leadership behaviors of school principals on teachers' job satisfaction. *Educational Management Administration & Leadership, 37*(5), 600–623.

Cha, S. E., & Edmondson, A. C. (2006). When values backfire: Leadership, attribution, and disenchantment in a values-driven organization. *The Leadership Quarterly, 17,* 57–78.

Chapman, J., & Thompson, J. (2006, February 15). *The economic impact of local minimum wages.* Retrieved from http://www.epi.org/publications/entry/bp170.

Chatbury, A. A., Beaty, D. D., & Krick, H. S. (2011). Servant leadership, trust and implications for the "Base-of-the-Pyramid" segment in South Africa. *South African Journal of Business Management, 42*(4), 57–61.

Chief Human Resource Office (2014, January 24). *Performance management. Just cause standards for represented employees.* Retrieved from http://www.oregon.gov/DAS/CHRO/pages/manual/perf/disciplinary_standards.aspx.

Choudhary, A., Akhtar, S., & Zaheer, A. (2013). Impact of transformational and servant leadership on organizational performance: A comparative analysis. *Journal of Business Ethics, 116*(2), 433–440.

Chung, J. Y., Jung, C. S., Kyle, G. T., & Petrick, J. F. (2010). Servant leadership and procedural justice in the U.S. national park service: The antecedents of job satisfaction. *Journal of Park & Recreation Administration, 28*(3), 1–15.

Cocker, F., M., A., & Sanderson, K. (2012). Managerial understanding of presenteeism and its economic impact. *International Journal of Workplace Health Management, 5*(2), 76–87.

Collins, J. (2001). *Good to great.* New York: Harper Collins.

Cordeiro, W. (2009). *Leading on empty.* Minneapolis, MN: Bethany House.

Covey, S., Merrill, A. R., Merrill, R. R. (1994). *First things first: To live, to love, to learn, to leave a legacy.* New York: Simon and Schuster.

Cropanzano, R., Byrne, S., Bobocel, D. R., & Rupp, D. E. (2001). Moral virtues, fairness heuristics, social entities, and other denizens of organizational justice. *Journal of Vocational Behavior, 58*(2), 164–209.

Dalton, D. R., & Metzger, M. B. (1993). "Integrity testing" for personnel selection: An unsparing perspective. *Journal of Business Ethics, 12*(2), 147–156.

D'Arcy, J. (2012, February 1). A homemaker's real salary. *Washington Post* [Web log post]. Retrieved from http://www.washingtonpost.com/blogs/on-parenting/post/a-homemakers-real-salary/2012/02/01/gIQAh7czhQ_blog.html#pagebreak.

De Cremer, D., Brockner, J., Fishman, A., van Dijke, M., van Olffen, W., & Mayer, D. M. (2010). When do procedural fairness and outcome fairness interact to influence employees' work attitudes and behaviors? The moderating effect of uncertainty. *Journal of Applied Psychology, 95*(2), 291–304.

De Meuse, K. P., Bergmann, T. J., Vanderheiden, P. A., & Roraff, C. E. (2004). New evidence regarding organizational downsizing and a firm's financial performance: A long-term analysis. *Journal of Managerial Issues, 16*(2), 155–177.

de Waal, A., & Sivro, M. (2012). The relation between servant leadership, organizational performance, and the high-performance organization framework. *Journal of Leadership & Organizational Studies, 19*(2), 173–190.

Deci, E. L., & Ryan, R. M. (1985). *Intrinsic motivation and self-determination in human behavior.* New York: Plenum Press.

Deckop, J. R. (1995). Pay system effects on altruism motivation. *Academy of Management Proceedings August 1995,* 359–363.

Deckop, J. R., & Cirka, C. C. (2000). The risk and reward of a double-edged sword: Effects of a merit pay program on intrinsic motivation. *Nonprofit and Voluntary Sector Quarterly, 29*(3), 400–418.

Deming, W. Edwards (1986). *Out of the Crisis.* Cambridge, MA: MIT Press.

Dennis, R. S., & Bocarnea, M. (2005). Development of the servant leadership assessment instrument. *Leadership & Organizational Development Journal, 26,* 600–615.

Digeorgio, R. (2004). Winning with your strengths: An interview with Ken Tucker of the Gallop Organization. *Journal of Change Management, 4*(1), 75–81.

Ding, D., Lu, H., Song, Y., & Lu, Q. (2012). Relationship of servant leadership and employee loyalty: The mediating role of employee satisfaction. *I-Business, 4*(3), 208–215.

Drucker, P. F. (2006). *Managing the nonprofit organization.* New York: Harper Collins.

Ebener, D. R., & O'Connell, D. J. (2010). How might servant leadership work? *Nonprofit Management and Leadership, 20*(3), 315–335.

Ehrhart, M. G. (2004). Leadership and procedural justice climate as antecedents of unit-level organizational citizenship behavior. *Personnel Psychology, 57,* 61–94.

Elise, J. C., & Kolenikov, S. (2014). Flexible work options and mothers' perception of career harm. *Sociological Quarterly, 55*(1), 168–195.

Farling, M. L., Stone, A. J., & Winston, B. E. (1999). Servant leadership: Setting the stage for empirical research. *The Journal of Leadership Studies, 6*(1/2), 49–72.

FedEx (2013, January 23). *FedEx attributes success to people-first philosophy.* Retrieved from http://www.fedex.com/ma/about/overview/philosophy.html.

Feldman, J. M. (1981). Beyond attribution theory: Cognitive processes in performance appraisal. *Journal of Applied Psychology, 66*(2), 127–148.

Ferch, S. R. (2010). Consciousness, forgiveness and gratitude. In D. van Dierendonck & K. Patterson (Eds.), *Servant leadership: Developments in theory and research* (pp. 77–89). New York: Palgrave Macmillan.

Figart, D. M. (2001). Ethical foundations of the contemporary living wage movement. *International Journal of Social Economics, 28*(10–12), 800–814.

Fiscal Policy Institute (2011, May 5). *Top ten reasons a living wage makes sense in New York City.* Retrieved from http://fiscalpolicy.org/wp- content /uploads/2011/07/TopTenReasonsALivingWageMakesSenseForNYC _20110505.pdf.

Fisher, R., Ury, W., & Patton, B. (1991). *Getting to yes: Negotiating agreement without giving in.* New York: Penguin Books.

Folger, R., & Cropanzano, R. (1998). *Organizational justice and human resource management.* Thousand Oaks, CA: SAGE.

Fried, Y. & Ferris, G. (1987). The validity of the job characteristics model: A review and meta-analysis. *Personnel Psychology, 40*(2), 287–322.

Gallup (2013, October 8). *Worldwide 13% of employees are engaged at work.* Retrieved from http://www.gallup.com/poll/165269/worldwide -employees-engaged-work.aspx.

Garber, J. S., Madigan, E. A., Click, E. R., & Fitzpatrick, J. J. (2009). Attitudes towards collaboration and servant leadership among nurses, physicians and residents. *Journal of Interprofessional Care, 23*(4), 331–340.

Goleman, D. (1998). *Working with emotional intelligence.* New York: Bantam.

Golonka, S., & Matus-Grossman (2001, May). *Opening doors: expanding educational opportunities for low-income workers.* MDRC. Retrieved from http://www.mdrc.org/publication/opening-doors-expanding-educational-opportunities- low-income-workers.

Graham, J. W. (1991). Servant leadership in organizations: Inspirational and moral. *Leadership Quarterly, 2*, 105–119.

Green, D. & Roberts, G. (2010). Personnel implications of public sector virtual organizations. *Public Personnel Management, 39*(1), 47–57.

Greenleaf, R. K. (1977). *Servant leadership: A journey into the nature of legitimate power and greatness.* New York: Paulist Press.

Gross National Happiness (2014, January 28). *Gross national happiness.* Retrieved from http://www.grossnationalhappiness.com/.

Gross-Schaefer, A., Trigilio, J., Negus, J., & Ro, C. (2000). Ethics education in the workplace: An effective tool to combat employee theft. *Journal of Business Ethics, 26*(2), 89–100.

Groysberg, B., Nanda, A., & Nohria, N. (2004). The risky business of hiring stars. *Harvard Business Review, 82*(5), 92–100.

Hackman, J. R., & Oldham, G. R. (1976). Motivation through the design of work: Test of a theory. *Organizational Behavior and Human Performance, 16*(2), 250–279.

Halawi, L. A., Pires, S., & McCarthy, R. V. (2009). An evaluation of E-learning on the basis of bloom's taxonomy: An exploratory study. *Journal of Education for Business, 84*(6), 374–380.

Hale, J. R., & Fields, D. L. (2007). Exploring servant leadership across cultures: A study of followers in Ghana and the USA. *Leadership, 3*(4), 397–417.

Hamersma, S. (2003). The work opportunity and welfare-to-work tax credits: Participation rates among eligible workers. *National Tax Journal, 56*(4), 725–738.

Hamilton, F., & Bean, C. J. (2005). The importance of context, beliefs and values in leadership development. *Business Ethics: A European Review, 14*(4), 336–347.

Hamilton, J. H. (2010). Optimal tax theory: The journey from the negative income tax to the earned income tax credit. *Southern Economic Journal, 76*(4), 860–877.

Han, Y., Kakabadse, N. K., & Kakabadse, A. (2010). Servant leadership in the People's Republic of China: A case study of the public sector. *Journal of Management Development, 29*(3), 265–281.

Handlin, H. C. (1992). The company built upon the golden rule: Lincoln electric. *Journal of Organizational Behavior Management, 12*(1), 151–163.

Hellgren, J., Sverke, M. & Isaksson, K. (1999). A two-dimensional approach to job insecurity: Consequences for employee attitudes and wellbeing. *European Journal of Work and Organizational Psychology, 8*(2), 179–195.

Herbst, M. (2007, September 14). The Elite Circle of $1 CEOs. *Bloomberg Businessweek*. Retrieved from http://www.businessweek.com/stories /2007-09-14/the-elite-circle-of-1-ceosbusinessweek-business-news -stock-market-and-financial-advice.

Herman, R. (2008). Servant leadership: A model for organizations desiring a workplace spirituality culture (Doctoral dissertation).

Hicks, D. A. (2003). *Religion and the workplace: Pluralism, spirituality, leadership*. Cambridge: Cambridge University Press.

Hillman, O. (2014, February 16). Spiritual strongholds [Web log post]. Retrieved from http://www.marketplaceleaders.org/spiritual -strongholds/.

———(2000, July 6). Our work versus our value [Web log post]. Retrieved from http://www.intheworkplace.com/apps/articles/default.asp?articlei d=72527&columnid=6525.

Hirschman, A. O. (1970). *Exit, voice and loyalty*. Cambridge, MA: Harvard University Press.

Hodgkinson, G. P. (2003). The interface of cognitive and industrial, work and organizational psychology. *Journal of Occupational and Organizational Psychology, 76*, 1–26.

Hu, J., & Liden, R. C. (2011). Antecedents of team potency and team effectiveness: An examination of goal and process clarity and servant leadership. *Journal of Applied Psychology*, 96(4), 851–862.

Hu. W. (2010, May 19). Teachers facing weakest market in years. *New York Times*. Retrieved from http://www.nytimes.com/2010/05/20/nyregion/20teachers.html?pagewanted=all&_r=0.

Hunter, E. M., Neubert, M. J., Perry, S. J., Witt, L. A., Penney, L. M., & Weinberger, E. (2013). Servant leaders inspire servant followers: Antecedents and outcomes for employees and the organization. *Leadership Quarterly*, 24(2), 316–331.

Ibarra, H., Carter, N. M., Silva, C. (2010, September). *Why men still get more promotions than women*. Retrieved from http://hbr.org/2010/09/why-men-still-get-more-promotions-than-women/ar/1.

Ilgen, D. R., Fisher, C. D., & Taylor, M. S. (1979). Consequences of individual feedback on behavior in organizations. *Journal of Applied Psychology*, 64(4), 349–371.

Irving, J. A. (2010). Cross-cultural perspectives on servant leadership. In D. van Dierendonck & K. Patterson (Eds.), *Servant leadership. Developments in theory and research* (pp. 118–129). New York: Palgrave Macmillan.

Irving, J. A., & Longbotham, G. J. (2007). Team effectiveness and six essential servant leadership themes: A regression model based on items in the organizational leadership assessment. *International Journal of Leadership Studies*, 2(2), 98–113.

Jackson, S. E., & Schuler, R. S. (2006). *Managing human resources through strategic partnerships* (ninth ed.). Mason, OH: Thomson South-Western.

Jain, S., & Nair, S. (2013). Research on work-family balance: A review. *Business Perspectives & Research*, 2(1), 43–58.

Jaramillo, F., Grisaffe, D. B., Chonko, L. B., & Roberts, J. A. (2009a). Examining the impact of servant leadership on sales force performance. *Journal of Personal Selling & Sales Management*, 29(3), 257–275.

———(2009b). Examining the impact of servant leadership on salesperson's turnover intention. *The Journal of Personal Selling & Sales Management*, 29(4), 351–365.

Jenkins, M., & Stewart, A. C. (2010). The importance of a servant leader orientation. *Health Care Management Review*, 35(1), 46–54.

Jex, S. M. (1998). *Stress and job performance: Theory, research and implications for managerial practices*. Thousand Oaks, CA: SAGE.

Jones, D. (2012a). Does servant leadership lead to greater customer focus and employee satisfaction? *Business Studies Journal*, 4(2), 21–35.

———(2012b). Servant leadership's impact on profit, employee satisfaction, and empowerment within the framework of a participative culture in business. *Business Studies Journal*, 4(1), 35–49.

Joseph, E. E., & Winston, B. E. (2005). A correlation of servant leadership, leader trust, and organizational trust. *Leadership & Organization Development Journal*, 26(1), 6–22.

Jungins, K., & Wiggins, M. E. (2011). Family-friendly human resource policy: Is it still working in the public sector? *Public Administration Review,* *71*(5), 728–739.

Kacmar, K. M., Wayne, S. J., & Wright, P. M. (2009). Subordinate reactions to the use of impression management tactics and feedback by the supervisor. *Journal of Managerial Issues, 8*(1), 35–53.

Kanter, R. M. (1979). Power failure in management circuits. *Harvard Business Review, 57*(4), 65–75.

Keeling, K. A., McGoldrick, P. J., & Sadhu, H. (2013). Staff word-of-mouth (SWOM) and retail employee recruitment. *Journal of Retailing, 89*(1), 88–104.

Kool, M., & van Dierendonck, D. (2012). Servant leadership and commitment to change, the mediating role of justice and optimism. *Journal of Organizational Change Management, 25*(3), 422–433.

Lakshman, C. (2008). Attributional theory of leadership: A model of functional attributions and behaviors. *Leadership & Organization Development Journal, 29*(4), 317–339.

Laub, J. (1999). Assessing the servant organization: Development of the Servant Organizational Leadership (SOLA) instrument. *Dissertation Abstracts International, 60*(2), 308 (UMI No. 9921922).

——— (2005). From paternalism to the servant organization: Expanding the Organizational Leadership Assessment (OLA) model. *International Journal of Servant Leadership, 1*, 155–186.

——— (2010). The servant organization. In D. van Dierendonck & K. Patterson (Eds.), *Servant leadership: Developments in theory and research* (pp. 105–117). New York: Palgrave Macmillan.

Lefkowitz, J. (2000). The role of interpersonal affective regard in supervisory performance ratings: A literature review and proposed causal model. *Journal of Occupational and Organizational Psychology, 73*, 67–85.

Leung, R. (2003, July 3). The Mensch of Malden Mills. CEO Aaron Feuerstein Puts Employees First. *60 Minutes.* Retrieved from http://www.cbsnews.com/news/the-mensch-of-malden-mills/.

Liden, R. C., Panaccio, A., Hu, J., & Meuser, J. D. (2014). Servant leadership: Antecedents, consequences and contextual moderators. In D. V. Day (Ed.), *The Oxford handbook of leadership and organizations* (pp. 357–379). Oxford: Oxford University Press.

Liden, R. C., Wayne, S. J., Zhao, H., & Henderson, D. (2008). Servant leadership: Development of a multidimensional measure and multi-level assessment. *Leadership Quarterly, 19*(2), 161–177.

Likert, R. (1961). New patterns of management. New York: McGraw-Hill.

Long-Zeng, W., Eliza Ching-Yick, T., Pingping, F., Ho Kwong, K., & and Jun, L. (2013). The impact of servant leadership on hotel employees' "servant behavior." *Cornell Hospitality Quarterly, 54*(4), 383–395.

Luthans, F., & Peterson, S. J. (2002). Employee engagement and manager self-efficacy: Implications for managerial effectiveness and development. *The Journal of Management Development, 21*(5), 376–387.

Lydon, R., & Walker, I. (2005). Welfare to work, wages and wage growth. *Fiscal Studies, 26*(3), 335–370.

Macdonald, J, & Beck-Dudley, C. (1994). Are deontology and teleology mutually exclusive? *Journal of Business Ethics, 13*(8), 615–623.

Maier, N. R. F. (1958). *The appraisal interview: Objective methods and skills.* London: Wiley.

Malik, K. (2013). *Human development report 2013.* United Nations Development Programme. Retrieved from http://hdr.undp.org/sites /default/files/reports/14/hdr2013_en_complete.pdf.

Marchand, A., & Blanc, M. (2011). Occupation, work organisation conditions and the development of chronic psychological distress. *Work, 40*(4), 425–435.

Markova, G., & Ford, C. (2011). Is money the panacea? Rewards for knowledge workers. *International Journal of Productivity and Performance Management, 60*(8), 813–823.

Mayer, D. M. (2010). Servant leadership and follower need satisfaction. In D. van Dierendonck & K. Patterson (Eds.), *Servant leadership: Developments in theory and research* (pp. 147–154). New York: Palgrave Macmillan.

Mayer, D. M., Bardes, M., & Piccolo, R. F. (2008). Do servant-leaders help satisfy follower needs? An organizational justice perspective. *European Journal of Work and Organizational Psychology, 17*(2), 180–197.

McCuddy, M. K., & Cavin, M. C. (2008). Fundamental moral orientations, servant leadership, and leadership effectiveness: An empirical test. *Review of Business Research, 8*(4), 107–117.

McFarlin, D. B., & Sweeney, P. D. (1992). Research notes: Distributive and procedural justice as predictors of satisfaction with personal and organizational outcomes. *Academy of Management Journal, 35*(3) 626–637.

McGee-Cooper, A., & Trammell, D. (2010). Servant leadership learning communities: Incubators for great places to work. In D. van Dierendonck & K. Patterson (Eds.), *Servant leadership: Developments in theory and research* (pp. 130–144). New York: Palgrave Macmillan.

McGregor, D. (1960). *The human side of enterprise.* New York: McGraw-Hill.

Meade, A. (2014, March). How to study a Bible passage. Sermon presented at Vineyard Community Church, Virginia Beach, VA.

Melchar, D. E., & Bosco, S. M. (2010). Achieving high organization performance through servant leadership. *Journal of Business Inquiry: Research, Education & Application, 9*(1), 74–88.

Mehta, S., & Pillay, R. (2011). Revisiting servant leadership: An empirical study in Indian context. *Journal of Contemporary Management Research, 5*(2), 24–41.

Meuser, J. D., Liden, R. C., Wayne, S. J., & Henderson, D. (2008). Is servant leadership always a good thing? The moderating influence of servant leadership prototype [Presentation]. *Paper presented at the meeting of the Academy of Management.* San Antonio, TX.

Meyer, H. H. (1980). Self-appraisal of job performance. *Personnel Psychology, 33*(2), 291–295.

Mittal, R., & Dorfman, P. W. (2012). Servant leadership across cultures. *Journal of World Business, 47*(4), 555–570.

Morgan, T. (2006, August 10). Leadership summit: Andy Stanley. Message posted to http://tonymorganlive.com/2006/08/10/leadership-summit-andy-stanley/.

Murphy, K. R., & Cleveland, J. (1995). *Performance appraisal: Social, organizational, and goal-based perspectives.* Thousand Oaks, CA: SAGE.

Neubert, M. J., Kacmar, K. M., Carlson, D. S., Chonko, L. B., & Roberts, J. A. (2008). Regulatory focus as a mediator of the influence of initiating structure and servant leadership on employee behavior. *Journal of Applied Psychology, 93,* 1220–1233.

Ng, K. Y., & Koh, C. S.-K (2010). Motivation to serve: Understanding the heart of the servant- leader and servant leadership behaviors. In D. van Dierendonck & K. Patterson (Eds.), *Servant leadership: Developments in theory and research* (pp. 90–104). New York: Palgrave Macmillan.

Northouse, P. G. (2013). *Leadership: Theory and practice* (sixth ed.). Thousand Oaks, CA: SAGE.

Nutt, P. C, & Backoff, R. W. (1995). *Strategic management of public and third sector organizations.* San Francisco, CA: Jossey-Bass.

O'Boyle, E. H., Jr., Humphrey, R. H., Pollack, J. M., Hawver, T. H., & Story, P. A. (2011). The relation between emotional intelligence and job performance: A meta-analysis. *Journal of Organizational Behavior, 32*(5), 788–818.

Obukhova, E., & Lan, G. (2013). Do job seekers benefit from contacts? A direct test with contemporaneous searches. *Management Science, 59*(10), 2204–2216.

O'Halloran, P. L. (2012). Performance pay and employee turnover. *Journal of Economic Studies, 39*(6), 653–674.

O'Reilly, C. A. III., & Pfeffer, J. (2000). *Hidden value: How great companies achieve extraordinary results with ordinary people.* Boston, MA: Harvard Business School Press.

Ortberg, J. (2002). *The life you've always wanted.* Grand Rapids, MI: Zondervan.

Paine, L. S., & Santoro, M. (2003). Sears auto centers. *Harvard Business School Case 394–009.*

Parris, D. L, & Peachy, J. W. (2012). Building a legacy of volunteers through servant leadership: A cause-related sporting event. *Nonprofit Management & Leadership, 23*(2), 259–276.

———— (2013). A systematic literature review of servant leadership theory in organizational contexts. *Journal of Business Ethics, 113*(3), 377–393.

Patterson, K. (2003). Servant leadership: A theoretical model. *Dissertation Abstracts International, 64*(2), 570 (UMI No. 3082719).

———— (2010). Servant leadership and love. In D. van Dierendonck & K. Patterson (Eds.), *Servant leadership: Developments in theory and research* (pp. 67–76). New York: Palgrave Macmillan.

Pekerti, A. A., & Sendjaya, S. S. (2010). Exploring servant leadership across cultures: Comparative study in Australia and Indonesia. *International Journal of Human Resource Management, 21*(5), 754–780.

Peterson, S. J., Galvin, B. M., & Lange, D. (2012). CEO servant leadership: Exploring executive characteristics and firm performance. *Personnel Psychology, 65*(3), 565–596.

Poon, J. M. L. (2004). Effects of performance appraisal politics on job satisfaction and turnover intention. *Personnel Review, 33*(3), 322–324.

Prosser, S. (2010). Opportunities and tensions of servant leadership. In D. van Dierendonck & K. Patterson (Eds.), *Servant leadership: Developments in theory and research* (pp. 25–38). New York: Palgrave Macmillan.

Prottas, D. J. (2013). Relationships among employee perception of their manager's behavioral integrity, moral distress, and employee attitudes and well-being. *Journal of Business Ethics, 113*(1), 51–60.

Pynes, J. E. (2013). *Human resource management for public and nonprofit organizations* (sixth ed.). San Francisco, CA: Jossey-Bass.

Raines, R. (2012, March 29). Companies that invest in employee education reap multiple benefits. *ajc.com*. Retrieved from http://www.ajc.com /news/business/companies-that- invest-in-employee-education-reap-m /nQSd4/.

Rao, A., Schmidt, S. M., & Murray, L. H. (1995). Upward impression management: Goals, influence, strategies, and consequences. *Human Relations, 48*(2), 147–167.

Reed, L. L., Vidaver-Cohen, D., & Colwell, S. R. (2011). A new scale to measure executive servant leadership: Development, analysis and implications for research. *Journal of Business Ethics, 101,* 415–434.

Regent University Center for Entrepreneurship (2014). Retrieved from http://www.regententrepreneur.org/.

Reichers, A. E., Wanous, J. P., & Austin, J. T. (1997). Understanding and managing cynicism about organizational change. *The Academy of Management Executive, 11*(1), 48–59.

Reinke, S. J. (2004). Service before self: Towards a theory of servant-leadership. *Global Virtue Ethics Review, 5*(3), 30–57.

Rezaei, M., Salehi, S., Shafiei, M., & Sabet, S. (2011). Servant leadership and organizational trust: The mediating effect of the leader trust and organizational communication. *EMAJ: Emerging Markets Journal, 1*(1), 70–78

Roberts, G. E. (2010). A guide to practical human resource management research. In S. Condrey (Ed.), *Handbook of Practical Human Resources Management* (third ed.), (pp. 735–768). San Francisco, CA: Jossey-Bass.

Roberts, G. E. & Hess-Hernandez, D. (2012/2013). Religious commitment and servant leadership: The development of an exploratory conceptual framework. *International Journal of Servant Leadership, 8/9*(1), 299–330.

Roberts, G. E. & Pavlak, T. P. (1996). Municipal government personnel professionals and performance appraisal: Is there a consensus on the characteristics of an effective appraisal system? *Public Personnel Management, 25(3)*, 379–408.

Rubin, B., & Rubin, R. (2007). Service contracting and labor-management partnerships: Transforming the public sector. *Public Administration Quarterly, 31(2)*, 192–217.

Rubin, R., & Rubin, B. (2006). Labor-management relations: Conditions for collaboration. *Public Personnel Management, 35(4)*, 283–298.

Schaubroeck, J., Lam, S. S. K., & Peng, A. C. (2011). Cognition-based and affect-based trust as mediators of leader behavior influences on team performance. *Journal of Applied Psychology, 96(4)*, 863.

Schawbel, D. (2014, March 5). Douglas Stone: The importance of feedback in business communications [Web log post]. Retrieved from http://www.forbes.com/sites/danschawbel/2014/03/05/douglas-stone-the-importance-of-feedback-in-business-communications/.

Schneider, S. K., & George, W. M. (2011). Servant leadership versus transformational leadership in voluntary service organizations. *Leadership & Organization Development Journal, 32(1)*, 60–77.

Searle, T. P., & Barbuto, John, E. (2011). Servant leadership, hope, and organizational virtuousness: A framework exploring positive micro and macro behaviors and performance impact. *Journal of Leadership & Organizational Studies, 18(1)*, 107–117.

Sendjaya, S. (2010). Demystifying servant leadership. In D. van Dierendonck & K. Patterson (Eds.), *Servant leadership: Developments in theory and research* (pp. 39–51). New York: Palgrave Macmillan.

Sendjaya, S., & Pekerti, A. (2010). Servant leadership as antecedent of trust in organizations. *Leadership & Organization Development Journal, 31(7)*, 643–663.

Sendjaya, S., Sarros, J. C., & Santora, J. C. (2008). Defining and measuring servant leadership behavior in organizations. *Journal of Management Studies, 45(2)*, 402–424.

Showkeir, J. D. (2002). The business case for servant leadership. In L. C. Spears & M. Lawrence (Eds.), *Focus on leadership* (pp. 153–156). New York: John Wiley & Sons.

Skarlicki, D. P., & Folger, R. (1997). Retaliation in the workplace: The roles of distributive, procedural, and interactional justice. *Journal of Applied Psychology, 82(3)*, 434–443.

Snell, S., & Bohlander, G. (2013). *Managing human resources* (sixteenth ed.). Mason, OH: Southwestern.

Spears, L. (1998). *Insights on leadership: Service, stewardship, spirit, and servant leadership.* New York: John Wiley & Sons.

Stewart, S. M., Gruys, M. L., & Storm, M. (2010). Forced distribution performance evaluation systems: Advantages, disadvantages and keys to implementation. *Journal of Management and Organization, 16(1)*, 168–179.

Stogdill, R. M. (1974). *Handbook of leadership: A survey of theory and practice.* New York: Free Press.

Stone, D., & Heen, S. (2014). *Thanks for the feedback: The science and art of receiving feedback well.* New York: Viking.

Sturm, B. A. (2009). Principles of servant-leadership in community health nursing: Management issues and behaviors discovered in ethnographic research. *Home Health Care Management & Practice, 21*(2), 82–89.

Sun, P. T. (2013). The servant identity: Influences on the cognition and behavior of servant leaders. *Leadership Quarterly, 24*(4), 544–557.

Swenson, R. (2004). *Margin: Restoring emotional, physical, financial, and time reserves to overloaded lives.* Colorado Springs, CO: Navpress Publishing Group.

Taggar, S., & Neubert, M. (2004). The impact of poor performers on team outcomes: An empirical examination of attribution theory. *Personnel Psychology, 57*(4), 935–968. Retrieved from http://0 search.proquest .com.library.regent.edu/docview/220141766?accountid=13479

Takamine, K. S. (2002). *Servant-leadership role in the real world: Re-discovering our humanity* in the workplace. Frederick, MD: PublishAmerica.

Tan, K., & Newman, E. (2013). The evaluation of sales force training in retail organizations: A test of Kirkpatrick's four-level model. *International Journal of Management, 30*(2), 692–703.

Taylor, T., Martin, B. N., Hutchinson, S., & Jinks, M. (2007). Examination of leadership practices of principals identified as servant leaders. *International Journal of Leadership in Education, 10*(4), 401–419.

Tolar, M. H. (2012). Mentoring experiences of high-achieving women. *Advances in Developing Human Resources, 14*(2), 172–187.

Tsui, A. S., Pearce, J. L., Porter, L. W., & Tripoli, A. M. (1997). Alternative approaches to the employee-organization relationship: Does investment in employees pay off? *Academy of Management Journal, 40*(5), 1089–1121.

Tversky, A., & Kahneman, D. (1974). Judgment under uncertainty: Heuristics and biases. *Science, 198*, 1124–1131.

Uru Sani, F. O., Caliskan, S. C., Atan, O, & Yozgat, U. (2013). A comprehensive research about academician's servant leadership style and its consequences. *Ege Academic Review, 13*(1), 63–82.

van Dierendonck, D. (2011). Servant leadership: A review and synthesis. *Journal of Management, 37*(4), 1288–1261.

van Dierendonck, D., & Jacobs, G. (2012). Survivors and victims: A meta-analytical review of fairness and organizational commitment after downsizing. *British Journal of Management, 23*(1), 96–109.

van Dierendonck, D., & Nuijten, I. (2011). The servant leadership survey: Development and validation of a multidimensional measure. *Journal of Business & Psychology, 26*(3), 249–267.

van Dierendonck, D., & Rook. L. (2010). Enhancing innovation and creativity through servant leadership. In D. van Dierendonck & K. Patterson (Eds.), *Servant leadership: Developments in theory and research* (pp. 155–165). New York: Palgrave Macmillan.

Varma, A., Pichler, S., & Srinivas, E. S. (2005). The role of interpersonal affect in performance appraisal: Evidence from two samples—the US and India. *The International Journal of Human Resource Management*, *16*(11), 2029–2044.

Walumbwa, F. O., Hartnell, C. A., & Oke, A. (2010). Servant leadership, procedural justice climate, service climate, employee attitudes, and organizational citizenship behavior: A cross-level investigation. *Journal of Applied Psychology, 95*(3), 517–529.

Washington, R., Sutton, C., & Feild, H. (2006). Individual differences in servant leadership: The roles of values and personality. *Leadership & Organization Development Journal, 27*(8), 700–716.

Widén-Wulff, G., & Suomi, R. (2007). Utilization of information resources for business success: The knowledge sharing model. *Information Resources Management Journal, 20*(1), 46–67.

Wilkes, C. G. (2008). *Jesus on leadership: The man with the miracle touch*. Nashville, TN: Lifeway Press.

Wilson, K. Y., & Jones, R. G. (2008). Reducing job-irrelevant bias in performance appraisals: Compliance and beyond. *Journal of General Management, 34*(2), 57.

Winston, B. (2002). *Be a leader for God's sake*. Virginia Beach, VA: Regent University-School of Leadership Studies.

Wong, P. T. P., & Davey, D. (2007). Best practices in servant leadership [Presentation]. *Paper presented at the Servant Leadership Roundtable, Regent University*. Virginia Beach, VA.

Wong, P. T. P., & Page, D. (2003). An opponent-process model and the revised servant leadership profile [Presentation]. *Paper presented at the Servant Leader Research Roundtable, Regent University*. Virginia Beach, VA.

Zainaldin, J. S. (2004, July 27). Eastern air lines. *New Georgia Encyclopedia*. Retrieved from http://www.georgiaencyclopedia.org/articles/business-economy/eastern-air-lines.

Zapalska, A., & Brozik, D. (2006). Learning styles and online education. *Campus-Wide Information Systems, 23*(5), 325–335.

Zhang, H., Kwan, H. K., Everett, A. M., & Jian, Z. (2012). Servant leadership, organizational identification, and work-to-family enrichment: The moderating role of work climate for sharing family concerns. *Human Resource Management, 51*(5), 747–767.

Zigarelli, M. (2003). A Christian approach to firing people. *Regent Business Review, 8*, 4–9.

Zigarelli, M. A. (1993). Catholic social teaching and the employment relationship: A model for managing human resources in accordance with Vatican doctrine. *Journal of Business Ethics, 12*(1), 75–82.

Zottoli, M. A., & Wanous, J. P. (2000). Recruitment source research: Current status and future directions. *Human Resource Management Review, 10*(4), 353–382.

Index

Printed in the USA
CPSIA information can be obtained
at www.ICGtesting.com
LVHW010806220824
788957LV00002B/226